"Kate Braestrup is funny, reflective, and—above all—honest. In *Anchor and Flares* she has proven, once again, that she is a writer upon whom nothing is lost, even when her mind is reeling."

—Phyllis Theroux, author of *Night Lights: Bedtime Stories for Parents in the Dark*

"Kate Braestrup is at the very top of her game with *Anchor and Flares*. She's working to understand the very heart of parenthood—the weave of attachments that make it almost impossible to do what we know we must: let go."

—Kelly Corrigan, author of *Glitter and Glue* and *The Middle Place*

"Reading *Anchor and Flares* is like having a fiercely compassionate and comically no-nonsense best friend meandering with you through meditations on faith, war, death, and parenting. 'Why? Why? Why?' Braestrup asks a million times, in a million different ways. Sometimes the answer is courage or grief or hope. But usually it's love."

—Catherine Newman, author of *Catastrophic Happiness*

"Braestrup cuts an intriguing figure in her warm, thoughtful chronicle of her time in the trenches as a parent and on the job. Braestrup's compassion, grace, and wisdom come through loud and clear." —*Publishers Weekly*

"Braestrup confronts issues of love and independence, fate and violence, faith and service.... She is a thoughtful mother and writer, and many readers will find in her a kindred spirit as she comes to terms with her son's choice, often by exploring biblical stories of war and soldiers.... Braestrup leavens her musings with humor... and brings a relentless curiosity to every topic she raises. But the book's at its most powerful when she lingers at her story's quietest moments."

— Kate Tuttle, *Boston Globe*

"Sensitive and wholesomely charming, the book is refreshingly free of preachy proselytization and instead addresses the bittersweetness of parenthood and perennial nurturing. Braestrup delivers another appealing, tenderhearted memoir braiding faith and family."

— *Kirkus Reviews*

"Braestrup's straightforward, empathic writing folds in many well-considered thoughts. She speaks from experience, and her viewpoint will serve parents, grandparents, and all those struggling to deal with maintaining their nests as they empty."

— Eloise Kinney, *Booklist*

"Both a personal story and a universal one.... Braestrup's self-deprecating humor and strong respect for the dignity of all of her subjects, from her son's recruiter to a violently abusive man she meets in the line of duty, make *Anchor and Flares* an honest, revealing, moving book."

— Paul Montgomery, *Manchester* (NH) *Union Leader*

Anchor
&
Flares

A MEMOIR
OF MOTHERHOOD, HOPE, AND SERVICE

KATE BRAESTRUP

BACK BAY BOOKS
Little, Brown and Company
New York   Boston   London

ALSO BY KATE BRAESTRUP

Onion

Here If You Need Me

Marriage and Other Acts of Charity

Beginner's Grace: Bringing Prayer to Life

Back Bay Books / Little, Brown and Company
Hachette Book Group
1290 Avenue of the Americas, New York, NY 10104
littlebrown.com

Originally published in hardcover by Little, Brown and Company, July 2015
First Back Bay Books trade paperback edition, April 2016

Back Bay Books is an imprint of Little, Brown and Company, a division of
Hachette Book Group, Inc. The Back Bay Books name and logo are
trademarks of Hachette Book Group, Inc.

The publisher is not responsible for websites (or their content) that are
not owned by the publisher.

The Hachette Speakers Bureau provides a wide range of authors for speaking events. To find out more, go to hachettespeakersbureau.com or call
(866) 376-6591.

ISBN 978-0-316-37378-4 (hc) / 978-0-316-37377-7 (pb)
Library of Congress Control Number: 2014960211

10 9 8 7 6 5 4 3 2 1

RRD-C

Printed in the United States of America

Dedicated to Peter Braestrup and
W. Zachary Griffith

Semper Fi

Prayer for a Little Child

God keep my jewel this day from danger;
From tinker and pooka and black-hearted stranger.
From harm of the water, from hurt of the fire.
From the horns of the cows going home to the byre.
From the sight of the fairies that maybe might change her.
From teasing the ass when he's tied to the manger.
From stones that would bruise her, from thorns of the
*   briar.*
From red evil berries that wake her desire.
From hunting the gander and vexing the goat.
From the depths o' sea water by Danny's old boat.
From cut and from tumble, from sickness and weeping;
May God have my jewel this day in his keeping.

Winifred M. Letts

Anchor
&
Flares

CHAPTER ONE

When I was a little child, I lived in hot places (Algeria, Thailand, Washington, DC) but I prefer the hazards, inconveniences, and forced modesty of a cold climate, so now I live in Maine. Blizzards and black ice are easier for me to cope with than cholera and political turmoil, and I like knitting sweaters more than sweating, so though my first (late) husband, Drew, was a Southerner, our children were reared where the climate provides, as Mainers say, two seasons: winter and July.

Simon's children also call Maine home. Simon is my second husband. Between us, we have a total of six (four of mine, two of his; three boys, three girls), so, one way and another, separately and together, Simon and I have done a fair amount of parenting.

Now Zach, our eldest, and his wife, Erin, are going to have a baby. *All the bliss, none of the hassle,* proselytize our grandparent friends, and we are beside ourselves with anticipation and joy.

The newest family member (whom I refer to for the time being as our *grandfetus*) is now big enough to startle his dad-to-be with kicks and bumps visible on the outside of his mother's belly. I've got booties to knit and children's books to purchase in case *Goodnight Moon* and *Charlotte's Web* go out of print in the next four months. And I am trying hard to remember what I did right and wrong as a parent so I can pass my experiences along to Zach and Erin as Useful Advice.

When I was having babies, the sex of a child wasn't necessarily something one found out ahead of time. Should some other potential problem necessitate an amniocentesis, the answer to "XX or XY?" might be provided, but only incidentally. Nowadays, it's normal to know, so Simon and I know that our grandfetus is a boy.

The baby squirrel who fell out of one of our huge, old oak trees last week was a boy, too. Did he fall or was he pushed? My theory was that the heat affected the mother squirrel the way it affects me: in winter (which is to say, most of the time in Maine), she and I are serene, cheery, cozily accommodating...but not in July.

Summer had brought a return of all our beloved sons and daughters from far-flung places. The thrill of reunion had long since waned. We all were forced to relearn the skills of parent-child cohabitation, but with new handicaps. Our college-age children had spent nine months making messes and mistakes out of range of the parental eye, while Simon and I had gotten used to greeting the morning in a clean kitchen and storing our towels in the bathroom closet rather than on our daughters' bedroom floors. Then there were the girlfriend/boyfriend questions—who sleeps where, and for how many nights? Must they, too, be fed and permitted to hoard towels? What is the etiquette for occasions in which, for example, a significant hookup brings a dog? Or when, on the following morning, that dog pukes up a condom under the breakfast table?

One hot day, the mother squirrel and I both had the urge to kick our offspring permanently from the nest, the difference being that I yelled at everyone and retired to the back porch with a book while she followed through on her impulse.

The baby squirrel survived his rapid descent from nest and favor without apparent ill effects. Oh lordy, was he cute! And snuggly, wrapping his little front paws around my thumb with the faith of the defenseless, willing to accept me as surrogate squirrel-mom no matter that I was large, fur-free, and proffered only a single, enormous nipple that tasted of rubber and leaked. He was, frankly, a lot more fun to mother than the dipsomaniacal towel-thieves now occupying my premises.

I am a law-abiding citizen, an ordained minister, and I serve as chaplain to the Maine Warden Service, Department of Inland Fisheries and Wildlife. It's my job to provide support and comfort to the families of folks who've gone missing when the wardens are called out for search and rescue operations; snowmobile, ATV, and boating accidents and drownings; plus suicides or homicides that take place in or around the Maine woods. But comforting a squirrel was new: I don't ordinarily have much to do with the fish-and-wildlife part of the game wardens' work. Even so, I can't blithely pretend that I didn't know that keeping wild animals as pets is illegal.

But I was entranced by the warm, quivering little creature curled in my hand, so I tried to play up my connections. I telephoned several game wardens, hoping to find one who would tell me, "Oh, it's okay! Keep the squirrel, Kate! Being chaplain to the Maine Warden Service is ample qualification for rehabilitating wildlife!"

None did.

They were sympathetic—these guys like animals—but firm.

"It's better for the squirrel to go to someone who knows what she's doing," said Warden Chris Dyer. "A baby squirrel grows into a bigger squirrel, and he'll need space to practice climbing and leaping. The certified wildlife rehab folks have cages big enough to protect him from predators while he builds those skills."

Besides, he told me, when squirrels reach adolescence, they become moody and disagreeable.

"I know all about moody and disagreeable," I said.

"Well, and that's the ideal moment to release 'em into the wild, but if you send the little bugger out to seek his fortune in, say, October, the squirrel may be eager to go. But he'll be facing the winter without the caches of nuts that his wild relations will have spent months setting aside."

"Fine. I get it," I said sadly.

"He's a wild animal. He needs to be wild to be happy."

Your squirrel is not your squirrel. Isn't that what Kahlil Gibran wrote? *"They are the sons and daughters of Life's longing for itself."*

So I drove the squirrel over to the Belfast Animal Hospital, which has a sideline in taking care of lost wild things. I signed forms. One affirmed my understanding that if the veterinarian's humane and expert judgment so decreed it, my—that is, *the*—squirrel would be euthanized. ("Not likely," said the receptionist cozily, "but we have to say it, don't we?") The other form stated plainly, in black and white, that the squirrel would not return to me. I signed and with a last, longing fingertip caress of his soft little head, I reluctantly took my leave, and went home to miss him.

CHAPTER TWO

Zach himself was born in another, even hotter July. His father and I had been living in Washington, DC, where we had family, but Drew had just been hired by the Maine State Police, so we were headed north ASAP. The photographs of our very new family show all three of us sweating profusely, surrounded by cardboard boxes.

I arrived in Maine with a newborn, a still-healing cesarean wound, a painful case of mastitis, and a husband who would, for the next four months, be home only on weekends. During the week, he would be training at the Maine Criminal Justice Academy, and Zach and I were to occupy one of two cruddy little apartments fitted into the space above a convenience store. The advantage of our new dwelling was that it was cheap, but there were certainly a few disadvantages.

The convenience store's parking lot turned out to be

where local drunks gathered when feeling convivial, and the odor of their urine rose from the asphalt to mingle with a background reek of fried food and cigarettes. The neighbors in the adjacent apartment enjoyed whim-based lifestyles in which sketchy lovers, toddlers, fights, and ferrets came and went. If all this weren't discouraging enough, Drew was earning far less than he had been and I'd left my job behind in DC along with everything and everyone else, so even the low rent wasn't really low enough to allow the new ends to meet.

Zach was healthy and reasonably happy: I'd love to be able to say that my awareness of our good fortune in this regard helped me to bear the unfamiliar isolation, loneliness, and relative poverty with grace. But I bitched. I wept and whined more or less continuously, to my sister by phone during the week, and to Drew on weekends. I bitched to myself, lamenting aloud my still-smarting incision and aching boobs, until my neighbors—usually inclined to forbearance by substance abuse and their own sins—got fed up and thumped the walls. At least I was lucky enough to be spared the truly crippling form of postpartum depression that can interfere so painfully (if generally temporarily) with a woman's ability to respond to her offspring.

Indeed, in that first year of Zach's life, I was so besotted that motherhood felt like a spiritual pilgrimage. I persuaded myself that the elders of my family—aunts and uncles who had made this holy journey before me—could desire nothing more than a chance to relive this most self-evidently defini-tive period of human life.

I sent a letter around, inviting them to contribute stories and advice to a parenting manual (by family, for family) I was hoping to put together. Zach happened to be the first grand- and great-grandchild, but there was no reason to think he'd be the only. Mine is a large and reasonably close-knit family yet, oddly enough, I didn't get a single reply.

However old they might have seemed to me, my aunts and uncles were in their forties and fifties, women and men in their prime, not venerable sages. They were *busy.* This was probably sufficient explanation for their reluctance to contribute, though I imagined I detected a more specific ambivalence.

I wondered: *What if my aunts and uncles aren't sure about whether their parenting has actually been a success? I mean, yeesh! Just look at how some of my cousins have turned out!*

There's irony here. For every cousin dutifully chugging down the good-college-good-career track, there was another like, well, *like me,* who would have to bloom late if she bloomed at all. In spite of an expensive parental investment in my higher education, I'd married young, gotten knocked up, and was now completely dependent on the earnings of a man employed by what was, at the time, the lowest-paid State Police in the country. Drew and I qualified for *food stamps,* for God's sake (which, frankly, I wish I'd known: food stamps would've helped). And we kept on reproducing with the monotonous regularity of woodlice; I wasn't exactly a post-feminist success story. At family reunions, I was probably not the kid my folks boasted about.

But maybe *no one* was boasting? My cousins and I were in our late teens and early twenties, right around the age my kids are now. It is a stage of life my husband Simon has vividly dubbed "perineal." Just as the terrible-two teeters between baby and child and the thirteen-year-old shifts uneasily from kid to teen and back again, so the late adolescent/young adult is *'taint this, 'taint that.*

My Aunt Ellen's son and daughter were Ivy League college students the first time I heard her declare that you can't really tell how a child has turned out until he or she is forty. Lise and Tom were offended, but one's kids take everything parents do and say so *personally.*

For instance, my own kids get prickly when I admit that their conceptions were accidental and unwise, even though obviously it's not Zach, Peter, Ellie, and Woolie specifically whose conceptions a wiser person might have avoided. To the extent that their father and I used birth control, it was in an attempt to control *our lives,* not theirs.

Similarly, when Aunt Ellen made the "don't count your chickens until your eggs turn forty" remark, I think she was identifying the moment that her own human life began to reveal its trajectory—she was the one who was forty, after all, not her daughter or son. She had "turned out."

At forty(-ish), Simon and I met and married just in time

to share the parenting—for better or worse, for richer, for poorer, in sickness and in health—of a half-dozen perineal persons, three sons and three daughters all sauntering, sprinting, staggering, tiptoeing, and/or being yanked up to and across the threshold of adulthood. Their transition will, willy-nilly, be our transition, too. Once grown-up, they won't need parents and we'll be finished, perhaps in all senses of the word.

In the meantime we, too, are going to be a little "perineal," another pair of 'taints waiting to go where our elders and their elders, all the way back to the beginning of human time, have gone before.

My aunts and uncles' silence makes more sense to me now. I, like my Aunt Ellen, am not yet prepared to render judgment about whether, on the whole, my childrearing has been successful—nor even what success might look like when and if it comes. On the other hand, given the impending arrival of the first representative of the next generation, it would be nice to think that Simon and I might have at least a few practical tips to offer and a little wisdom to pass along.

A useful recipe for Play-Go

2 cups ordinary white flour (cheapest available)
2 cups warm water
1 cup salt
2 tablespoons vegetable oil
1 tablespoon cream of tartar

a drop of food coloring
a drop of peppermint oil

Mix all ingredients together in a saucepan and cook over low heat, stirring constantly. The mixture will thicken and look sort of like mashed potatoes. When the dough pulls away from the sides of the pot and forms a ball—or, my favorite test, when you can pinch it and it doesn't stick to your fingers yet it holds its shape—turn it out onto the counter and let it cool a bit. Then knead it.

—∿—

Dear Zach,

You and your siblings liked to play with this while it was still warm. It is a soothing activity for fractious, cranky little ones. While this dough isn't a particularly good medium for real sculpture, it's a lot of fun to squash, roll, poke, and smash. Yes, you all took a bite of it at least once, but the taste proved discouraging enough to make parental intervention unnecessary. Still, I put peppermint oil in as a scent instead of vanilla because it seemed cruel to make the dough smell like cookies. And by the way, you were the one who called it Play-Go.

CHAPTER THREE

When my children were very small and learning how to speak, there were glitches. Zachary, for example, was very fond of *lurgik*. Forced to estimate, I would say Zach said *lurgik* for maybe six weeks, until his ear and tongue aligned and he began asking for *yogurt*. His father and I, on the other hand, went on saying *lurgik* for years. We were charmed into it the way we were charmed into repeating Peter's equally short-lived but adorable "I *yuv* you, Mama!"

Surely we weren't the only parents to find our offsprings' transient speech impediments irresistible and catchy? Nor could ours have been the only family in which the jargon of one member's occupation turned up in ordinary conversation? I'll bet my local pharmacist's family proclaims its affection in doses and warn one another of side effects.

As "PKs" (preacher's kids), my children grew accustomed to being greeted, soothed, and lambasted with biblical verses, and since I am also a law enforcement chaplain and their dad was a State Trooper, our family's slang is strongly tinged, too, with the language of police work.

I can (mostly) keep myself from referring to our family car as a "vehicle" and I've yet to answer the question "Do you have children?" with "Affirmative, three Caucasian males, three Caucasian females, last seen headed southbound..." but I have been known to answer Simon's suggestion that we meet up for lunch with a brisk "10–4, what's your 20?"

Like soldiers, truckers, and anyone who communicates over occasionally untrustworthy radio waves, American police use numeric codes to supplement or replace the spoken word. The codes vary from place to place: "10–4" always and everywhere means "affirmative." But in Maine, the code for "subject has mental health issues" is "10–44," whereas officers with the LAPD would describe him as "51–50."

The last words I heard Drew utter weren't actually words at all. It was early morning and he was leaving for work. His State Police cruiser was still in the driveway, the driver's side door ajar, his German shepherd K-9, Rock, turning circles in the backseat, "flattening the grass" and settling in for a day on patrol.

I was standing on the driveway in my bare feet, though it was April and a light snow had fallen the night before. The strong spring sunlight was already starting to melt the snow off the black asphalt, which was beginning to warm. "4–12 Augusta, I'm 10–8," Drew said to the dispatcher. Neither the dispatcher nor I needed to translate this remark into

English (*Trooper James Andrew Griffith is on duty and ready for service*).

The dispatcher answered, "10–4, 4–12," and I mused affectionately to myself, *What a cool job he's got. No wonder he loves it,* as I went back into the house to finish getting ready for the day—though not for the day it would turn out to be.

A little more than an hour later, the dispatcher was advising units statewide of a 10–50 involving a State Police cruiser and a box truck fully loaded with ice: she was calling for a 10–57. I heard the sirens and looked out the window in time to see the flashing red lights of the first ambulance racing down Route 1 on its way to the accident.

For eleven years, I had been 10–8, 24/7 as Drew's A-unit and mother of our four little B-units. Suddenly I was a State Trooper's widow, which doesn't have its own code.

Feeling called to explore new ways to understand and serve the human needs he had encountered as a law enforcement officer, Drew had made plans to attend seminary and, eventually, to seek ordination as a minister. Without knowing it, he'd left a trail for me to follow toward my own service, one made not of breadcrumbs but of brochures and application forms for the Bangor Theological Seminary. A year and a half after his death, I entered and began work toward a master's degree in Divinity.

Meanwhile, finding itself in need of a chaplain, the Maine Warden Service asked Lieutenant Bill Allen to telephone that

State Trooper's widow, the one who, rumor had it, was going to seminary and becoming a minister.

Bill has an appropriately deep, Hebrew prophet–like voice, and though he probably asked in English if I wanted the job, I received and accepted my literal "call to ministry" in spiritual Creole: *10–4, God. 412-A will be 10–8.*

Simon is an artist and a teacher, but when he married me, he married into the Maine law enforcement family and was even new baptized—as my spouse, he's 2107-A. Along with adding four children to his life, he's had to adjust to such novelties as the occasional armed, uniformed person showing up at the house just to be friendly (or maybe to use the bathroom).

His relationship to the world at large has changed, subtly or not so subtly: "Does your wife attend executions?" acquaintances ask, upon hearing that he is married to the Chaplain of the Warden Service.

"She works with game wardens, not prison wardens."

"So, what does she do? Bless the moose?"

I bless 'em whenever I get the chance, along with bears, deer, and the occasional otter, not that these four-legged denizens of the woods actually require (let alone request) my benedictions. More often, Simon explains, the chaplain's blessings are joined to the much more urgent, practical assistance given by game wardens to the two-legged, wandering, accident-prone, and occasionally fratricidal species that makes up the citizenry of Maine and our seasonal visitors.

I offer comfort and support to the anxious families and

friends of people who have met with an accident, gotten lost in the woods, or drowned in a lake or river. I provide pastoral care to the wardens themselves, who are tasked with rescue missions or, when rescue is impossible, with recovering remains and managing heartbreak.

In return for explaining the work and mission of Maine's game wardens to civilians, Simon gets a taste of the entertainment so reliably and generously offered by the public to off-duty law enforcement officers. He is given the dramatic details of the last speeding ticket his interlocutor received.

Simon's children, Ilona and Cobus, have meanwhile learned to greet their stepmother at the door with the compassionate query, "Did they find the body?"

With longevity comes the presumption of expertise, and I've been doing this work for quite a long time now, so I am often invited to speak about death and its related issues (grief, trauma, the care and handling of bereaved persons) around the country.

On a flight to one such speaking engagement in Mobile, Alabama, I was seated beside a woman who noticed that I was knitting a baby bootie. She struck up a conversation. Once the blessing of convicts versus the blessing of moose issue was out of the way, the woman began to tell me all about the father of her unborn and as yet unconceived child.

This happens a lot, by the way, and not just to me: clergy colleagues confirm that when a member of the traveling public finds out he or she is in the presence of a person of the cloth, they are moved to share their joys and deep concerns. A very old woman wonders whether she is morally obliged to tell her husband that one of their septuagenarian children isn't actually his. A muscular young European wonders aloud whether he might actually be a woman (and only then admits he's German).

Once, when I happened to be going through security wearing a clerical collar, I had a TSA officer follow me all the way to the departure lounge so he could tell me about the love of his life. She was a prostitute, he had been a young grunt on R & R from the Vietnam War, and in 1970 they had spent four days together in a hotel room in Bangkok.

"It wasn't how it sounds," the TSA guy said mournfully, shaking his grizzled head. "It was really special. And I never saw her again."

My flight was called then. All I could offer was a prayer; a request for God's blessing for him and his erstwhile lover, to be borne aloft along with the white-knuckled entreaties I'd be mumbling as the jumbo jet hauled itself into the sky.

The woman on the flight to Mobile was telling me about a man she'd never met. She felt as though she knew him. She was even, she said, at least a little smitten with him though she was (a) a lesbian and (b) old enough to be the guy's mother. Having read all about him in a catalogue of donors sent to her by a sperm bank in California, she'd sent away at once for what she called "his vials." Packed in dry ice, these were probably waiting at home now, in her mailbox, in Mobile.

I said, "Wow."

Southern accent aside, this woman was eerily like me. She had short, graying hair and a Birkenstocks-and-socks fashion sense. She was even, like me, a Unitarian Universalist, and though she wasn't a mother yet, she certainly wanted to be one, so we had that maternal instinct in common, too.

But while the genes and the timing for my children's births were pretty much chosen by the brainless force of youthful passion, here was a mature woman making these choices as deliberately and consciously as modern science allows.

Fascinated, I asked, "What do women look for in a sperm donor?"

She chuckled. "I can't speak for all women, of course. Everyone's different!"

Well, actually, she could've spoken for all women, or at least for a substantial majority of the customers of American sperm banks. She, like most, chose a donor who was white, tall, physically fit, mentally healthy, and intelligent (by which is really meant "has been to college").

The sperm banks locate themselves near college campuses for a reason. Their donors are mostly cash-hungry college students, and this apparently suits everyone just fine. Though no one mentions it, "college educated" is also a marker of social class; nobody, however liberal, seems to be trolling inner cities and trailer parks for potential sperm donors. In fact, women pay a premium for the genetic contributions of students with degrees from Ivy League schools.

I didn't raise this, or any of the many thorny issues I

might have otherwise been tempted to hash out with her, partly because it was going to be a long flight but mostly because I am a middle-aged, Birkenstocks-and-socks liberal and *we don't judge.* (Though I couldn't resist remarking that her donor sounded as much like George W. Bush as Bill Clinton.)

After meeting that mother-to-be on the plane to Mobile, I passed an idle afternoon online delving into the commerce of "reproductive material." For this I was punished in the all-too-familiar way: I am and shall be in perpetuity subject to frequent e-mail solicitations from several Californian sperm banks. They offer me "vials" from their most exciting new donors in blurbs that could have been cribbed directly from Match.com except that, unlike single men looking for a date (and possible LTR), sperm donors do not admit to human needs.

Call me Mr. Charming! Invited a recent sample. *5'11", Caucasian (German/Irish/English), hazel eyes, athletic build with a great smile, Virgo, loves animals...*

This pretty much described Drew. With just a few tweaks (Dutch, blue-green eyes), it could describe Simon as well. Obviously, I have a type.

Back when I was first dating Drew and beginning to meet his family, I noticed he didn't look all that much like his parents and siblings. I don't mean there wasn't a family resemblance: I suspected no secret adoption or hidden extramarital paternity. Drew just looked different.

Then one day I was browsing through family photo albums, and there, gazing calmly out of a sepia-tinted 1920s studio portrait, were Drew's eyes. There was his mouth and the shape of his chin. It was a photograph of Drew's great-great-uncle Lacey, whose traits had evidently jumped two generations.

So while the implication of the sperm bank's listing, clearly, is that would-be customers are to imagine themselves giving birth to a smiling, hazel-eyed, athletic animal lover, the kid could just as easily turn out to be a shy, gray-eyed ailurophobe like the donor's Aunt Clarice.

Moreover, when Drew was a twenty-year-old college student, he could have replied with cheerful negatives to sperm bank inquiries about the prevalence of cancer, heart disease, and mental illness among his close relations, since these had yet to fully reveal themselves. Had I decided, at twenty, to sell a few nice, fresh eggs, I could ignorantly but honestly have advertised these, too, as genetically Grade A.

So, okay, the control implied by a sperm-and-egg catalogue is an illusion. Reproductive science may reveal all eventually, but for the time being, every baby comes as the small, mysterious bearer of the genes of vanished eons.

The more interesting question is why, given this illusion, would seekers of donor sperm or eggs (or sometimes both) choose what they choose? The qualities my companion on the flight to Mobile openly declared herself to be seeking in a bio-dad weren't her own—though she was white, she wasn't tall, for instance, nor an Ivy Leaguer (I asked)—but more to the point, they are not the qualities the bumper stickers on her car would suggest she held most dear.

No, I didn't see her car. I didn't need to. I could look at the bumper stickers on my own car and draw what I'm sure were the right conclusions: peace, diversity, sharing and caring, the brotherhood and sisterhood of all humankind. Love is all you need.

I would have fallen into baffled silence if my companion on the airplane had announced she was in search of a spouse but was only interested in upper-class Caucasian supermodels. On the other hand, all other things being equal, I'd just as soon the grandchild for whom I'd been knitting that bootie was born handsome, healthy, and smart, if only to spare him the difficulties inherent in being homely, sick, and thick. So aren't I also hoping that, when the genetic cards are dealt, my grandchild will receive a winning hand, or at least the best the deck has to offer? Not my bunions and tendency toward melancholia, that is, but maybe his uncle's indefatigable good cheer or his grandfather's open-mindedness and nice, straight teeth?

When Woolie was about three, Drew and I began actively considering the adoption of a fifth child. I called a nonprofit adoption agency one day, and spoke to a nice woman about the process.

"My husband and I would like to maintain the present birth order in our family," I explained apologetically, "which means that we could really only consider adopting an infant under the age of three. Is that possible?"

Before we got to that, Drew and I would need to be evaluated and educated as adoptive parents, which was, she said, a fairly lengthy process that could take up to six months to complete. Once we'd passed muster, there were three adoption programs we could choose between.

"First, we've got what we call Healthy White Infant."

"We have four children already," I said. "So we feel we've done the Healthy White Infant thing pretty thoroughly. What else do you have?"

"Well, there's Overseas Adoptions."

"Aren't there other American babies who need a family?" I asked.

"Well, there is the third program," she said. "Special Needs."

"Really? But what about healthy nonwhite babies?" I asked.

"They're in Special Needs."

"You're kidding. You mean an essentially healthy, newborn African-American infant..."

"Yes."

"Put us down for that program, then," I said. "Because that's what we want."

"African-American newborns are among the easiest babies to locate and adopt," she said brightly. "Once you've passed your home inspection and completed the training, we could probably have an infant for you within three months. In fact, we have a little boy up for adoption who was born just yesterday in Jacksonville, Florida."

"Is the poor guy going to have to wait three months?" I said.

"No, no... you've misunderstood: the average wait is relatively short for Special Needs kids because the demand is low. In fact, the chances are quite good that this little boy won't be adopted at all."

"For God's sake!" I squeaked. "Send him up here—we'll take him!"

The agency woman laughed. She thought I was kidding.

Not long after this conversation, Drew died, and even I could grasp that this meant the end of the adoption idea. But to this day, I think about that little boy down in Florida, hoping some lucky family found and adopted him, and that he is well and waxing strong in spirit.

Being adopted, by itself, is statistically correlated with vulnerability to various difficulties—health and otherwise—and while these are neither inevitable nor insurmountable, one might as well acknowledge the risks and be prepared to address them.

This particular little boy—I call him Jacksonville, in my mind—would, like any child, have had his own, distinctive (and therefore "special" in the more general sense) requirements: Perhaps he'd take a little longer at potty training, or have to carry around an EpiPen in case of bee stings; maybe, as he grew, Jacksonville would demonstrate unusual precocity in mathematics, and have a "special need" for extra tutoring to keep him from getting bored in school.

I'm not naïve; I know that being an African-American child in a Caucasian family would present its own peculiar challenges, though my brother had already adopted my nephew, so little Jacksonville would have had at least one black cousin. There would have been at least a few African-American kids in his school, all of them the adopted children of Caucasians—I don't know if that would have been reassuring, misleading, or just plain weird.

A (white) Maine friend took his daughter to New York City, hoping to expose her to a wider range of cultures and experiences. Standing in the middle of the Metropolitan Museum of Art, the little girl gazed wide-eyed at the teeming, multiethnic multitudes. "Oh Daddy!" she exclaimed. "Look at all the *adopted people!*"

It might have been extra important for little Jacksonville to visit New York, and Washington, DC, and hang around our old friends whose whole families are African-American. And maybe being the adopted child of our family wouldn't have been the best imaginable situation for Jacksonville. But adoption, by definition, takes place because alternatives are believed to be worse or are unavailable for the child. I might not have been a perfect adoptive mother for Jacksonville any more than I have been the perfect biological mother for my biological kids, or the perfect stepmother to my stepchildren. But I would have done my best for him, in his biological mother's stead.

There's another "if only" to add to the list of good things that might have been if only Drew hadn't died.

Always scheduled for the week of May 16, Police Week is an annual gathering in which tens of thousands of law enforcement officers from the United States and abroad arrive in our nation's capital to participate in solemn ceremonies honoring the fallen. The families and friends of officers who have died in the line of duty are there as well, to find and trace the engraved names of a loved one on the polished granite of the National Law Enforcement Officers Memorial at Judiciary Square, and to be recognized and comforted in their loss.

I first went to Police Week as a widow in 1997. A decade later, I was invited as a chaplain to give the invocation at the annual candlelight vigil. This time, two game wardens, Jason Luce and Josh Smith, were with me as moral support and arm candy.

Jason is, like his chaplain, a history buff, happy to discuss the causes, conduct, and moral salience of, say, the Civil War or World War II for hours. He and I had entertained each other in this way on the long drive from Maine to Washington while Josh dozed peacefully in the backseat. Appetites whetted and with Josh in tow, we went to Arlington National Cemetery, the monuments, and the national Holocaust Museum between the scheduled law enforcement events. These sites were thronged with police officers, recognizable even in mufti by their clipped hair and ingrained habit of keeping their arms akimbo to accommodate a phantom gun belt. It was in the company of cops, therefore, that I visited my father's grave at Arlington, stood between the statue of Lincoln and the steps on which Martin Luther King Jr. described the Dream, and watched a film at the Holocaust Museum that made me cry.

In this film, two young soldiers ride a motorcycle along a street. The street is in one of the ghettos created by the Nazis to confine and starve thousands of victims prior to their eventual deportation and murder. Like so much of the photographic evidence we have of Nazi atrocities, this film was shot by German troops, presumably to show to friends and relatives back home, so as their motorcycle comes toward the camera, the two young men grin and wave. Over to one side, crouched in a doorway, are a small boy and girl. They are scrawny, hollow-eyed, and the little boy is having a seizure in his sister's arms.

The film is no more than a minute in length, and it is shown in continuous loop on a permanent screen, so the wardens and I could watch it again and again. Again and again, the two young men—healthy, smiling—ride toward the camera, again and again they pass the little kids in the doorway.

The first time I watched, my focus was on the children, suffering. *Those could be my babies.*

Then I looked at the handsome young men on the motorcycle and realized: *They could be my babies, too.*

*　　*　　*

I can't claim to be serenely immune to the kind of fear that prompts all of us to seek assurance and safety (or the illusion of it) amid the existential uncertainty of our own and our children's lives. All actual or potential parents have known this fear and sought to quell it through prayers to God or deals with the Devil or even by those attempts at "good breeding" that long predated high-tech reproductive technologies that some might think of as informal eugenics.

Parents try to immunize their kids against mediocrity with *Baby Einstein* tapes, soccer clinics, and SAT prep courses. How odd it is that for all of us, not just the customers of sperm banks, the characteristics we try to inculcate are not those we are, in the end, most proud of. In the choices we make about and for our children, we are often encouraged to be Richard Dawkins–style Darwinists seeking to maximize our children's ability to compete against their peers — socially, academically, athletically, and ultimately financially. But as I stood with my brethren before that awful film, these "advantages" seemed completely beside the point.

Dear Beloved Co-Parent Simon,

Our children are intelligent and healthy, and yours are even athletic. But have we adequately seen to the setting of each child's moral compass, have we fostered the courage to heed it? How can I be absolutely sure that our children will not end up like those healthy, smiling boys on the motorbike?

CHAPTER FOUR

As a community minister, I occasionally preach from a church pulpit about the usual theological themes, but the obvious sometimes bears repeating: I am never called to the scene of a woodland calamity to give a sermon. Chaplaincy, above all, is about showing up; demonstrating by sheer presence the truth of the line in the 23rd Psalm: *"Yea, though I walk through the valley of the shadow of death, I need fear no evil for thou are with me."*

A chaplain is called to seek and find the Word in the world, in the places and moments where human beings are wavering on the thin edge—by a hospital bed, in a prison cell, at the scene of an accident, at a fire, in the midst of battle, or on the shores of a cold body of water—where the theological rubber must meet and hold the road.

The chaplain's job is to be present, but those the chaplain serves with—nurses, doctors, law enforcement officers, firefighters, soldiers, or Maine game wardens—are there not to feel, believe, or be: they are there to *do something*.

One December day in central Maine, Warden Diver Tony Gray, for example, had to swim through winter water so thick with ice crystals it had the consistency of a Slurpee.

With thickly gloved hands, he gripped the handles of an underwater planing board tethered by a long, upward-slanting polypropylene towrope to the stern of the Warden Service dive boat. At little more than strolling speed, the boat traveled the surface of Masquinongy Pond, trailing Tony.

Relieved of the need to provide forward propulsion, Tony could spend his air and energy scanning the submerged landscape through the slightly fogged lens of his dive mask. He was hoping to discern a human form or catch the pearly gleam of Caucasian skin amid a crepuscular green-gray clutter of shoals, stones, and submerged tree limbs. Periodically, he glimpsed an undulation in the murk—the black flippers of his dive partner and fellow warden—and he could hear, through static, the deep voice of Warden Bruce Loring.

"Air check…air check…Tony…Rick…do you copy?"

Never entirely reliable, underwater communications gear (or comm gear) seems always to be most fickle when most urgently required: Tony's answer wasn't clearly heard the first time he gave it, nor the second, though naturally Warden Bruce Loring's muttered *"goddammit"* came through loud and clear.

Tony is a young man with an appealingly expressive face.

Once back on the boat, and warmed until his lips were no longer blue, he would hear my words of good news: *Tony, buddy, do you copy? This day, and your work, is holy!*

As a chaplain, I represent the love that is the will of God, but Tony and his comrades are the ones who actually do it, even on days like this when, beyond doubt, the man Tony had been searching for was dead. The Warden Service Dive Team couldn't give his family a rescue, only the hope that they might be allowed to know and tell the end of his life story, and it was definitely not the end they wanted.

"A son shouldn't die before his mom," the missing man's mother declared later that evening. "It isn't natural."

Clad in a T-shirt that revealed sundry intricate tattoos on her plump forearms, she was sitting on the living room sofa in her trailer, a box of Kleenex in her lap and a wastebasket half full of Kleenex by her feet. Her hair was the color of a manila envelope, gray at the roots, and her fingernails were scarlet.

I sat near her, on a squashy chair that smelled strongly, though not unpleasantly, of damp hay. Even stripped of all the layers I'd worn while out on the dive boat, I was sweating. The air was very warm. There was a Christmas tree in the corner, but it was artificial and had no scent. There was a faint—but very faint—whiff of cigarettes: smoking was prohibited in the trailer on account of the grandbabies and also because the missing man's mother was trying to quit.

"I haven't given up hope," she said.

"Can't give up hope," her boyfriend echoed, and sighed so lugubriously that it was clear he'd given it up long ago.

"Miracles happen. Don't they?"

"We would be so glad to find your son alive, Barbara," I said, aware that my expression probably conveyed just how unlikely this was.

"Call me Barbie. Everyone does."

I smiled. "Barbie," I agreed.

Barbie shot a glance at my clerical collar. "I'm praying," she said. "Not just when you're here, I mean. I tried to find my old rosary, even. Looked all through my dresser. Don't know where it is now, but I used to have one."

"I can bring you one if you like," I said. "Would you like for me to contact a Catholic priest?"

"Oh," she said. She looked around with an air of vague alarm, as if I might suddenly conjure a priest out of the warm air. "No. That's okay. I'm not really...I just, you know... *believe*. Still."

"Have to believe," muttered the boyfriend.

The boyfriend had no tattoos or other visible alterations to his flesh, and he spoke in sentences devoid of the profanity that was sprinkled lavishly in and among Barbie's utterances. Dropped in seemingly at random, Barbie's *f-* and *s-* and various *b*-words contributed little to her meaning, and I found myself automatically disregarding them the way I might a lisp or nervous tic. Still, the boyfriend's clean speech sounded strange by contrast.

"Keeping the faith," he was saying. "That's very important." He took a deep breath, coughed violently, and wiped his eyes.

"Yes, well, nevertheless, Barbie, if there's going to be bad news it's worth being prepared for it. Right now, all the evidence we have would indicate your son did not make it back to shore. I would love to be wrong about this, but…"

Barbie gave forth with a sob. While she wept, her boyfriend patted her back gingerly.

"I'll fuckin' kick that boy's ass," Barbie sobbed.

Late at night, two young men, Donald and Dick, decided to paddle a canoe across Masquinongy Pond. Their motivations were not entirely clear, possibly even to them. Alcohol was in the mix, of course, along with some other extralegal stimulants of holiday cheer. But the most credible chem-free reason for the undertaking would eventually be revealed by one of Donald's ex-girlfriends. Apparently, Dick and Donald planned to paddle a mile or so across the water, rob the little gas station/grocery at the boat landing on the other side, then leap back into the canoe to make their getaway. This was unquestionably stupid, but these were persons whose age and gender placed them at the statistical apogee of organic, human brainlessness so often mistaken for or exploited as courage.

By their own standards fully equipped (they brought a bottle and a dog, though no life jackets), Donald and Dick climbed into the canoe, skidded and smashed their way across the broad, white ribbon of shell-ice that edged the shore, and paddled out into deeper water where half-submerged tree limbs, ice floes, and other all-but-invisible hazards lay in wait.

Predictably, they hit something. Donald, the larger of the

two men, evidently forgot the rule about standing up in boats. He stood up. The canoe turned turtle, and the two men and the dog fell into the water.

Upon surfacing, the dog set off for shore and Dick had the presence of mind to grab her tail as she swam past. With the dog's guidance, he was able to swim for land. Staggering up the boat ramp by the little grocery store, Dick and the dog were spotted by the store clerk, who locked the animal inside his warm shop, turned the sign on the door to "Closed," and drove Dick to the hospital to be treated for severe hypothermia. En route, Dick managed to chatter out the information that he hadn't been alone in the disaster, and the store clerk called the police. The search for the still-missing Donald began.

"He was a good boy," Barbie told me, holding my gaze with watery eyes, imploring me to believe her in spite of what we both knew: that her good boy had not grown into a good man. On his official arrest record, along with petty thefts, assaults, driving-to-endanger, and OUIs (his license had finally been taken away, which explains—sort of—why Donald took a canoe to a robbery), were a couple of arrests for domestic violence. He'd hit his mom at least once.

The Maine Warden Service divers spent a couple of long, extremely cold days being towed behind the dive boat, searching for Donald. Other wardens, along with a number of hardy civilian volunteers, walked the snowy shoreline looking for evidence that Donald had somehow made it to dry land. Local police knocked on doors and checked empty lakeside summer cottages and camps in the hope that Donald might, in some hypothermic fugue state, have sought shelter.

I divided my time between perching on the gunwales of the dive boat, plump as a winter cardinal in snow pants and scarlet float coat, and, outer layers removed, nestling into that warm, squashy chair in Barbie's trailer. Enfolded by its slightly damp, smelly upholstery, I paged through photo albums.

"What a beauty," I said with perfect honesty. Donald had been a peachy little guy, with a curly tuft of dark hair and large, lustrous eyes. It was just possible to see the resemblance between the baby, wreathed in the heartbreaking, gummy smile so characteristic of a happy infant, and the adult, now bearded, scowling from the mug shot that was the most recent photo available for distribution to the searchers.

"Even then, I couldn't keep him out of trouble," Barbie confided. "Even when he couldn't hardly walk, he'd climb out of his little crib and I'd find him outside, chasing the cat around the dooryard with a stick."

In what would turn out to be the bare beginning of the long, purgatorial interval between "missing, believed dead" and "dead," Barbie asked me about her other children.

"Should I tell them? They'll fret."

"Ah," I said. Back in 1996, my daughter's kindergarten teacher gathered her pupils together to tell them sad news: Ellie's dad had been killed in a car accident.

When the teacher had asked for suggestions on how the class could help, a little boy instantly and earnestly said, "Well, don't *tell* her!"

Later, the teacher stopped by the house to drop off the carefully crayoned condolence drawings the children had made for my daughter, and we both smiled at the innocence but also the universality of the little boy's impulse to protect Ellie from the pain of bad news.

"It is the privilege of love to fret," I told Barbie gently. "They'll want to know."

She cried. I waited.

"Has Donald's father been told that he's missing?"

The boyfriend snorted contemptuously through his nostrils. "Couldn't handle it if he did know," he declared. "Useless, that's what he is."

"He never was much part of Donald's life," Barbie explained. "He's been in prison, on and off, and I don't know if he's in there to this day, tell you the truth. Donald tried, once, to get ahold of him, maybe visit, attempt a reconciliation, you know, but nothing came of it. He hasn't been in touch."

"We can find him. Don't worry about that."

Barbie fixed me with her sad eyes again. "One thing you can say about my Donald," she said. "Even when their moms didn't want nothing to do with him, at least Donald's babies would always know where to find him."

Barbie went outside to make some calls. Her boyfriend and I drank the cans of diet Moxie he fetched from the refrigerator. Through the far window, I could see the top of Barbie's head moving back and forth as she paced, the smoke rising with her breath in the cold air. Occasionally, a red-nailed, tattooed hand would appear, upraised to emphasize whatever point she was making to the person on the other end of the phone.

Between sips and breaths, her boyfriend told me that he and Barbie had been together for five or six years, and during that time the only problem they really had as a couple was Donald.

"He kept screwing up, you know, and she'd just keep forgiving him. She bailed him out of jail a couple times, and took out a loan to pay his lawyer—we don't have money even to live normal, and I really wanted her to spend some money on herself, maybe fixing up the trailer or getting herself a decent car." One eye on the top of Barbie's yellow head, still visible and in motion beyond the window, he spoke quickly. He clearly had a few things he wanted to get off his chest.

"Even that time when he hit her—and he hit her hard! Knocked her over—right there, next to the chair you're sitting in. Drunk, of course. I called the cops on him that time, and Barbie was mad at me. At me! I said, Barbie, what are you waiting for? He's going to kill somebody one of these days... well," he said, deflating suddenly. He wiped his hand across his forehead.

We heard the outside door open and close, and Barbie reappeared.

"The kids took it hard. My daughter especially."

She sat back down on the sofa and cried. Her boyfriend and I waited quietly.

"When we find Donald," I began, but she was still crying.

I waited.

Speak…weep…swear…inhale…exhale…sow…
reap…scatter the stones…gather the stones together…

At last, she sat upright. "You were saying that when you find him…?"

"Once we've made the recovery, when would you wish to see his body?"

No pause for tears on that one: "Right away," said Barbie.

Her boyfriend, shocked, put his drink down and remonstrated, "Oh, now, sweetheart, you don't want to see…"

Barbie pressed both hands to her mouth. "I mean…as soon as I can." Her eyes filled with tears again. "Am I weird?"

"Not at all," I said firmly. "You're his mom. It's perfectly normal that you'd want to see him."

"Barbie'll freak out," the boyfriend said. He sucked in a strained breath: "If you need someone to, you know, identify him, I could be…"

He fished around in his shirt pocket, withdrew an inhaler, and took a deep hit. He squared his shoulders and glared at me with red-rimmed eyes. "If it's necessary. So she doesn't have to," he said.

"That's very brave," I said. "Thank you."

"But I *want* to see him," Barbie insisted, her resolve growing stronger.

"Of course."

"You'll be there with me?" said Barbie.

"Right beside you."

"And can other people be there? Like, you know…" She

glanced at the man next to her, who wheezed dubiously and rubbed at his eyes.

"Anyone you want. It's up to you," I said.

But that day's search, like the first day's search, ended without result. That night, the temperature dropped and the lake began to freeze over, making exploratory diving impossible. The best that could be accomplished by the warden team was an in-and-out dive on a likely target, and we hadn't identified a target yet. The lake would soon be solid enough to drive a truck across. The dive team leaders and I met with Barbie and her boyfriend and gently told them what can seem the worst news of all: we had to suspend search operations. We would not be able to retrieve Donald's body until spring.

CHAPTER FIVE

When I was little, I wanted to be a boy. In those days—the 1960s and early 1970s—anyone who lacked a penis could not try out for Little League. Note to Freud: It wasn't the thing itself I envied, especially after the time my little brother got his stuck in a zipper. I just wanted to play ball. And I also wanted to be a cowboy, a policeman, and a soldier. Or was it a combat correspondent, like my father, that I was pretending to be, marching around the backyard in a little pair of fatigue pants?

Then, at the age of twelve, I read the seminal (ovulatory?) primer for the modern feminist movement, *Sisterhood Is Powerful*, edited by Robin Morgan and, cured of what was a merely situational gender dysphoria, I picketed the White House, marched for the Equal Rights Amendment, and arraigned the nearest available man—my father—for all the crimes of patriarchy.

"What good are men, anyway?" I demanded, in scornful summation.

"Men are here to protect women," Dad answered virtuously.

To which I promptly retorted: "Well, but what are you protecting us from? *Other men!* If there were no men, there'd be no problem!"

This might have hurt my father's feelings except that he got a real kick out of his children's rhetorical flourishes.

My boy babies would wear pink and flowered clothing; my girls would play with trucks and get their OshKosh B'Gosh overalls dirty. When I noticed that the kids' Playmobil play sets seemed to offer few obviously female "people" to play with, Drew and I spent a long evening switching the little plastic heads around on the bodies to create nurses in skirts with short hair, and police officers with ponytails and eyelashes. The three little pigs my kids heard about were named Marion, Adele, and Ermintrude; Little Red Riding Hood achieved victory over her nemesis-in-drag unaided, and it was a bored little shepherd girl who cried wolf.

Perhaps I went too far when I informed my sons that at least two of the four Teenage Mutant Ninja Turtles, statistically speaking, were probably female.

"They're all boys!" Peter insisted furiously. "They have boys' names. Raphael, Leonardo, Michaelangelo, and Donatello."

"Who named them?"

"Splinter!"

"That's the rat who adopted them after he found them in

the sewers when they were babies, right? Are you telling me a rat knows how to sex a reptile? Any mention of him checking out their little turtle cloacae?"

My avowed motivation in all of this was to keep open as many imaginative doors as possible, though the only concrete result on this occasion was that the kids learned the word *cloacae.*

Though I claimed to desire maximum freedom as much for my sons as for my daughters, I'll now admit to another possibility: absent deliberately nonsexist childrearing, would my dear little boys be in danger of growing up to be the limit-*ers*? Did I go so far as to imagine they might become "agents of oppression"? I hope not, but these were the 1980s, after all, and people like me often spoke that way.

Despite our best efforts, our sons demonstrated a few, strangely gender-specific inclinations. They were given toy babies but not toy weapons, but it didn't take them long to figure out that a Lego plowshare could be made into a Lego gun. All on their own, the boys stuck the little plastic blocks together into an approximate gun shape, then ran around the house, shrieking, "BANG!" and feigning death.

The perspicacious reader will point out that, toy gun rule or no toy gun rule, the boys' father carried a real one every day to work. Whatever we might have said to our children, guns were as obvious a feature of the adult lives they sought to imitate as babies were.

On the other hand, during this same period and a mere twenty miles away, my eventually-to-be second husband,

Simon, was rearing his own children, and he and his wife also did not buy toy guns. Simon was an artist and a teacher, his wife was a flautist, and yet their boy, Cobus, also made swords from sticks and guns from Lego.

Meanwhile, it was only when my daughters took a turn playing with the Ninja Turtles that the little plastic mutants got a break from otherwise constant combat and had a chance to chat. Was it just me or did Raphael and Leonardo seem suspiciously good at verbally exploring their relationships?

("They're *boys!*" shouted Peter.)

When I was a young mother, babies draped about my person like small, sticky ornaments on a bent, bedraggled tree, elderly women — I thought of them as elderly though they were probably younger than I am now — would gaze reminiscently at me and say, "Oh, enjoy this time! It will be gone before you know it!"

Clad in the shabby maternity wear I never really had time to put away, my shoulders sporting crusty epaulettes of spit-up, my breasts the common, pawed property of the whole fam-damn-ily, and my daily conversation consisting of phrases like, "It hurts the kitty when you bite her tail" and "Yes, you did do a nice job of wiping your bum," my early motherhood seemed to be passing with glacial slowness. But those older women were right: the days pass slowly but the years fly, and in the blink of an eye my little boys are becoming men. Once small, soft-skinned, and sweet, the boys now wear enormous shoes on hairy feet and loom above my head.

Peering upward, I offer advice and remonstrance to their bristling chins, and they make their rebuttals in baritones.

I don't think of myself as being especially feminine — indeed, I imagine I'm pretty butch, though that's a self-image mostly derived from childhood (during which friends and relatives were required to call me "Kit," as in Carson, or sometimes "Keith," as in Partridge). I'm reasonably, if reluctantly, muscular thanks to weight lifting, treadmill running, and various other gerbil-ish activities, and I go to work in a male-dominated field clad in a *muy macho* uniform that the poet Richard Blanco (he's a Mainer) once described as "SWAT-Team Pastorwear." My children's mother indeed wears army boots, but I could not be an adequate father figure to them.

This wasn't as obvious to me when the kids were small. Zach and Peter were nine and seven, respectively, when their dad died, and his sudden absence from our lives was more a problem of Drew-absence in particular rather than father-absence more generally. It took a while to recognize that there were deprivations my kids were subject to because they didn't have a father, in addition to the sorrow deprivation of their own beloved and specific dad.

Male relatives, friends, and assorted troopers were around as they had been before Drew died, though with a commendably heightened consciousness of how important their presence might be. Deliberately, they would visit, seek out my boys, talk to them, and take them fishing.

Once, when dropping Peter off to play with his friend Elias Jenks, I saw Elias's dad greet my son with a big smile, a soft punch, and a hug. A large, gentle man, he is also the local Episcopal rector, so it was a man in a clerical collar who met my boy on the threshold. Reverend Jenks would probably have assured me that the Father was with my son, always, but it was Reverend Jenks himself whom I was grateful for that day.

For my own father, too: in the pink shorts I dressed them in to combat gender stereotypes and "Semper Fi" T-shirts, Zach and Peter received sandbox lessons on battlefield strategy from my dad, whom they addressed as Morfar, Danish for "mother's father." Pipe clenched between his teeth, my father joined his grandsons in the sand and, with a bagful of plastic soldiers, showed them how to place an artillery battery, or prepare an ambush that would subject the enemy to blistering *enfilade*.

"Take and hold the high ground if you can, lads!" Morfar would say. "Guard your flanks!"

Violence and sex are two areas that often make the single-motherhood of boys especially tricky. Drew had explained sex to his sons so comprehensively before he died that I didn't need to contribute anything to their sex education other than a few repressive hisses when they demonstrated their impressive command of the details in public. Knowing that Drew had already covered this territory was very helpful, as I tend to be puritanical and squeamish about such things.

It wasn't just because they were boys: I wasn't really a whole lot better when it came to talking about sex with my daughters, though as my daughter Woolie points out appreciatively, at least I didn't try to persuade them that menstruation is beautiful.

Luckily, Ellie and Woolie spent quite a lot of time with Drew's sister, their Aunt Mary, and she was willing to be as frank and comfy about the details of human sexuality as the modern mom is meant to be.

"Aunt Mary, what is an orgasm?" Woolie inquired the day Aunt Mary took all of my children and hers to Six Flags Over Georgia. Woolie still retained a minor speech impediment, so what she actually said, according to the story that will probably be retailed yet again on Woolie's wedding day, was, "Aunt Mawy, what is an awww-gasm?" In any case, Mary spent the rest of their ride on the Great American Scream Machine explaining, whereas I, under the same circumstances, probably would have said something like, "Sweet pea, that's the sort of information best obtained from your peers."

One winter day, when Zach was about fourteen, I was driving him to a guitar lesson and forcing him to listen to The Capitol Steps' New Year's comedy show on NPR.

Zach was not enjoying it. He wasn't enjoying much of anything, really. He was fourteen. Scowling darkly at the winter sky, he was wishing he was somewhere else, throwing rocks at something maybe, or feeling up a girl, but even he started laughing when "Lirty Dies" came on. It's a routine that consists of a political commentary delivered in spoonerisms (just whip your flurds!) and this one was about *Clill Binton*, who at the time was in *trig bubble.*

Clill Binton had an affair with *Lonica Moo-insky*, the comedian declared, adding gravely that the president *tondled her fitties*…In no time, my son *Grack Ziffith* and I were laughing so hard that I had to pull onto the verge, where we could *gicker and snuffaw* safely.

Did a shared cackle at sexual innuendo count as effective parent–child communication? Was cultivating the knock-and-wait habit before walking into my boys' bedrooms or tactfully averting my eyes from any magazines that might be stashed beneath the mattress an adequate substitute for a frank chat about the natural virtues of masturbation?

In Denmark, where whole families frolic bollock-naked on the beach, my Danish cousins congratulate their sons when male secondary sex characteristics become evident. Not me. Peter began wearing his pants slung down around his hips and, when I objected, declared that this was so he could show off the hairs that had begun to sprout below his belly button.

"It's my happy trail, Mom-Dude," he declared proudly.

"The problem isn't seeing the trail, it's glimpsing the destination," I replied. "Get a belt."

Then came the day that Zach came staggering in from the backyard, howling.

"What is it? What's wrong?"

"My balls...Mom, something's wrong with my balls."

"You mean, your testicles?" Silly question. "Well, did you...you know, fall on...something?"

"They just started hurting! Ow, ow, ow...Mom, it *hurts!*"

Okay, even I know this much about testicles: the things are ridiculously delicate. They make you wonder why a Designer intelligent enough to tuck the ovaries away behind a wall of muscle and fat decided to dangle those gormless gonads out in the air, so vulnerable that male soccer players have to fold their hands across their crotches when guarding the goal from a PK and even little boys on T-ball teams have to wear a cup. But balls don't just spontaneously excruciate, do they?

"Sweetie, do you want me to, ahh...take a look?"

Zach dropped his trousers. When a fifteen-year-old boy is willing to show his mom his junk, it's bad. Without bothering to look, I took him to the emergency room.

En route to the experts, I stopped wondering what was causing the problem and began considering the process of diagnosis.

"Um...Honey-Bunny?"

"Yeah?" Zach's voice was muffled. He was curled in semifetal position in the passenger seat, emitting the occasional whimper when we went over a bump.

"When we get to the ER, the doctor is going to have to..." *How shall I put this?* "He...or possibly she...is going to have to look, you know, at your..."

"Omigod, Mom!"

"Well, and he'll have to..." I took a deep breath. "He'll have to *tondle your festicles.*"

Silence. Then Zach started to giggle. Then we were both snickering and guffawing, all the way to the ER door.

FYI, Moms-of-Boys: It turns out that beneath what the doctor referred to as a "tough membrane" called the *tunica albuginea* ("not tough enough," I muttered) the testicles are full of fiddly tubes and cords and whatnot, all prone to catastrophic kinks. The sudden onset of testicular pain should indeed be considered a medical emergency because it could signal a "testicular torsion" of the spermatic cord, from which the testicle is suspended. If that gets twisted, the blood supply can be interrupted, leading to tissue death and the need for amputation.

Zach, fortunately, was merely suffering torsion of the testicular appendix. "It can be treated with analgesics and rest," the doctor said reassuringly, "as it will likely resolve itself."

In order to arrive at this diagnosis, the doctor (male) indeed had to extensively examine Zach's intimate tackle and so did the nurse (female). And then they handed him off to a fetching ultrasound technician named Cindy, whose examination began with a liberal blob of warm K-Y Jelly.

"Not all bad, then," was my bright comment as we drove home together.

"It was really embarrassing. But sort of fun, in a way," Zach admitted.

"Quite an evening," I said.

"Yup. Everybody *tondled my festicles.* And Cindy *pondled my fenis,* too."

As the eldest, Zachary would be the first to launch from the familial nest into what I still determinedly thought of as adulthood rather than manhood. As he progressed through high school, the focus of my maternal anxiety began to shift from present to future: What if my darling, special boy wasn't accepted to the college of his choice? What if, having matriculated, he not only failed to make the dean's list but actually flunked? Even assuming some measure of academic success, could his studies prepare him for a good job or graduate school?

Those halcyon college years immerse a young person in a sea of demographically suitable potential spouses. Would Zach fall in love with yet another arts-and-letters type or might he find a girl whose scores on the math portion of the SATs promised numerate DNA to freshen the mix in the family gene pool?

Then, one fine winter afternoon, Zach arrived home from school with interesting news. "We had a career day at school, and I talked to the military recruiters," he said.

Zach was a gangly junior with the rest of this year and another after that before his graduation. There was plenty of time for him to make other plans, and it wasn't as if there was a draft to dodge.

Besides, the notion that Zach, of all people, might want to be a soldier was laughable to me. When the neighborhood kids organized Wiffle ball games, Zach was the one who argued for extra strikes for the small and klutzy. He wasn't an athlete. He avoided killing anything, even insects.

I was only paying partial attention to what Zach was saying, anyway: Barbie, the mother of Donald, had called that day. She was having a rotten new year so far, and the call concluded with her still in tears. I was going to call her back just as soon as I recalled the formula for predicting whether and when a drowned body would come up on its own, if only so I could provide her with something resembling concrete, useful information.

"An Army guy, a Navy guy, and a Marine are coming to visit me at home. Because I'm not eighteen yet, they will need a parent to be present."

"I'll be present," I said. "Don't worry."

And because I do remember the precise position of my son's hand on the door of the fridge, and the angle of his head as he peered into the fruit drawer where the apples were kept, I must somehow have felt fear, for fear is what can etch such small details so sharply into memory.

I said something like "uh huh," though, and Zach ate his apple.

An all-volunteer force makes enlistment a personal decision rather than a public duty. Like young widowhood or a child predeceasing a parent, donning a uniform, taking up a weapon, and setting off for war represent a once-common parting modern Americans have the luxury of finding strange, and even unnatural. But it isn't unnatural, not by the evidence of history. In every human culture, it is a transition marked and recognized, wherein the boy seeks to join the company of warriors and in so doing also and thereby severs the cord that has bound him to his mother, and enters into the world of men.

When olden-days cartographers found the limits of their knowledge, they left a blank space on their maps, inscribed simply: *Hic sunt dracones!* My son was thinking of joining the military at a time when American forces were involved in two wars, neither of which was going particularly well. On my maternal mental map, therefore, a similar blank space opened. Here, undoubtedly, were dragons.

Chapter Six

From the day of her birth, Ellie had a runny nose. Is that genetic?

Did Drew have a chronically runny nose? Did I? Is that why I had my adenoids out at the age of three, in that horrible Paris hospital where the nurses were thin and cruel, and administered anesthesia by placing a large, black toilet plunger over my face?

As a baby, Zach woke up at night screaming inconsolably.

It's probably because we moved when he was four weeks old, right? And then his father was gone for four months, and his mother was so stressed out, she walked around the cruddy little apartment over the convenience store, bitching aloud until the neighbors pounded the walls in alcoholic fury.

"He drank in stress with his mother's milk," I mourned.

"He was perfect when we got him," Drew concurred gloomily. "We've ruined him already."

Every parent begins as an amateur.

The experts horn in: everyone from the author of Prov-erbs ("Train up a child in the way he should go; even when he is old, he will not depart from it," 22:6) to cozy Peggy O'Mara ("The way we talk to our children becomes their inner voice"). It was some bona fide experts—guys in white lab coats—who informed my grandmother in no uncertain terms that breast-feeding was a bad idea.

"Your breasts are too small, you can't possibly make enough milk, and, besides, it is 1929, for God's sake, not the Middle Ages!"

Modern artificial baby milk was pure, hygienic, scientifi-cally formulated, and, they told her, just plain better than nature's primitive effluent.

My father's mother—Farmor, as her grandchildren would call her—had only recently arrived in the United States from Denmark, the young bride of a Danish physicist.

"In Denmark mothers still fed their babies from the breast," Farmor told me. My father's father (*farfar* in Dan-ish), a scientist himself, must have strongly identified with the white-coat guys, and both young immigrants surely wished to raise their new, American boy in the American way. So it was with what I can only think of as commendable determination that my grandmother insisted on breast-feeding. The doctor reluctantly agreed on condition that my grandmother follow a strict, scientific protocol.

"Before every feeding, I had to take all of your father's clothes off and weigh him. Then I could nurse and, when he was finished, I had to weigh him again. The difference between what the doctor thought he should weigh, and what he actually weighed, I had to make up with a bottle."

My grandmother managed to keep the strip-weigh-feed-weigh routine going, day after day (not to mention night after night) *for six months.*

Farmor told me this story for the first time as she watched her first great-grandchild suckling away, unstripped, unweighed, and uninterrupted, the scientific establishment having done a 180 on the value of breast milk between her day and mine.

Parents remain vulnerable to the advice of experts because, as a group, we're scared. If you've been lucky enough to get through your early life without anything disabusing you of the notion that the world is a reasonably safe and manageable place, the first glimpse of your own infant in all his absolute, appalling, and adorable vulnerability will do the trick. Feed! Clothe! House! Protect! Educate! And if, as a parent, you're human and fallible? Tough titty: failure is not an option.

Snuggling my firstborn, I imagined cruel peers, bigots, child molesters, nuclear warriors, and neo-Nazis. I, who once experimented with allowing mosquitoes to drink my blood and fly away, sated and unsquashed, vowed *I will kill you all* and I meant it.

As Zach's siblings came into the world, its perils changed. The focus of anti-bellum anxiety shifted away from Nicaragua and El Salvador and toward the Middle East, while nuclear winter yielded pride of place to global warming as the primary environmental plucker of the national nerve. Even so, the kids grew up and headed for high school during a period in which global prospects for peace and prosperity were so far advanced that British prime minister Tony Blair happily predicted that ours would prove "the first generation able to contemplate the possibility that we may live our entire lives without going to war or sending our children to war."

Based on the available data, both Tony Blair's boys and mine were far more at risk of becoming slackers than soldiers. This was true even after 9/11 and the invasions of Afghanistan and Iraq. The defeat of terrorism might be the great cause of our time, and Saddam Hussein a brute of Hitleresque proportions, but Uncle Sam wasn't pointing the "I NEED YOU" finger at our children. According to no less an authority than the U.S. secretary of defense, these were low-cost, cakewalk conflicts our professional soldiers would win without breaking a sweat. I might question their wisdom and the necessity of the conflicts as a citizen, but I need not fear them as a parent.

"How are you, ma'am?" the Army recruiter said to me, and answered himself in the next breath. "Great! Great! I've got some great stuff to show you, here, let me just sit you down, ma'am…"

He was a diminutive fellow with a salesman's enthusiasm. Soon the couch was covered with glossy brochures detailing (with floor plans) the lavish accommodations available to enlisted men at upscale military bases in Italy and

Germany. He talked about the great food at the dining halls, the great medical facilities, and the great, guaranteed comfort of an on-base T.G.I. Friday's. Army Guy clearly believed it was Mom who had to be won over. Zach peered over my shoulder as I examined dreamy photos of Venetian lagoons, rare Hawaiian bird life, Munich's museums and beer festivals.

"Great opportunities if he likes culture..." Army Guy pointed out.

"What about the war?"

"The Iraq thing? That'll be over in no time," Army Guy predicted breezily. "Now, let me show you some of the great educational benefits we'll be offering your son..."

Navy Guy had tender, brown eyes, and was endearingly soft around the middle of his white sailor suit. He confided to me, sotto voce, that the Navy had one of the lowest casualty rates of any branch of the military.

"All the mothers ask," he said, with a sad smile.

Navy Guy ended up staying for lunch. He confided in me about his girl troubles and laughed politely at my Village People jokes, while Zach leafed idly through a pamphlet showing happy sailors lounging on the deck of a destroyer.

"I don't know, Mom," said Zach, after Navy Guy left. "Maybe I don't want to be in the military after all. It seems kind of goofy."

Then we got a visit from the Marine.

The Marine was fit, spit-shined, and sharp. "My name is Sangster, ma'am. Rhymes with *gangster*." That was pretty much all he had to say to me. His pitch was aimed at Zach.

"The Marine Corps will make you puke, make you cry, and when that's over, you'll be sent to the most miserable, dangerous, godforsaken place on the planet. I'm not here to show you that the Corps is good enough for you. I'm here to see if you're good enough for my Corps. So let me ask you: Why should I let you join?"

I opened my mouth, but was quelled by a sharp look from Zach.

"Well...um, sir," he said. "I think I'm reasonably smart. I do well on tests, but I don't work very hard. I want you to teach me to work."

Sergeant Sangster looked at him for a long moment. He gave the barest hint of a smile. "We can do that," he said.

I had a couple of friends—both men—at seminary who were genuinely antiwar and day-to-day pacifists. One night, they found a bona fide burglar in their living room, and being the kind of Christians only seminarians can be, they sat him down on the futon couch and asked him earnestly whether, in addition to cash and the almost-new DVD player he'd tucked under his arm, there was anything else the burglar felt he needed? A nice meal, perhaps, or the shirt off their backs?

Interested, I asked, "What did he say?" but, disappointingly, the burglar had just mumbled, *"No, dude, whatever, I'm good,"* and skedaddled.

My friends had the guy outnumbered and he wasn't armed, besides which they didn't have kids in the house. They were only risking themselves.

Might we imagine that, having benefited from Christian

charity, the burglar renounced his wicked ways and sinned no more? If not, how would his next victims feel about my friends' willingness to refrain from calling the police?

Before we imitate Christ and turn the other cheek, shouldn't we first make sure that ours is the only cheek that's going to get slapped?

But I was still willing to be impressed: "That's the kind of thing I can imagine Zach doing," I said in talking this over with Simon.

"The one who is joining the Marines…"

"Um…yeah."

At twenty-four, new mother of a baby boy, I had counted Zach's sleeping breaths as if he might forget his need for oxygen. When he was ten months old, I gave him walking lessons. If I couldn't trust my son to breathe and become bipedal, how could I possibly trust him to hold on to his soul's sweetness in the Marine Corps?

Like with the night terrors, I tried to blame Zach's interest in donning a uniform on his father. No matter what overt messages about nonviolence we tried to offer our children, Drew wore a uniform and carried a gun.

Then I blamed it on my own father.

The first song I learned to play on the piano was the Marine Corps Hymn. Dad taught it to my kids, too, as they played with plastic soldiers in the sandbox: *From the halls of Mont-uh-zoo-ooh-muh to the shores of Tripoli; We fight our country's ba-ah-ttles in the air, on land, and sea!*

"My father was a Marine," I told Sergeant Sangster.

"Yes, ma'am," said Sangster. "So Zach informs me."

"I'm proud of him," I said, confusedly.

"Semper fi," said Sangster.

"You wear a uniform, too," Simon pointed out afterward, when I described this interchange to him. "You may not carry a gun, but the guys you work with do."

Damn. That's true.

In the normal course of things, I don't have nearly as much to do with violence as, say, the State Police chaplain does. While a fatal hunting accident is technically considered a homicide (that is, the killing of another human being), deliberate assaults and murders aren't a primary investigative responsibility of game wardens. We get involved only when wild land or fresh-water are part of the picture—if, for example, a murder has taken place in the woods or a body has been disposed of in a river, and the troopers need help locating and interpreting the body and other evidence. Given that Maine boasts a lot of wild land and water, the Warden Service gets involved more often than one might think. But I am still able to assure my worried loved ones that the deaths I am exposed to are mostly the result of human foolishness and frailty rather than deliberate human cruelty. And yet what I am exposed to is sufficient: even when it comes to murder, I know more than it is comfortable to know.

Fictional killers generally come in two varieties. There's the serial killer, depicted as amoral and coldly intelligent rather than pathetically bonkers as such persons are wont to be in real life. Then there's the rational murderer, motivated by self-interest, eliminating witnesses to his crimes, or bumping off Uncle Charles so as to inherit his fortune.

When fictional or filmed, the criminal mastermind will be a mercenary rather than an ideologue, his (he's virtually always male) lackeys driven by greed and fear rather than, say, the will of God.

On the other hand, the most common explicit motivation for real-life violence from barroom brawls to genocide is moral outrage.

"They disrespected me," the perpetrator earnestly explains. Or, "His ancestors massacred mine," or "She's a whore," or "He cheated on me."

"What did she *expect* me to do?" a murderer wails, positive that the destruction he was driven to, if not exactly virtuous, should be understood as the lesser of two evils.

One evening, over dinner with a friend, a divorced man confidently declared, "My wife and kids and I, we're all going to be together again."

The friend interpreted this to mean that the man planned to reconcile with family members who had made it clear in every possible way that they considered themselves not so much estranged as escaped from him. Reconciliation seemed highly unlikely (if not downright delusional), but the man's friend didn't say so. Instead, he changed the subject.

Two days after expressing complete confidence in a family reunion, the man went to his ex-wife's house and shot her, his son, and his daughter with a shotgun, then shot himself in the head. A local police officer, spotting the car that everyone in the community knew to keep an eye out for, arrived at the house just in time to hear the final shot.

When the first urgent plea for reinforcements came over the radio, it happened that the Warden Service firearms team was en route to a training session. Being close to the relevant exit off the interstate, they beat the State Police tactical team to the scene, provided backup to the local officer, established a perimeter, and secured the crime scene. Their chaplain arrived not long afterward.

Crime scene tape surrounded the little frame house, with its side porch and bay window. One end of the yellow tape was tied to the pole that hoisted a basketball net above the driveway. The medical examiner was there amid the half-dozen or so State Police crime scene specialists, clad in blue coveralls, their faces somber as they went in and out of the house.

I waited outside, exchanging the snippets of information with various wardens, cops, and EMTs that first responders tend to offer one another in inadequate condolence.

"D'you know she taught kindergarten?"

"One of the guys is over at the school right now, trying to figure out how to tell the kids…"

"She's a friend of my wife's. She was wicked nice. A sweetie pie."

"My daughter's in middle school with her boy."

"This sucks."

"Where did he get the gun?" I asked. No one had an answer.

The medical examiner emerged from the house, having made a preliminary examination of the bodies. He was peeling off vivid-purple latex gloves.

"Dr. David," I asked. "When they bring the bodies out, would it be all right with you if I said a blessing for each one before they are loaded for transport?" I was prepared to explain: *You see, Dr. David, I want to be able to tell the family...*

What family? There would be no immediate family to comfort. Everyone was dead.

But surely there were uncles and aunts, and grandparents. And there were those little kindergarteners and their parents, there was the community as a whole: everyone was going to be shocked and sad.

The police officers present at the scene, their pale faces held carefully expressionless as their gloved hands tugged and turned, and their discerning eyes considered and measured, were here, forestalling grief, so that they might give justice. God knows, giving justice is an act of love. I wanted to name this for them, for everyone, for myself.

As it turned out, I didn't have to explain any of this.

"Absolutely! Absolutely!" the doctor said at once, and when the first body bag was taken from the house and hoisted onto the gurney, he loudly proclaimed to the assembled personnel, "Okay, people! Kate's going to say a blessing!" The scene fell silent. The officers and wardens folded their gloved and bloodied hands and bowed their heads.

"This is the head end?" I asked as I stepped up to the gurney.

Dr. David nodded.

There was some blood and brain tissue on the outside of the body bag.

I raised my hand, preparatory to placing it gently on whatever remained of the forehead under the heavy vinyl. *May the words of my mouth and the meditations of my heart be acceptable to you, my strength and my redeemer.*

My hand was descending when Dr. David spoke again, calmly, without particular emphasis.

"Now, that's the shooter."

Later, one of the game wardens told me he saw my hand halt abruptly in the air above the body bag. It hovered, just for a moment, before resuming its downward motion and coming to rest on the smeared black bag.

"I wondered what you were praying," he said. "All I could imagine was, 'Sorry, you bastard. You're on your own...'"

"It was all I could do not to snatch my hand away," I admitted.

"Yeah, well, good. You're human."

Had I found the threshold at which love stops short? God's love, that is, but translated, as it must be through the actions of human hands and voices. If not at this—the murder of innocents—then at what point can one honestly say that love no longer makes its absolute, implacable, and holy demand? *Love one another.*

The shooter's father would defend his son in the coming days, loudly insisting that his son was a good husband whose playful threats had been misinterpreted by his wife, an affectionate and dedicated dad pushed over the edge by a system weighted too heavily in favor of women.

I think of my love for my children as being unconditional, so perhaps I should've been better able to identify with the shooter's father? Maybe, in similar circumstances, I also would continue to proclaim my son's essential (if not material) blamelessness, continue to denounce the victim and the system rather than the boy I raised…

Would I be able to do it if my grandchildren were among the casualties?

With my hands gently resting on the "head end" of one after another of the body bags containing the murdered wife, then the murdered son, and then the murdered daughter, I said: "Bless you, beloved, and go peacefully to God. Your life has not been lived in vain: you gave love, received love, are loved, and will be remembered. Amen."

I didn't know what to say for the shooter. The best I could come up with was, "Oh God, I'm sorry."

When Peter was two years old, I took my mind and eye off him at an inopportune moment, and the next thing I knew, he'd disappeared. With the taffy-mired slowness of emergency time, fourteen seconds of frantic searching passed before I heard a shout: my brother-in-law, Peter's Uncle Jeff, had spotted him toddling happily and speedily toward a very busy road.

Peter wasn't hit by a car that day. If he had been, it would definitely have been my fault. Claiming, in my defense, that I was preoccupied with his infant sister, while true, wouldn't have had the slightest effect on the appalling suffering I would inflict and experience through my negligence. Thank God Uncle Jeff saw him. Thank God Peter stopped and turned, rather than toddling onward, giggling, when he heard his uncle call his name. But it wasn't God who saved Peter. It was Uncle Jeff, and luck.

The sense of overwhelming responsibility and anticipatory guilt got worse after Drew died. If anything bad happened to my children, there would be no one to blame but me. *God, keep my jewel this day from danger…*

"People are stupid," Warden Jesse Gillespie said. "So incredibly goddamned stupid."

Sometimes, when law enforcement officers say things like this, they mean *other* people. They mean the miscreants, criminals, "frequent fliers"—the ones who make needless, catastrophic messes of the kind that cops get called to clean up. But on that particular night, I don't think the warden was excluding any of us from his unhappy condemnation.

"We don't know yet what happened," Lieutenant Nate Robertson had said matter-of-factly, earlier that evening. He was calling from his truck en route to the scene of what had been described as an accidental shooting with juveniles involved, and he had me on speakerphone.

"Hey Kate," said his passenger.

"Hey Jesse!" I responded, recognizing Gillespie's voice.

"Given there's kids involved, Gillespie here suggested you might as well get started over this way," the lieutenant continued. His voice was calm. In my mind's eye, he was lifting his uniform cap and rubbing his head so that his chronically cowlicky hair stuck out in some new direction.

"It's going to be bad," said Jesse.

I got my gear together.

Two eighth grade classmates, close in age, became brothers—sort of—when the divorced father of the elder moved in and set up housekeeping with the divorced mother of the younger. After dinner that autumn evening, the boys asked if the father would take them out to the field behind the house all four now shared to do some target shooting in preparation for deer season.

"You boys go out and practice," the mother said, perhaps jealous of her time with her still-new man. "Dad'll take you hunting when the season starts."

With the rifle and several pockets full of ammunition, the boys went out into the gathering dusk. Later, the older boy would claim they shot only at trees and twigs, though the wardens suspected they'd at least tried to shoot some little birds. They weren't particularly good shots, however, so they hadn't hit anything.

"I gotta take a whiz," the younger one had announced and, seeking privacy, he made his way down along the field edge until he reached a spot perhaps fifty yards away. There, he turned his back and unzipped his pants.

What combination of Bruce Willis/John Wayne/Jim Carrey hero stories surged up together in the older boy's mind, ready to fill the space between impulse and calamity? No one can say, least of all the boy who lifted the rifle stock to his shoulder. Waiting only until the stream of his stepbrother's pee was audible, he aimed at the air a foot or so above the other boy's bent head and pulled the trigger.

Bad things happen. Yet boys of a certain age can't bring themselves to believe this, partly because of hormones but mostly because of inexperience. It is a demographic vulnerability nations exploit when it comes to making war. But you don't need a war to reveal that vulnerability: a case of beer will do it, or a dark country road with a frost heave that, approached at sufficient speed, might just launch a carload of laughing friends into the air. Or a YouTube video that shows how a snowmobile can actually be made to skim across open water if you just give the thing enough gas. Or a gun.

The bullet was supposed to whistle harmlessly through the branches of the trees, through still-unfallen leaves above the younger boy's head, startling him, frightening him even, but it was a prank intended to be just scary enough to be funny.

The older boy failed to account for the effect of gravity on a bullet's trajectory. It flew, struck, and penetrated just above the younger boy's right ear and traveled through, destroying the brain stem so absolutely and instantaneously that the child dropped like a stone.

"This is going to be a bad one," Jesse predicted, and it was.

Absurdly small, the body lay in the frosty grass, the small, curled hands glowing white in the beam of a warden's Maglite.

Surely even a thirteen-year-old knows better than to aim a firearm in the direction of a human being? *What were you thinking?*

The shooter was struck dumb; he did not answer. He also looked awfully small, as if the enormity of what he had done had literally diminished him.

Surely no parent could be foolish enough to send a couple of mere children out, unsupervised, to play with a loaded gun? *What were you thinking?* The father was too busy shouting his belated, obscenity-laden lessons on gun safety at his son to answer, and the mother was now childless and screaming.

Surely a good God would not permit a parent's mindless error or a child's resultant blunder to be so catastrophically transformed into what the medical examiner would sadly marvel was "a perfect sniper's shot"?

The mother clutched the dead boy's jacket to her nose and desperately inhaled his scent.

People are often stupid. Myself included. After Peter almost but not actually toddled into a busy road to be run over and killed, I took the Dorothy Law Nolte poem (quoted at the end of this chapter) off the fridge. But it didn't matter. I'd memorized it by that time. What parent can be serene when the possibility of failure is everywhere and the stakes are so goddamned high?

When Zach casually informed me that a friend's dad had offered to take him along to a shooting range to try out his marksmanship, I instantly and strenuously forbade it.

"Mom, the Marines shoot guns!"

"You aren't a Marine yet. At the moment, you are still a minor, and guns are dangerous."

"Mom, you don't understand!"

Unfairly, perhaps, I demanded how much, exactly, Zach understood? Like God answering the plaints of Job, I thundered: "Do you know what havoc a bullet wreaks in flesh, or the tender places flies will lay their eggs to grant their larvae an easy feast? Do you know how a body smells and what it looks like after lying for a day, or two days, or ten days in the sun? Have you seen the varying hues of bone and blood or inhaled the disturbingly appetizing barbecue smell we human beings give off when we accidentally get cooked? Have you held a dead woman's charred teeth in your hand?"

My voice was probably loud enough for the neighbors to hear even if there wasn't a shared wall they could thump to quell me. Even I could tell when the energy behind my voice shifted from righteousness to shrill fear.

"You want to see what a stupid, avoidable death looks

like? I can show you the pictures, Zach." My throat was sore, now. "I won't need to look at them myself because the pictures are permanently stored in my head. I don't want you to have pictures like those in your head. Do you understand me?"

"Mom..."

"I love you," I said.

Because people I love have died, I am forced to recognize that being loved by me offers no immunity. Denial, in my case, is thus limited to a refusal to actually utter the words: *I don't want you to die.* Instead, I said what is also true: "I don't want you to go to war, I don't want you to have to see awful things."

"But Mom, *you* see awful things," Zach said.

Dear Zach and Erin,

Ubiquitous throughout my early motherhood, a poem by Dorothy Law Nolte was xeroxed and magneted to innumerable refrigerator doors (including ours) and calligraphed, framed, and hung reverently on the walls of childcare centers, pediatricians' offices, and Sunday school classrooms. It was called "Children Learn What They Live" and went like this:

If a child lives with criticism, he learns to condemn.
If a child lives with hostility, he learns to fight.
If a child lives with fear, he learns to be apprehensive.
If a child lives with pity, he learns to feel sorry for himself.
If a child lives with ridicule, he learns to be shy…

And so on, for another thirteen or so lines in the same spirit. Inspiring at first, as you and your siblings grew the poem increasingly began to impose responsibilities upon me that I did not feel I had the power to fulfill. At times, it read as an indictment: If any of you turned out to be shy, envious, or impatient adults, the fear, ridicule, and intolerance of their mother would be thereby revealed. If you were harmed by water, hurt by fire, eaten by pookas, or gored by cows it would be my fault. So though you'll probably come across the poem on your own, I don't think I'm going to recommend it to you.

Chapter Seven

After Drew died, the State Police offered to let us keep his K-9, Rock, for a family pet.

We eagerly accepted: Rock had been part of the family, and although a 105-pound German shepherd is a bit of a handful, losing him would have added another loss to kids who'd had enough. Besides, Rock was trained. I could direct him to sit, stay, and search a field for a missing Wiffle ball, among other spiffy tricks, using hand gestures alone. Actually, though I didn't think of this at the time, knowing Rock was trained to signal the presence of illicit drugs might have deterred unwise experiments on the part of some. But Rock was a working dog and, missing Wiffle balls aside, he was now suddenly jobless, the purposive adventures with his dear, departed master replaced by piddling boredom in the backyard.

During his training, Rock's inner wolf had been deliberately awakened and harnessed to the cause of officer protection. It was a role he took seriously. The officer might be gone but the wolf was not, and so, predictably, Rock mistook the mailman for a felon, and bit him.

Within minutes of my call, a State Police handler arrived and whisked Rock away. "What will become of Rock?" the kids asked mournfully. "They won't put him to sleep, will they?"

No, I assured them. A good friend and training partner of Drew's was a guard at the supermax prison. Rock would go to work with him, and live usefully and very happily ever after.

Is Marine Corps boot camp designed to, in effect, bring out the inner wolf in its recruits? Zach was one of the kindest people I knew, but he definitely had an inner wolf and I worried about the ways in which boot camp might awaken it irreversibly.

One afternoon when he was perhaps fourteen, Zach materialized before me out of a cloud of testosterone and, in a voice that veered violently between bass and soprano, made a truculent announcement: "I am going to watch *Gladiator*. Right now."

"C'mon, Zach," I said. "You know you can't watch movies in the middle of the week, and today is Wednesday. You are too young to watch an R-rated movie, and even if I allowed you to see this one on the grounds that it is somehow historical, your siblings are making forts out of the living room furniture, and they definitely are not going to be watching *Gladiator*, today or ever."

Zach exploded. To the best of my recollection, his remarks ran along time-honored lines — *You're stupid, I hate this family, all my friends get to watch R-rated movies whenever they want.*

I would, occasionally, allow a decision to be changed by a child's reasoned argument, but this rant did not qualify.

"You're being ridiculous," I said, and ranted back: "*Knock it off! Stop shouting at me! What's the matter with you! Go to your room!*" And at some point during this unhelpful mutual tantrum, Zach hit me.

He didn't hit me hard. Like Rock, who could've taken the mailman's leg off, this was a mere nip, a feeble half-punch aimed at my shoulder while his expression slid miserably between defiance and shame. But by closing his hand and striking me, Zach triggered this response: *My son must not become a man who hits women.*

Next thing we knew, I was gripping him by the front of his sweatshirt, and he was off the ground, pinned against the wall, his sneakers dangling above the floorboards. Baring my teeth like one of the more unprepossessing cinematic psycho-killers, I hissed, "If you ever hit me again, if you hit any woman, ever, I will kill you. Do you understand me?"

A sharp awareness of the mind's capacity to entertain more than one line of thought at a time is a curious feature of any stressful moment. Even as my hand closed around the fabric of his shirt and my biceps contracted to lift him, I was pondering my own hypocrisy as well as wondering whether my injunction ought to be more inclusive: I didn't want Zach hitting men or children, either.

Never mind: I, the liberal Democrat, ordained minister, certified nice-person, and tenderhearted mother, had literally threatened my own son with murder.

As soon as I let him go, Zach ran off to his room, and the scene ended leaving us shaken and bewildered, still angry, and yet already sick with regret. For years, whenever I thought about this confrontation, I would cringe, appalled by the violence I had visited upon my son.

CHAPTER EIGHT

The church had white clapboards and a splendid spire, box pews, and tall, shining, clear glass windows. Inside, the old plaster walls were painted a soft, robin's-egg blue. The place was so pretty, I briefly entertained a fantasy of being a real church minister...but I was just a guest in the pulpit on a winter Sunday, filling in for the regular pastor, who had the day off.

Before I could be introduced to give the sermon, the normal weekly business of the congregation was dealt with: announcements of the Lenten prayer schedule, news from the committee in charge of finding a replacement for Pastor Frank (long serving, long loved, and soon to be honorably retired), plus an enlivening hymn, and the lesson for the children.

The church's religious education teacher—young and full of vim—bounded to the front of the sanctuary. She bore a large basket containing props that she swiftly decanted onto the altar table: a cardboard Ark, twinned sets of plastic animals, and a plastic Mr. and Mrs. Noah who were, perhaps, six inches tall. I don't know about anyone else, but this Mr. and Mrs. Noah did not conform at all to my mental image of the original Survivors. Noah's tunic was open to his sternum, displaying tanned pecs (though no bling); Mrs. Noah was white-haired but pert-breasted. The pair looked like retiree versions of the action figures my kids played with when they were little.

The Graying of the Mainstream Liberal Church being what it is, there was only one child on hand to hear the teacher's story. He was about five and, evidently well-trained, he marched up the aisle when the lesson was announced and waited dutifully while the teacher set up the Ark and positioned Mr. and Mrs. Noah in welcoming attitudes on either side of the plastic gangplank.

Then the little boy agreed to line the animals up two by two while she read the story of the Flood out loud. When at last, "in the seventh month, on the seventeenth day of the month, the Ark came to rest on top of Mount Ararat," the religious educator pulled the final surprise out of her basket — six long, brilliantly colored strips of silk attached to a dowel, which the little boy was given to wave above the scene. This he did with vigor, and the plastic doves were knocked off the Ark roof before he got the hang of making the silk ribbons float and dance in the air.

"What a beautiful rainbow! The rainbow represents God's promise," the religious educator announced. "Isn't that wonderful?"

"Yah!" said the little boy, and flailed the ribbons enthusiastically.

"God is promising that he will never, ever destroy the whole world again...Well," she amended, "not by flooding, anyway."

The little boy looked at her expectantly, still waving the rainbow above his head.

"From 2 Peter 3:7, we Christians know," the teacher went on brightly, "that by the same word the present heavens and earth are reserved for fire, being kept for the Day of Judgment and destruction of ungodly men."

The little boy was looking puzzled, and the silk ribbons had settled to the floor by his feet, so the religious educator wisely decided to end the lesson there. "You did a good job with the rainbow, Evan! I hope you'll remember that story. Now, let's help the adults sing the next hymn, and then you can bring Mr. and Mrs. Noah and all the animals to our Sunday school classroom!"

So we sang the hymn, and then the little boy helped his teacher push all the animals back into the basket. She led the way out of the sanctuary, and he skipped along behind her, holding Mrs. Noah up in the sky so the matriarch could fly, to the accompaniment of airplane noises, good and loud.

Considered with detachment, the stories we tell our

children—whether scriptural or secular—are frequently weird. Planted like scattered seeds, some set roots and later bloom, often in unanticipated ways.

One rainy afternoon, for instance, my friend Tonya and I took our small children to see the film version of one of my favorite childhood books, *Harriet the Spy*.

What I would have good reason to recall from this occasion was the single serving of Coca-Cola contained in a plastic cup the size of a beer keg that the children somehow persuaded us to let them share as a treat. As promised, they shared nicely, passing the cup hand to hand, up and down their row for the duration of the movie. Predictably (though obviously, Tonya and I hadn't predicted it), they would all come down with an identical, disgusting stomach virus within the week.

What Zach remembered, however, was my explanation of a bit of mysterious movie dialogue. He was only nine, so when one of the girls on screen said dismissively of another, "Oh, well, she spent the summer growing breasts," he leaned over to his mother and whispered, "*What does that mean?*"

Bored by the movie, and inclined to mischief, I whispered, "When a girl decides she wants to have breasts, she collects chicken bones and grinds them up into a smoothie with milk, daisy petals, and fresh raspberries. She drinks some of it every day until her breasts grow."

Zach went back to watching the movie, and I went back to enriching Tonya's cinema experience with my muttered critique.

More than two years later, Zach came home from his first day in sixth grade and earnestly informed me that the girls in his class had been doing that chicken bone and daisy-petal thing.

It took a long time to figure out what the hell he was talking about, and while Tonya laughed herself down to the carpet when she heard about it, I felt horribly guilty. For my own, mindless entertainment I'd thrown out a bit of what I imagined to be obviously outré satirical humor. But young children don't really get outré satire, sarcasm, or irony. What other cleverness and falsehoods had been taken in as gospel and now lay implanted in my children's little psyches?

A few more indeed bloomed over the years: Peter came home fuming after an argument with the elementary school music teacher because she was teaching the kids to sing "There Is Nothing Like a Dame" for a school concert of Broadway show tunes. Though I had forgotten it, at some point I persuaded my kids that this was a hymn of Danish patriotism: *There is nothing like a Dane...nothing in the world...there is nothing you can name that is anything like a Dane...*

"My teacher thinks *everything* has to be about love and women," was Peter's scornful conclusion.

The late British naturalist and prolific author Gerald Durrell wrote delightful memoirs about his lifelong and very happy obsession with animals. His books were favorites of mine, passed down to and enjoyed by my children in their turn. Taken in sequence, Durrell's books reveal his developing understanding of the modern zoo as not merely a house of curiosities for people to gawk at, but as a critical tool in the effort to thwart animal extinctions. The metaphor he uses is that of Noah's Ark. For Durrell, a modern zoo can be a "stationary Ark" that offers refuge to breeding stocks of endangered species and, potentially at least, might permit restocking of native ecosystems.

Given who and what I am, I react to the story of Noah's Ark by resisting its murderous characterization of God. But for Durrell the story was a useful inspiration and parable for his life's work.

On the Sunday I spent at the white clapboard church (the day little Evan heard the story of Noah's Ark from his religious education teacher), I offered a sermon on the Parable of the Good Samaritan. As the following Monday was Martin Luther King Day, I quoted Dr. King's last speech, in which he, too, talked about the Good Samaritan.

King used the parable to illustrate "dangerous unselfishness," a sacred inclination that can't be confined to the lofty plane of philosophy and theology King called "mid-air" but must be worked out on the ground, where — though Dr. King didn't actually use the phrase — the theological rubber meets the road.

He said: "[T]he first question that the Levite asked was, 'If I stop to help this man, what will happen to me?' But then the Good Samaritan came by, and he reversed the question: 'If I do not stop to help this man, what will happen to him?' That is the question before you tonight."

At the time, Dr. King was exhorting his listeners to support the Memphis Sanitation Workers' strike, but I don't think he would mind that I chose another historical episode by which to illustrate the principle. For my (Danish-American) family, the rescue of the Danish Jews is a parable.

Before they were old enough to hear the true, historical version, my kids were told the young'uns legend.

"When the Nazis told King Christian that all the Jews in Denmark must wear the yellow star, King Christian obeyed... but followed this decree with another of his own: 'All citizens in Denmark, including the king, must wear a yellow star!' And so the Jews of Denmark remained safe, for they were hidden in the sea of stars now proudly worn by all the Danish people and their king," I triumphantly concluded, before leading my children in a chorus of that old, patriotic Danish hymn, "There Is Nothing Like a Dane."

The children's story is apocryphal, but it contains the essence of the truth.

In the spring of 1940, Nazi Germany invaded Denmark. Shots were fired — but not many. The Danish army was in no condition to resist the armies of the invincible German Reich. Its constitutional monarchy, led by King Christian X, capitulated almost immediately.

Denmark would be known as a "model protectorate" of the German state: the Danish government remained in place as a reward for surrender. More to the point, the Danes were permitted to be a little *peculiar* when it came to the eight thousand or so Danish Jews.

"First a human being, then a Christian: this alone is life's order," Denmark's greatest and most influential theologian, N. F. S. Grundtvig, had written more than a century before. "People are bound to one another with ties more profound than any of the barriers human history, including the history of religion, may have constructed."

Danish culture, long infused with Grundtvig's ecumenical spirit, enabled Danes who might profoundly disagree on other issues to speak in virtual unanimity on the matter of Jewish Danes. Speaking through king, parliament, and church, the Danes insisted that their Jewish countrymen must remain unmolested.

Astonishingly, the Germans acquiesced. No yellow stars, no separation and isolation, no confiscation of property or dismissal from jobs: in Denmark, Jews were subject to none of the harsh, oppressive measures imposed (and acceded to) in every other occupied country. The unusual arrangement persisted for some three and a half years.

At last, however, the provocations of the Danish Resistance became more than the Germans could take. They imposed draconian measures on the populace, the Danish government promptly resigned, and a secret order for the liquidation of Denmark's Jews was sent from Berlin.

The liquidation order was intercepted by a German cultural attaché by the memorable name of Duckwitz. Duckwitz

222

(described by witnesses as "trembling with shame") met with members of the erstwhile Danish government to warn them. In turn, the Danish leadership warned leaders of the Jewish community.

What could they do? Where would they hide? How could they leave, and where would they go?

The short answer was this: the Danish gentiles hid the Danish Jews. And the Danish gentiles brought them—almost all of them—across the water to Sweden.

Danes of all descriptions—men and women, old and young, rich and not so rich—participated in the rescue. Once word got out that the deportation of the Jews was scheduled to commence, Danish Jews found themselves accosted in the streets by strangers who thrust the keys to apartments and summer houses into their hands, offered spare bedrooms, or sofas, attics or cellars, food, money, and transport.

There was an ambulance driver who drove around Copenhagen with an open telephone book in his lap, looking up the addresses listed beside Jewish-sounding names, and offering the occupants a ride to the hospital, where hundreds of Jewish Danes were being tucked into bed as "patients" or disguised as nurses, doctors, or orderlies.

Meanwhile, the fishing and pleasure fleets of this seagoing country, their holds stuffed with a frightened human cargo, had begun to navigate the waters between Denmark and Sweden.

Within two weeks, nearly all of Denmark's Jewish population was safely beyond the reach of German persecutors.
About five hundred Jews were captured and deported from
Denmark to the Theresienstadt ghetto in Czechoslovakia,
but owing largely to persistent protests from their government, these Danish inmates were never sent from Theresienstadt to the death camps, as most others would be.

To understand the scope of what has been called the
Danish Miracle of October 1943, it helps to consider the fol-
lowing somber list of estimates of the Jewish victims of the
Holocaust from Nazi-occupied Europe:

Between 7,000 and 8,000 Italian Jews were murdered by
the Nazis.

Austria, Bohemia, Bulgaria, and Greece each lost roughly
50,000 to 75,000 Jewish men, women, and children.

France — 77,000.

The Netherlands — 100,000.

The Germans murdered 100,000 of their own.

Lithuania lost 140,000; the Soviet Union, 1 million.

Poland? Three million.

The nation of Denmark lost a total of 60.

"*Six zero?*" asked a parishioner from the pew in the clapboard church, making sure he'd heard correctly.

"Six zero," I confirmed.

A skinny fourth grader once asked me the same question,
in just that way: "Six zero?"

On that occasion, I was telling the story of the Danish

rescue of the Danish Jews—or Jewish Danes—to my son Peter's social studies class. The story held them spellbound for forty-five minutes, at the end of which this little blond guy had allowed as how he was a lobsterman.

"I'll bet I could fit all kinds of Jews in my lobster boat and hide 'em out on Matinicus Island!" he said stoutly, and my eyes unexpectedly filled with tears.

It would be easy to imagine that the Danish Miracle was accomplished by people with superior genes—Danish genes, that is, versus German ones. But that is not the case, as shifting borders have rendered Danish and German genes virtually identical. This is what makes the story of the rescue of the Danish Jews such a perfect repudiation to Nazism in particular, and racism more generally: those who demonstrated moral courage were, broadly speaking, genetically identical to those who failed so catastrophically to do so.

"It has been said that if we were putting together a Bible today, the story of the Danish rescue of the Danish Jews would be included in it," I told the congregation of the clapboard church. They seemed impressed. Still, it is only when the one who hears the tale recognizes himself in it and acts, that the illuminating power of a parable is revealed.

"Mom, I need thread!" cried Zach.

My eleven-year-old son was rummaging through my sewing basket.

"What for?"

"I need it to sew a patch..."

"Here," I said, reaching past him to pluck the thread from its place. "What do you mean, you need a patch? Did you get a hole in your pants?" Not that holes had ever bothered him before, but he was in sixth grade now, and who knew what sartorial standards tweenie culture had imposed?

"It's not that," said Zach. "The other boys at school have been hassling kids they think are gay. And they use 'gay' as an insult when they think someone is stupid or lame. So I'm going to sew this rainbow patch onto my book bag."

"But that rainbow patch is a symbol for homosexuality," I said, unintelligently.

"Right."

"If you sew that onto your book bag, the kids are going to hassle you."

"Right," Zach repeated, and then added, helpfully, "They're *really* mean about this, Mom."

An uneasy roiling had begun in the pit of my stomach.

Zach, one eye squinched shut and his tongue protruding from the corner of his mouth, was trying to thread a needle. "Can you help me?"

Memories sputtered in my mind like fat in a pan...gruesome scenes of middle school...hadn't my own utter unpopularity begun in sixth grade?

It might have had something to do with my tendency to emit rhetorical flourishes only a dad could love, or even the fact that I still, occasionally, wet my pants. Or it might have been because adolescent girls can be real turds. All I know is that it was in defense of no brave principle that I'd sat alone in the cafeteria while the other girls giggled and whispered behind their hands, rolling their eyes in the classic manner of aggressive femininity.

"Mom?"

I swallowed hard and handed him a thimble.

CHAPTER NINE

While most religious traditions follow a standard lectionary or at least expect the minister to read from the Bible, the Unitarian Universalist worship-leader can choose passages from any of the world's religious writings and from secular sources, too.

However, I studied at a Christian seminary, and so it is images and stories from Jewish and Christian sacred literature that are ingrained and thus leap to mind whenever I ponder life's persistent questions.

War definitely poses a few of these, even if your son isn't planning to join the Marines. Unlike some other issues so vexing to modern life (global warming, euthanasia, the obesity epidemic), when it comes to war and warriors, the Bible has a lot to say. You don't have to resort to drawing inferences or finding metaphors when consulting the Good Book on the subject unless, of course, you're hoping to prove that God is a pacifist.

When atheists mount an attack on the moral values of Scripture, they are inclined to cite stories like this one: after Joshua fought the Battle of Jericho and the walls came tumblin' down, every man, woman, child, and animal in the city was slaughtered by Joshua's army as a thank-you gift to God.

In what was probably a bit of boastful exaggeration, Joshua reported the number of "civilian dead" at thirty thousand. Only after his troops were defeated at Ai did Joshua pause to wonder whether he was acting in strict accordance with God's wishes. He concluded that God objected not to wholesale murder, but to Joshua's habit of consorting with people of other faith traditions.

In Christian hagiography, Joshua is not repudiated: indeed, Joshua—the name is pronounced *Yeshua* in Hebrew, and *Jesus* in Greek—is considered a precursor of his namesake.

But these days, even the most excitable old-school Judeo-Christian is unlikely to suggest that, having conquered Baghdad, American troops should turn the place into an abattoir in God's honor. The closest anyone will come is to suggest, in the aftermath of some grim disaster, that God performed His own bit of butchery, for reasons the cognoscenti can not only accurately discern but must enthusiastically endorse.

After 9/11, for instance, Reverend Jerry Falwell held a televised conversation with his fellow Christian evangelist Pat Robertson in which he blamed "...the pagans and the abortionists and the feminists and the gays and the lesbians and the ACLU" for setting the scene for the still-unfolding carnage at the World Trade Center and at the Pentagon. Reverend Robertson concurred. As another paid-up member of a worldwide fundamentalists' interfaith consensus, Osama bin Laden affirmed that, along with the objections he had to U.S. Middle East policy, he also disliked our "separation of religion from policies" and our "immoral acts of fornication, homosexuality, intoxicants and gambling." And though he left out the civil libertarians, bin Laden nonetheless confirmed that America is a "despicable" state and "the worst civilization witnessed by the history of mankind."

We religious professionals are allowed, are even expected, to wax theological about anything and everything: weather, pop culture, great art, literature, music, history, anthropology, astronomy, sociology, paleontology, biology, neurology, medicine, politics, statistics—no fact of life can be excluded from the discussion of that which creates, sustains, and redeems it. Everything must arise in the course of our discourses. Everything must be examined through the lens of faith.

Admittedly, the lens of faith can distort as much as it reveals. Hard facts can (and should) be used to scrape that lens clean, or even carve and refine its shape so that it may transmit and refract more light.

"If I have to receive another folded flag on behalf of a grateful nation," I warned Sergeant Sangster, in one of my more histrionic arguments against my son's enlistment, "I'm going to fling it across the friggin' room."

"Mom!" the kids chorused, genuinely shocked.

"Well, no, I won't," I conceded.

This was the plain, hard fact that was scraping painfully against my faith: if I had once worried that Zach's rainbow patch would make him a target in sixth grade, what would an American uniform do for him in Iraq?

Sangster-rhymes-with-gangster was hanging out at our house quite a lot by this point. As part of the requirements for the Marine Corps Delayed Entry Program, Zach met with his recruiter weekly, and attended meetings with the other would-be Marines from around the state. Sangster would pick Zach up at our house, often arriving in plenty of time to share our lunch. I would give the man soup and a hard time.

"I'm a patriot."

"Yes, ma'am."

"And I'm proud of Zach."

"Yes, ma'am."

"Me, too," said Woolie, while Ellie confessed that her brother's enlistment had set a new standard to which the other boys and young men were now held...and found wanting.

"They talk about stupid things," she said. "About how wasted they were at the party last night, or how drunk they're planning to get on Saturday. Compared with Zach, they just seem so selfish."

While she was proud of her brother, this wasn't an entirely comfortable realization. She was speaking of her friends, classmates, and cousins.

"It's not even that they have chosen not to go," Ellie said. "They don't even *think* of it."

I empathized: their parents weren't thinking of it, either, even the ones who declared themselves in favor of the war(s).

As a Marine, Zach could be deployed to either of our wars. Why, then, when Sangster told me that the Marines might send my son to language school, did I tell Zach to opt for Pashto rather than Arabic? Why did my anxiety focus so much more on Iraq than Afghanistan? All the risks he faced in one war were present in the other: death or serious injury, the risk of witnessing horrors, the risk of exposure to moral wounds.

I wasn't the only one. I'd discovered a website for the Proud Parents Of Marines, and in the chat rooms many admitted that the war in Afghanistan made a little more sense to them than the conflict in Iraq. Osama bin Laden had launched an attack against innocent Americans from Afghanistan. It was Afghanistan where he was being sheltered, and the Taliban (who had already buggered their chance of getting sympathy from me by oppressing women and blowing up ancient statues of Buddha) refused to spit him out.

Still, to express a preference for a child's risking his life and mortal soul in Afghanistan rather than Iraq felt either obviously natural or seriously warped. Maybe the other Proud Parents and I were unconsciously bargaining with the gods: *Okay, you can have our kids if you promise to send them to a war we understand.* As if it were our bargain to make.

In an attempt to ensure that Zach knew what he might be getting into, I gave him a reading list (Tim O'Brian, Thomas Ricks, Michael Herr, James Webb, Winston Churchill). Some of the books made going to war sound exciting and noble; others described it as a dull and pointless hell. Zach was going to do this with his eyes wide open, but, unfortunately, that meant my eyes had to be open, too.

Denial has a long pedigree as the principal ally of anyone who would send other people's children into combat, and while it's harder to deny the obvious when it's your own kid, we Proud Parents did our best. "The statistics are with us," one communicant on a website assured himself and the rest of us one day. "Relatively few troops die in combat these days. The chances are excellent that our kids are going to be just fine."

My father, who died the year after Drew did, was buried with military honors at Arlington National Cemetery in a ceremony that the Maine State Police obsequies closely resembled. (The kids would be perplexed and disappointed by their great-grandmother's memorial service, held a few years after that: where were the uniformed men marching, the twenty-one-gun salute, and the folded flag?)

Dad was sixty-eight, young by modern standards. He died of a heart attack, and though the stress he endured as a combat marine and, later, as a war correspondent almost certainly contributed to his death (there is abundant evidence linking traumatic stress with cardiac disease and other illnesses), visiting Dad's white marble marker does not provoke the terrible, tender ambivalence of these:

JUSTIN DAVIS
1987–2006
KEMAPHOOM A. CHANWONGSE
1981–2003
PRINCESS C. SAMUELS
1985–2007

Their graves are found in Section 60, the part of Arlington National Cemetery where the dead from Iraq and Afghanistan are buried amid that vast, undulating sea of graves.

From a distance, the headstones are identical as Chiclets gleaming white in the sun. Closer up, diversity is discernible in what is called the "emblem of belief" inscribed at the top of each stone. Sixty symbols have been approved by the United States Department of Veterans Affairs including, most recently, the Wiccan Pentacle. In Section 60, I found stones engraved with the Crescent and Star of Islam, the Star of David, the Hindu Ohm, and the Buddhist Wheel, plus a Humanist "reaching-human" sprinkled among the Christian crosses in all their denominational variety.

I imagined thousands and thousands of mothers and fathers—Christian, Muslim, Buddhist, Jewish, Hindu, Humanist—all crushed to the Virginia turf by grief. Some would address their prayers to God by any of God's theonyms

(Allah, Shangdi, Gitche Manitou), while the yearning thoughts of atheists and secular rational materialists drifted eastward across the Potomac to where the White House, the Library of Congress, or maybe the Natural History Museum might hold answers.

What do we want for our children?

Not this.

Dad was too young to serve in the Second World War, but he spent his boyhood Saturdays playing at military drills with the neighborhood kids, and his evenings lying on the living room carpet, listening to the war news and marking out Allied positions on large maps of Europe and the Pacific.

After graduating from college, Dad joined the Marine Corps. There was a draft in those days, but for young men who wished to avoid service in Korea (as in Vietnam, a generation later), there were ways to get out of active duty. My father's combination of poor eyesight and chronic, serious psoriasis would almost certainly have excused him on medical grounds.

As the first-generation son of Danish immigrants, Dad had the new American's fierce patriotism, plus the old-fashioned conviction that when one's country calls, the relatively privileged should be the first to respond.

So when my bespectacled, twenty-two-year-old future father spotted his medical report among the other papers on the Marine recruiter's desk, he held it aloft: "Would you get in trouble if this particular piece of paper disappeared from my file?"

And the Marine (whom I now pictured as closely resembling Sergeant Sangster) replied, laconically: "Paperwork gets lost all the time."

Off Dad went to Parris Island and then to Korea where, presumably, he shot at people and/or (as a first lieutenant) ordered others to shoot. One night, a grenade landed in his foxhole and blew up. He survived, though it was a near thing. For years, Dad would entertain his kids by rolling up his shirtsleeve to show us where a piece of Chinese shrapnel could still be seen, shifting back and forth beneath his skin.

Dad had gotten to know many young Marines and soldiers through his manifold associations with war and warriors. Though my friends tease me about my "uniform fetish," I know that my instinctive sense of kinship for law enforcement officers is a gift originally bestowed on me by Dad, who loved his Corps.

How odd it is to realize that young strangers—Justin, Kemaphoom, and Princess—would have important things in common with my father, stories to share and ways of understanding, should they all happen to meet at that great, overcrowded VFW in the sky.

I believe that my father would have been deeply moved by Zach's desire to serve, and proud, even if—knowing war as intimately as he did—ambivalence would also have been in the mix. More than this, though, Dad would have found comfort and comradeship in meeting his grandson on this new, common ground.

"I miss Morfar more now than ever," Zach told me.

"I'll bet you do, Zackie."

"I want to get together with him and talk about being a Marine."

"Yes," I said, with a lump in my throat. "He would have enjoyed that very much."

Dad did not play in the sandbox with me when I was little, and while I could blame this on the fact that I was not a "lad" (even then, Dad was the only person I knew who used the word), the simplest explanation was that he was gone. In the mid-1960s, Dad was covering the war in Vietnam for the *Washington Post.*

My mother, sister, brother, and I stayed in Thailand because it was as close as Dad wanted us to be to the action. Dad caught military flights home to Bangkok on odd weekends, bearing odder gifts (he brought me a Viet Cong entrenching tool and a handful of spent bullets), and in between, he sent postcards from "Lovely! Lively! Saigon!"

Thailand didn't have a war going, and we got to have a monkey for a pet, a perk that makes my children groan with envy. The climate was very hot and humid except during the rainy season, when it would be slightly less hot but even more humid. Plus, in those days, at least, Thailand was really germy.

We had all been immunized to within an inch of our lives before leaving the United States, but once a month or so, my mother would nonetheless have to take my sister, brother, and me to have cholera boosters.

Plenty of American expatriates went to the American

Embassy for their shots, but Dad's journalistic principles declared that a reporter shouldn't receive extra favors from the government whose actions he was reporting on, lest this compromise his real or perceived neutrality. So instead of joining the other ex-pat families at the Embassy, my mother took us to the Snake Farm for our immunizations.

The Snake Farm was, actually, a snake farm: it held captive specimens of Thailand's many poisonous snakes. These would periodically have their mouths "milked" to obtain the venom from which antivenom was manufactured. In the middle of the Snake Farm's green grounds was a yellow brick building, and there, once a month, bright and early, a Chinese doctor and a Swedish nurse would set up shop at one end of a long, sunny auditorium.

The doctor would seat himself on a folding chair before the floor-to-ceiling windows that looked out onto a verdant lawn dotted with palms. The nurse stood next to a little enameled table upon which she'd placed a number of glass vials and a pan full of those old-fashioned, gleaming steel syringes.

The clients—mostly mothers and children—who were waiting outside the door would be ushered in, and we would line up first-come-first-serve around the perimeter of the room. At a signal from the nurse, the first child in line would step forward, the nurse would fill a syringe and hand it to the doctor, the doctor would jab the needle into the kid's arm, and firmly depress the steel plunger.

The needle had to be large, because cholera serum is

thick. The shot was slow, and it hurt like hell. The first kid's eyes would go wide and round with shock and his mouth would open very wide. Screams would spill forth, and all the kids in the room would begin screaming, too, in terrified sympathy.

It did us no good to scream, nor to weep and beg. We had to have our shots. With my baby brother on her right hip, Mom would have her shot first, to show us that it really wasn't all that bad. Her bright, game smile would buckle into a grimace when the doctor pressed the plunger down. Then Mom would have to shift my howling brother to her now-aching left arm. She couldn't put him down or else he'd bolt for the door on his fat little toddler legs, and she needed all the strength of her right arm to drag my older sister forward for her turn.

I did not bolt, nor did I have to be dragged. I would march forward, jaw clenched, to present my naked tricep to the doctor and his needle. This was a courage born of sibling rivalry: As the oldest, my sister had assumed all the good roles in the family before I was even born. She was the smart one, the polite one, and the one who did well in school. My brother was the baby, and a boy.

If I couldn't be good or male, I would be brave. I still have (and, secretly, still prize) the picture book my mother bought after one of these Snake Farm days, inscribed in her handwriting: *To Katie, who was the Bravest Braestrup, November 20th, 1967.* And my mother told my father about it, too, when he came home from Vietnam. He was proud of me.

When the nightmare was over, for the month anyway, we got to have a tall glass of a Kool-Aid–like beverage we called Jubidee Goose and take a tour of the Snake Farm. Rubbing our aching arms, we would peer, fascinated, down into concrete pits filled with cobras and kraits, before visiting the bamboo cage containing Suzie, the Burmese Python. Suzie was thirty feet long and very beautiful. You could reach through the bamboo bars and stroke her smooth, shiny skin. Sometimes there was a bump in her that used to be a chicken.

Slapping a bowl of vegetarian chili onto the table in front of Sangster, I said, "I'm proud of my father's courage."

"Ooo-rah, ma'am," he replied, picking up a spoon.

"But I don't think much of your commander-in-chief."

"Mom…" said Zach.

"I don't always agree with the president, either, ma'am," said Sangster smoothly. "I serve a country, not a person."

At the tender age of seventeen, my father-in-law, Drew's dad, volunteered to serve his country and spent months in a submerged cigar-tube being depth-charged by the Japanese. During the same period, my maternal grandfather, a forty-four-year-old father of five, was in the thick of naval combat at Leyte Gulf.

Then there's my dad who (like George W. Bush) graduated from Yale but then (unlike George W. Bush) enlisted for the combat service he, too, could so easily have avoided.

Explaining this to Sangster, I could see triumph in his smile.

The standard the president had failed to meet was the standard set by the men of my family, the standard my son was enlisting to live up to. *Damn.*

Simon's parents immigrated to the United States from Holland, and his father arrived after having endured the German occupation, the last months of which were made even more miserable by food shortages so acute that Simon's dad was given tulip bulbs to eat. Though Simon's relatives have been noncombatants as far back as anyone can recall, they nonetheless remember and honor the American troops who arrived to liberate the Netherlands.

On our first trip to Holland, Simon and I visited Margraten, near the southern city of Maastricht, to see the Netherlands American Cemetery and Memorial. Yet more rows of white tablets, inscribed with names and emblems of belief: Simon and I made a point of seeking out the guys from Maine among the over 8,300 Americans buried there.

Even in a search made cursory by a downpour, we found quite a few familiar Maine surnames: Bernier, Sirois, Stackpole. It wasn't hard at all to picture the mother of Army Sergeant Leverett L. Young (Plot J, Row 19, Grave 22) standing in the doorway of an Aroostook County farmhouse holding a telegram from the War Department ("We regret to inform you...") in her hand. There's no real reason to imagine Sergeant Young as a farm boy; he could as easily have been the son of a doctor or a state senator. In his war, everyone was called to serve.

It is not true as is sometimes claimed that nowadays

most, or even many, of the soldiers we send into harm's way are poor people whose desperation recruiters are wont to take advantage of. For any number of reasons, the very poor often fail to meet the minimum requirements in terms of health, education, criminal history, and drug use, though admittedly such standards tend to slacken a bit when the economy is robust and offers more alternatives or when America has overextended itself by fighting wars in Afghanistan and Iraq simultaneously, for example. Also contrary to popular belief, minorities comprise a smaller percentage of the military population than of the general population (as, less surprisingly, do women).

There are certainly financial motivations for military service. But the Army, Navy, Air Force, Marine Corps, and Coast Guard offer additional attractions for young men and women, not the least of which is the chance to participate in one of the few remaining institutions in American life in which words like "service," "honor," and "courage" are used without irony. I know this was one of the attractions for Zach.

One evening, Zach and I were invited to attend an informational meeting offered to the parents of would-be Marines by our local recruiting office and the VFW.

Backs sagging into curves carved by too much time spent before a screen, our kids did their best to stand at attention. They gasped their way through maybe a half-dozen push-ups, while an impeccable, steel-spined, bona fide Parris Island drill instructor rapped out orders.

It was the quality of the drill instructor's voice that struck me—literally struck me: each word had a palpable, percussive impact, a thud beneath my sternum.

How long does it take a drill instructor to learn that voice? I wondered. And how much time in the presence of that voice will be required before the sweetness in my son's soul is drummed right out of him?

Zach was given a Marine Corps Frisbee to take home with him. I imagined it whirling across our backyard, the motto spinning like the prayer in a Buddhist's prayer wheel:

... *Thechangeisforeverthechangeisforeverthechangeisforever*...

"I'm not a pacifist," I explained to the drill instructor as the informational meeting broke up. "And my father was a Marine. But my son..."

He smiled pleasantly at me.

"You see," I said helplessly, "Zach is a very special boy."

To his credit, the drill instructor did not laugh. Nor did he say what was true, which is that the United States Marine Corps, and indeed the whole of the U.S. military, is chockfull of very special boys and girls.

"He'll be a good Marine," he agreed, in a friendly, normal, human voice.

CHAPTER TEN

During the three years or so that our family lived in Thailand, my siblings and I often glimpsed the bald and barefoot Buddhist monks wandering past in their saffron robes, but it wasn't just the monks who were Buddhists. The men and women my parents employed to keep house and manage daily life in Bangkok for us were Buddhists, too.

"Within yourself, foster a limitless concern for every living creature," Buddha said. So when our neighbor's gardener was chomped by one of Suzie-the-Python's relatives the gardener had found lurking in the backyard *klong,* or pond, the cooks, drivers, housekeepers, night watchmen, and laundry girls from all neighborhood dwellings gathered for an animated debate about whether killing the snake could be consistent with Buddhist ethics.

Mind you, the python had not just remained on the scene—it was still *attached* to the gardener. Because its teeth aimed backward, once it had embedded itself in the flesh of the gardener's forearm, the snake couldn't let go even if it wanted to. So the snake and the man sat there, eyeing each other unhappily, while the discussion went on around them.

At last it was decided that since the python was stuck and would die in any event, it could be sacrificed. Someone fetched a machete and chopped its head off. The gardener was taken to the clinic with the python's head—eyes still open in the traditional, basilisk glare—clamped to his arm. The head had to be completely disassembled by the doctors, and the teeth dug out one by one.

Had everyone involved been a Christian or, for that matter, an atheist, the ending of the story would have been the same: the snake decapitated, the human gardener's life and arm preserved. Yet the fact that the snake's life was considered valuable enough to demand a moral consensus before it was taken is impressive in its way, though of course the suffering of both reptile and gardener were prolonged by the exercise.

What a cynic might spot as a more recognizable religious impulse—namely, hypocrisy—was evident in the sale of animals at the Bangkok Sunday Market.

The Market was a sort of weekly street fair. My siblings and I were taken there to spend the *baht* we received as allowance and watch little Thai kids fly their kites. The kites swooped and clashed in the humid sky and snipped one another's strings with their tiny, cleverly affixed blades.

We often returned home with animals. Some were intended

to be kept as pets — we got a small white puppy at the Sunday Market whom I named Lacey (she died of distemper within a few weeks), and I recall at least a couple of bunnies, plus, of course, there was the monkey. But the majority of our live acquisitions were birds — red-ringed doves, Eurasian finches, flycatchers and kingfishers, selected from the stacks of fluttery, tweeting, cooing cages piled up in the bird seller's stall.

Mom wasn't the only customer. The freeing of a caged bird is considered good for a Buddhist's karma and so, our chauffer Chimoy explained, these creatures — captured in the wild, perhaps hundreds of miles away — were destined to be released in urban Bangkok.

Clicking her tongue disgustedly, my mother would select some especially dehydrated, damaged specimen to bring home and nurse back to health. Once she even brought home a tiny owl.

I don't know whether opening a cage door and letting an exhausted, starved kingfisher stagger free into polluted city air could make up for any specific form of moral lapse, but in Bangkok circa 1967 there were undoubtedly sins aplenty to be atoned for.

Was the monkey — a baby and also, technically, an ape — also supposed to be set free by his purchaser? If so, freedom would have been of little use to him without a mother.

A siamang gibbon, he had soft, gray fur framing an anxious, black face. He wore diapers and slept in a basket. He had long, long arms for holding on to his mother, and long digits on hands and feet for clinging to her fur.

I tried to teach him to walk on his hind legs, but he quickly grew tired of this and would swarm up my body and wrap his arms around my neck as his little, hand-like feet gripped the sweaty cotton waistband of my play dress. Falling was to be feared: gravity is no friend to the tiny primate.

Left over from our own monkey-times, this Moro reflex was one of the earliest urgent communications Zach offered as an infant. Feeling himself beginning to fall, he'd fling his little arms wide and gasping, grasping, would try vainly to find purchase in nonexistent fur. But the gesture did provoke a protective response even from so inexperienced a mother as I: pressing him to my chest, I'd murmur, *It's okay. Don't worry. Mama's got you.*

"Parental nurture offers an infant a foundational lesson in the availability and reliability of love," one of my seminary professors memorably intoned. "And it is thus his first experience of God."

Zach learned eventually to cope independently with gravity. The lessons along the way were punitive. If he toddled wrong, gravity whacked him in the head with the coffee table or scraped the skin off his knees with the concrete sidewalk.

Possibly in preparation for such exercises, Zach (and then each of his siblings in turn) discovered the ubiquitous mealtime game known as drop-the-spoon-and-watch-Mom-pick-it-up. An exercise in elementary physics as well as alimentary hygiene, it is punitive only for the parents.

Inquiring minds wanted to know: *If I drop the spoon, will it always head toward the floor or might it sometimes float up to the ceiling? How much dirt sticks to the applesauce on the spoon?* It was an investigation into other natural laws, as well: *How many times can I get Mom to pick up the spoon? Does Mom laugh when I drop it, or does it piss her off? Which reaction do I prefer?*

Parents provide the human infant with all kinds of foundational lessons. Drew and I often wished we could have been the sort of saintly parents whose every response to a child's experimental "cause" conveyed a perfectly modulated, peace-promoting, and truthful effect. Dorothy Law Nolte's poem — *if children live with this, they will be that* — had persuaded us that a child's mind is just so much fertile but empty soil and the parent sows all the seeds. We wanted to sow nothing but peace seeds and loving-kindness seeds. But we ended up scattering a few that looked more like this, too: *People get mad when you bite them.*

"If an adult were to seize another adult and slap him, it would be grounds for a charge of assault," I said to my husband once, after reading a polemic against spanking. The logic seemed unassailable, but Drew had just returned home from an exhausting shopping expedition with his toddler sons and seemed in the mood to assail.

"Well, if another adult came up to me at Shop 'n Save, screamed in my face, and buried his teeth in my arm, popping him one on his tiny butt would count as self-defense," he retorted, showing me the mouth-shaped bruise on his forearm.

I have friends who can honestly say they never spanked their children (I can't). And yet I've been present in their homes on occasions in which a child's behavior called for discipline, and I couldn't help but notice just how hard some of those little bottoms landed on the wooden seat of the time-out chair. Can there really be a parent capable of serene diplomacy when a toddler's sharp little teeth are embedded in her flesh?

It would be easier to hold our tempers if the lesson our children learned was guaranteed to be *big people don't have the right to push smaller people around*. But what if, instead, the child learns something like this: *A grown-up is a person anyone is allowed to abuse*. And if Mom holds her temper and Dad doesn't, might the child learn that a woman, in particular, must not or cannot defend herself from aggression, even the aggression of someone less than half her size?

"Why would any little girl want to grow up to be a mother?" my friend Tonya lamented, when some experts writing for *Mothering* magazine denounced even the time-out chair as "violence."

To cheer her up, I told Tonya about the pediatrician who advised us to deal with Zach's persistent bouts of wee-hours screaming by letting him "cry it out."

"If picking him up and holding him isn't working," the doctor said reasonably, "then you might as well see if he can find a way to soothe himself."

So when that night's rest was rent by anguished cries, Drew and I did not rush to retrieve Zach from his crib. Instead, we lay there, side by side in the darkness.

I was thinking: *The baby is crying because I'm a bad mother.*

Drew was thinking: *The baby is crying because the baby is an asshole.*

Tonya laughed, but then, she knew Drew and how devoted he was to his children. And one virtue of Drew's reaction was its implicit recognition that his son was a being separate from himself: was not my guilty anguish all about me?

Years later, I picked up a pamphlet in our pediatrician's waiting room entitled "Why Do Babies Cry?" I didn't have babies anymore, just kids, and the fact that I was out in the waiting room reading rather than present in the examining room argues that at least one of these was a teen. Yet I read that pamphlet cover to cover.

—◊◊◊—

It wasn't just diapers, crying, and Legos gone astray. Woolie was Baby Number Four and sheer experience had made her parents more relaxed about everything. But here's a question: if baby Woolie announces that she wants to join the Marines, will I be "relaxed" about that, too?

As soon as the idea occurs, I recoil in anticipatory dread, but this time it isn't only because Woolie is my child, nor even that she's the youngest. Watching the list of American combat fatalities scroll by at the end of the nightly news broadcast, I find I am jolted by the occasional Susan or Michelle amid the Jareds, Dustins, Brandons, and Shawns.

I grew up in the 1960s and '70s, when all soldiers were (as far as I knew) male, but I'm not convinced this is a merely generational divide. After all, it is only her male friends that Ellie measures against the standard of service set by her brother. For all my efforts to make every knights-and-dragons story gender neutral (even the Mutant Ninja Turtles were armored-up girls in drag!), Ellie does not consider her female friends weak or wanting because it doesn't occur to them that they should, or even could, enlist.

"You know," Simon observes. "This thing—Zach joining the Marines, that is—is really challenging. On many levels."

"It is, isn't it?" I say.

Dear Zach and Erin,

It turns out that, well, babies cry. Sometimes the crying makes sense: the kid is tired, or hungry, or overstimulated, or has a diaper pin stuck in him.

Your sister Woolie once screeched for twenty minutes before I figured out that one of her siblings had dropped a Lego down her diaper. (Once the Lego was extricated, she stopped.) If the baby goes on crying after you've checked all of the obvious things, it could be because…babies cry.

You, my darling firstborn son, cried a lot. Peter was a crier, too. When he came along, your father and I were awake so much at night that we began to drink a lot more coffee during the day, which might have had something to do with your breast-fed brother's jittery personality.

Ellie didn't cry much, or at least I don't remember her doing so, and Woolie's infancy is a total blank. I only remember the incident of the Lego in the diaper because your father was changing her diaper later that day, and he let Ellie demonstrate her budding math skills by counting the six small circular bruises the Lego left on Woolie's teeny patootie.

Having pulled that memory up in my mind, I can see your father vividly, seated on the living room floor, baby Woolie on a waterproof mat between his outstretched legs (we never bothered with a changing *table). He gathers Woolie's ankles in one expert hand and lifts her backside, sliding the diaper beneath her. He and Ellie keep up a friendly, nonsensical patter that distracts—indeed, enchants—the baby. Ellie counts the bruises—"one...two...free..."—and then Drew pins the diaper, snaps the onesie, and picks up both little girls in his arms and carries them into the kitchen.*

CHAPTER ELEVEN

One of the few promises Sergeant Sangster made as he ushered Zach through the process of joining "his" Marine Corps was that the Corps would teach my boy manners. I could only imagine what the Marines' methods of teaching etiquette to barely adult boys might be.

"He already has good manners," I snapped and Sergeant Sangster, caught out in what was clearly one of his more successful routine sales pitches, admitted that yes, he'd noticed that. My kids might not have always been perfectly, peacefully behaved, but they knew how to be polite. Ilona and Cobus have nice manners, too, which endeared their father to me that much more.

Teaching a small child to be polite doesn't actually take much effort, which is why even I managed to do it. "Please" and "thank you" enter the vocabulary as easily and naturally as other expressions by imitation, on one hand, and on the other by the discovery that if you don't attach a "please" to a request, the desired object will not be forthcoming. Reinforcement was provided by the reactions of strangers—waitresses, for example, who were so reliably and often profitably charmed by a tiny customer's lisped "fank 'ooo!" (Smiles! Lollipops! Extra dessert!) Should the child forget, a hissed reminder was sufficient prompt.

But were the hissed reminders more common and more threatening than I recall? Recently, my stepson, Cobus, and I were having supper together in a restaurant and he was ordering a (legal) beer. I hissed, *Say please,* as automatically as, en route to the pub, I had flung a protective arm across his chest when bringing the car to a sudden stop.

In 2004, while he was still in the process of persuading me to let him join the Marines, Zach gave a speech at my ordination ceremony, in which he assured the congregation that his soon-to-be Reverend Mother "is a good person, however terrifying and God-like she might seem when she is angry." Was Zach talking about the hissing or maybe the moment I lifted him by his shirt and threatened him with murder? A child's first experience of God doesn't come only through the parents' tender nurturance: the God of wrath and judgment will be in there, too.

Drew could demonstrate God-like wrathfulness a lot more impressively than I ever could, and he noticed more bad behavior than I did (my mind wanders and I miss a lot). When Drew was loud, he was very, very loud, and his expressions of displeasure were memorable. This meant that he didn't have to express displeasure all that often. After Drew died, I had to do a whole lot of hissing, screeching, and punishing to get moderations in my children's behavior that Drew could've gotten by raising his eyebrows. Maintaining the discipline necessary for all five of us to enjoy at least a minimum of peace and safety was very hard work. Failure seemed a distinct possibility. I don't remember being terrifying. I remember being *terrified*.

Drew had consistency, a loud voice, and those scary eyebrows, and I could hiss, quote Scripture, and screech, but no one does discipline like a Marine Corps drill instructor.

Well, and why not? I was merely a mother teaching children to be reasonably civilized citizens. To become a warrior, a young man must be trained in violence, through violence, for violence. To become a warrior, a young woman also has to be trained this way, but an American woman warrior is still comparatively rare. When we think of war, we don't generally think of women attacking women, but of men fighting men.

In an essay included in a collection entitled *What Makes a Man?* filmmaker Michael Moore writes: "In the past few centuries, things seem to have taken a fatal turn for our gender. As is our wont, we commenced work on a series of projects that stunk everything up and made a mess of our world. Women? They deserve none of the blame. They continued to bring life into this world; we continued to destroy it whenever we could. How many women have come up with the idea of exterminating a whole race of people?" I think we all know the answer.

Presumably, Moore is talking Hitler. Hitler's longtime comrade Elenore Baur participated in Hitler's early, bloody, and unsuccessful attempt to seize power by force that was known as the Beer Hall Putsch (for which she was honored with the Nazis' prestigious Blood Order). She helped found the National Socialist German Workers' Party (NSDAP/Nazis), and had a major role in the construction and administration of the Dachau concentration camp.

About 10 percent of concentration camp guards were women. Their behavior was no less brutal or sadistic than that of their male counterparts.

Though the Nazis were reactionary about gender roles, it was nonetheless women who, as nurses, carried out the euthanasia program aimed at eliminating the mentally ill and genetically suspect. It was women who, as secretaries in concentration camps and SS offices throughout the Reich, typed up the lists of murdered innocents and mailed them off to female secretaries in Berlin for tidy filing. Female teachers withdrew their nurturance and support from the Jewish children in their classrooms and administered lessons to the rest of the class in the scientific and moral legitimacy of racism. And it was wives and mothers who unpacked the crates of plundered goods that flowed in from the lands their menfolk conquered; women who, for the duration of the war, were able to feed their German families well on the spoils of war even as other European families went hungry. It was women who dressed their young in the wee clothes of murdered Jewish children.

When Linda Gordon, professor of history at the University of Wisconsin, reviewed Claudia Koonz's history of women in Nazi Germany, *Mothers in the Fatherland*, she discovered in it the "disturbing" and thus presumably novel message that "…women are *not* necessarily morally or emotionally superior to men…"

That italicized *not* is in Gordon's original, but that comforting modifier struck me: not *necessarily!* Even after reading an exhaustive, five-hundred-page study of all the ways German non-Jewish women endorsed, encouraged, acquiesced in, and profited by the Nazi movement, Professor Gordon inexplicably retained the hope that the moral and emotional superiority of the female sex might yet be legitimately postulated.

If, consciously or otherwise, you share Moore's assumptions or Gordon's hopes, you'll be surprised by how many American women were implicated at every level in the Abu Ghraib scandal.

Lynndie England wasn't the only female soldier standing around the bloodied concrete floor of Cellblock A. Sabrina Harman and Megan Ambuhl also smiled their pretty smiles at ugly acts. General Janis Karpinski was the commander of all detainee operations in Iraq, while Captain Carolyn Wood, fresh from a stint at Bagram air base in Afghanistan (she would have the dismal privilege of being featured in Alex Gibney's Oscar-winning documentary about detainee torture, *Taxi to the Dark Side*) is credited with writing General Ricardo Sanchez's famous memo authorizing various take-the-gloves-off interrogation "enhancements" for use at Abu Ghraib. One could legitimately include Secretary of State Condoleezza Rice in the list of implicated females, since Rice was certainly aware of the torture memos and aware, too, that there were big problems at Guantánamo Bay, Bagram, and Abu Ghraib.

When I mention the surprising number of women who, having been given the opportunity for full participation in the military, went on to take star roles in the Abu Ghraib abuse scandal, female friends get defensive.

"Well, but these were women who were trying to get by in a male environment," they insist. "They were trying to fit in."

"They weren't just trying. They were succeeding."

"Yeah, but you just know that they had had to prove themselves and show they were just as tough as the boys. They couldn't rock the boat!"

"Lynndie England claims she went along with the abuse because she didn't want Charles Graner to stop liking her."

"Well, okay, but wasn't she from sort of a deprived background? I mean, she was pretty powerless…"

Power is a relative thing. Compared to Condoleezza Rice, Lynndie England was indeed one of America's social weaklings. On the other hand, compared to the guy on the other end of the leash, she had all the power anyone could ask for.

*   *   *

At some point during the vivid, almost painfully beautiful autumn that followed 9/11, I received my fall issue of *Tricycle* magazine. *Tricycle* is published by and for American Buddhists and, though I am not a Buddhist, I usually find much that is interesting and useful within its pages. The occasional illustration of a monk in saffron robes reminds me agreeably of my childhood. Yet I had not been looking forward to this issue.

On the cover was a dark image of the twin towers. Inside, I knew I would find admonitions to peacefulness, nonviolence, acceptance, forgiveness of enemies, and probably that story about the Tibetan lama whose greatest fear was that he would forget to be compassionate toward his cruel Chinese captors.

I like acceptance and forgiveness, I like Tibetan lamas, but cops in New York, a few of whom I knew personally, were digging the remains of their comrades from the rubble of the World Trade Center. I just wasn't in the mood.

What I had forgotten, however, is that the editorial offices for *Tricycle* are located in lower Manhattan. The editors had been deeply, personally affected by that day. One of them, Stephen Batchelor, refrained from reiterating the old understandings, and refreshingly confessed to a new one. After decades as a Buddhist committed to nonviolence, he had watched police officers running past him in the streets, moving toward and not away from the place of greatest danger. He now understood that his ability to practice nonviolence without risking his life had been predicated on the willingness of the state — in the form of police officers and soldiers — to use violence to protect him. Batchelor recognized that our relationship with violence is considerably more complicated than we might wish.

Batchelor's insight could be expanded beyond the peaceful American Buddhist's dependence upon the protection of soldiers and police officers. We could recognize all kinds of ways in which gentle, peaceful people who wouldn't hurt a fly are in reality only allowing others to do the dirty work.

"War is not healthy for children and other living things" the bumper sticker from Another Mother For Peace declares. Well, but it depends on whose children and which living things, doesn't it?

Blowflies, rats, vultures, crows, and microbial saprophytes flourish during wartime, and viruses, too. The Spanish flu was delighted to exploit the unsanitary, crowded, and stressful living conditions created by World War I, and was soon luxuriating in a worldwide pandemic. In an especially disgusting scene in Günter Grass's novel *The Tin Drum,* a fisherman declares that the eels were especially fat and abundant after the war, with so many men lost at sea. War was not healthy for mariners, perhaps, but it was salubrious for eels.

More to the point, while the children of the conquered suffer, the children, grandchildren, and great-grandchildren of the victors prosper with their parents. Joshua's war was good for the children of Israel, not so good for young Canaanites.

My children grew up in a colonial house situated on a half acre of land. The house isn't just "colonial" in style; it was actually built when Maine was still part of the English colony of Massachusetts. It's old enough to retain vestiges of the eighteenth-century's version of a safe room. In what is now the living room, the walls were thickly reinforced between the beams with handmade bricks capable of stopping arrows during an Indian attack. Though the original floor has long since been replaced, it would have been equipped with a trapdoor leading to a tunnel, through which the colonial family could escape if Indians set the house on fire.

No record exists of a battle waged over the particular half acre we now refer to as "the backyard," but we can nonetheless be perfectly certain of who won. European-American men forcibly wrested all the land in the vicinity from Passamaquoddy and Micmac men. European-American wives and children waxed fat at the expense of their Native American counterparts and, numerous as stars, continue to do so down to the present day.

The women and children did not do the violence themselves, for the most part. But we have benefited from it. If the European women settling in and around New England in the seventeenth century had refused to countenance violence, had refused to make their homes on stolen land or feed their children from the spoils of war, Native Americans would still own my land.

Could white women in the American South have refused

to participate in and profit by the enslavement of black women and men? Could German gentile women have refused to go along with the persecution of the Jews? While it's true that in virtually all societies women have less power than men, "less" is not the same as "none at all." The citizens of Denmark had very little power relative to occupying German forces, and still managed to leverage what they had into a great moral good.

Besides, if women personally commit less violence than men, it is no more proof of natural pacifism than the paucity of female mathematicians is proof of women's natural inability to do math.

It seems to me that we—whether male or female—tend to overlook or endorse others' violence when it's convenient, either because we are organisms seeking to maximize our prospects for reproductive success, or because we are fully human beings with the usual complex stew of inspirations, ambitions, fears, bigotries, blind spots, and bad and good ideas.

Spared in the mass murder of the Canaanites at Jericho was Rahab, a prostitute. She had evidently heard enough from the anxious guests of her brothel to conclude that the Israelites were going to win the coming battle. Rahab could have run away, or taken up arms, but instead she exhibited the "tend-and-befriend" response described by UCLA researchers as an especially feminine alternative to fight or flight. She helped a pair of Israelite spies in exchange for their promise of protection for herself and her extended family.

Rahab is a Hebrew heroine, and is named in the New Testament as one of Jesus's honored ancestors. Had the Canaanites won the Battle of Jericho, Rahab might have received the kind of treatment the French meted out to women they accused of being "horizontal collaborators" with the German occupiers. French women who had formed sexual relationships with German soldiers had their heads shaved, and were paraded naked in the streets.

Eighty thousand babies were born to French women and German fathers during the occupation. For that matter, five thousand Danes gave birth to children sired by German soldiers. In a wartime poll, 51 percent of women in courageous, exceptional little Denmark confessed to finding German men more attractive than Danish ones. Female friends express bewilderment at this. Male friends understand instantly. ("The Germans were the victors," Warden Jason Luce said, succinctly.)

Rahab accurately read the writing on the wall, predicted a bloodbath, and allied herself with the winning side. It might have been the better side—more virtuous, or more correct about the nature of God—but Rahab doesn't make that claim.

By the evidence of history and of my own life, I'm convinced that women, as a group, are no more naturally moral than men. Should one of my daughters decide to join the armed forces or, for that matter, become a police officer, she will be faced with the same complex choices such service poses to her brother or to anyone who accepts responsibility for meeting and managing the reality of violence in the world.

To claim that the mere possession of ovaries streamlines my daughter's moral decision making does not honor her, nor could it inspire others to emulate her. Ironically, it is Lynndie England's leash that lets us grasp the full heroism of the female soldiers who lie buried with my father at Arlington and the female law enforcement officers whose names are engraved with Drew's on the memorial in Judiciary Square.

CHAPTER TWELVE

I'm in the gym at the Maine Criminal Justice Academy, watching wide-eyed as Warden Chris Dyer invites a younger warden to demonstrate a choke hold on his neck. He wants the rest of us—students for the day in Chris's Defensive Tactics class—to observe how quickly compression of the carotid artery leads to loss of consciousness.

When Chris's eyeballs roll back in his head, the guys laugh. It's a sympathetic laugh, a glad-that's-not-me laugh, and the same laugh that spontaneously erupts when some brave police recruit volunteers to let another try out the Taser on him.

"Defensive tactics" is an umbrella term covering a variety of skills designed to help a police officer survive and prevail in a physical struggle with a suspect.

The polished floor is covered with large, blue wrestling mats upon which the wardens have been practicing takedowns, wristlocks, bar-arms and arm-bars, and the various routes by which handcuffs can find their ways onto human wrists.

I'm attending Defensive Tactics class because, should I happen to be on hand when an arrest becomes, in the parlance, "hands-on," I might be more helpful if I'm familiar with the actions an arresting officer is likely to take.

In my dozen years as a law enforcement chaplain, I've witnessed plenty of arrests, but few involved actual grappling. Contrary to the impression given by television cop shows, most suspects comply with arrest and need not be punched in the nose or flung violently over the hood of a car. (The ones who don't comply are usually mentally ill, drugged, or drunk.)

Might it be a good idea for the chaplain to learn a few self-defense techniques for her own sake and safety? I don't have to control and arrest anyone—I can merely focus on escaping unhurt, a far simpler proposition. If I insist on being left alone with a criminal, it will be because said criminal is grief-stricken, and therefore unlikely, at least in that moment, to express his darker proclivities. Still, it never hurts to be prepared for the worst.

Chris tells me that the biggest handicap facing a female recruit is simply the fact that she has never been hit. "Unless she's been a pretty aggressive soccer player, or has a bunch of older brothers, she's never had the experience of being punched in the face or knocked to the ground, so the experience is new and shocking as well as painful. Men by and large have been slammed around more, so they are more likely to take it in stride and can continue to think and respond."

Chris is fun to watch the way a gymnast or a dancer is: he neatly, almost elegantly, drops Dave, another, larger instructor, to the mat, then pins him there with catlike speed.

In realistic imitation of a recalcitrant arrestee, Dave stays on his stomach with his clenched hands hidden under his breastbone.

"Give me your hands, sir," Chris orders, kneeling beside him.

"Screw you, dude!" squeaks Dave, and we all laugh.

Chris administers a swift blow with his knee into Dave's side. Dave will describe this for us as an "upper dorsal nerve attack," one that targets the subscapular nerve that is vulnerable here, at the edge of the *latissimus dorsi*. But he won't describe it right away. Instead, he'll say "OOOF!" and wince, and everyone will laugh again, except the chaplain, who'll squeak, "Oh Dave!"

Chris, triumphant, plucks Dave's now unresisting hand out from under his chest.

"He didn't actually injure me," Dave elucidates later, as Chris swiftly snaps the handcuffs around his wrists. "That thump hurts just enough to 'change the channel': the subject's brain reacts to the pain by redirecting its attention, hopefully long enough for you to pull his hands out and get him cuffed up."

"Changing the channel" can also be accomplished by a

light but painful smack on the nose or side of the head. When Dave does this to Chris, Chris cries, "OUCH!" and we all chuckle sympathetically, including me.

After the class ends, I ask Warden Dyer whether he enjoys defensive tactics training.

"Hell, yes!" says Chris. "I love it."

"And do you feel…" I falter, diffidently, "sort of hopped up or adrenalized for the rest of the day?"

"Sure I do!" says Chris merrily. "I'm pumped!"

One of my kids' strongest memories of their father (even for Woolie, who was only three and a half when Drew died) is of play-fights: Dad hiding in the dark living room and grabbing them as they ran shrieking past; Dad tossing, rolling, holding, squashing, tickling, confining their little bodies in his powerful arms and then releasing them.

"More, Dada!" they'd cry. "More!"

In this heuristic play-violence, the strength and power in a man's body could be vividly experienced. *Dad can pick me up off the ground, over his head! Dad can toss me in the air and catch me! Dad doesn't hurt me, though he could. Dad protects me.*

I used to joke (rather grimly) that, even as an infant, a child somehow intuits that there is a large disparity between the investment of time, blood, and pain his mother has made in him and the moments (pleasant ones, at that) his father has expended.

If I make Mom mad, she might yell or spank, but if I piss Dad off, he'll eat me and start over...

This is, perhaps, a bit extreme. Still, I do wonder whether the authority Drew (and later Simon) exerted so effortlessly with our sons—effortless, at least, compared with my exertions—drew on the boys' intimate knowledge not of their father's anger or commitment but simply of his strength, demonstrated again and again through the play-violence the kids actively sought and demonstrably craved.

Forced to predict which of my sons would join the Marines, I would've chosen Peter. He was always my wild boy—even in utero he was always moving, dancing, testing the strength of the gentle cage formed around him by his mother's aching ribs. He was the sort of kid that those older women behind me in line at Shop 'n Save would identify, smiling, as "all boy." While the term's sexism grated, it was hard not to notice that coping with his relentless joie de vivre was a lot of work for one mere woman—or at least for this mere woman.

This was especially true because Peter wasn't mean-spirited or mindless, even when he was stormy. The line between creativity and mischief is a fine one, like the line between blessing and curse. When Peter decided he wanted to play the drums, he bought himself a drum set and with that same, relentless energy taught himself to play well with little encouragement or support from his unmusical mother.

When I arrived home from work to discover that our

entire backyard had been systematically relandscaped so that the G.I. Joes could engage in trench warfare, Peter was the usual, well, actually, the only suspect. Wrathfully, I yelled at him for digging up the yard. Then, of course, I felt guilty for being too harsh: Oh, look at him! Poor fatherless boy, out there in the yard, meekly filling in the trenches! Does the lawn really matter all that much? At the time, I couldn't even fathom how "creative" my darling boy had been. Long after the fact, he confessed: As a budding filmmaker armed with the family's battered video camera, Peter had taken full advantage of my absence and filled those backyard trenches with lighter fluid so as to record the kind of thrilling explosions that might have blown his hands off, or set the house on fire, but made his amateur war movies awfully realistic. Only years later would he admit he'd filled the trenches in so meekly, and thoroughly and quickly, so I wouldn't catch the lingering whiff of petrol or notice the scorched grass and immolated plastic soldiers.

Around the time his elder brother had begun being courted by military recruiters, Peter started getting up early on Sunday mornings. He dressed himself carefully in a jacket and tie and walked up the street to St. John's Episcopal Church in time for the eight-thirty service. I didn't pay this too much heed (as usual) until the rector, Reverend Jenks, informed me with considerable triumphant hilarity, that Peter had become an acolyte. Robed in white, a solemn expression on his freckled face, Peter had been given a shiny brass cross to carry up the aisle to the altar.

"Maybe Peter will become a bishop!" Reverend Jenks crowed.

The reverend's son, Elias, was (and remains) one of Peter's great buddies. Peter—fatherless and with Zach's departure looming—liked going to church with Elias and he *really* liked spending time with Elias's dad (the familiar, large, cozy man even the adult congregants sometimes referred to as "Father"). Within Reverend Jenks's church's sanctuary, despite the Episcopalians' best efforts at gender-inclusive language, everything spoken and enacted underlined paternal authority.

Thanks to life insurance, Drew's death added no new economic burden to our family's woes. Unlike that of the children of divorcing friends, my children's childhood home was not sold in a division of assets. They didn't have to move to a new city or even a new neighborhood and they did not have to change schools.

Losing a loved one in a car accident brings sympathy and casseroles rather than even the subtlest social stigma. And yet, the strong statistical correlation between father-absence and behavioral, academic, and emotional problems in children as described, for example, in Barbara Dafoe Whitehead's *The Divorce Culture,* rang uncomfortably true to me. My children weren't just sad; they were becoming anxious, inattentive at school, and badly behaved. Especially the boys.

When a boy in a story sets out to become a knight, he may begin by pulling a sword from a stone, but we all know that what the boy truly needs is a mentor. Eli, Merlin, Yoda, and Professor Dumbledore: each takes a proto-knight under his protection, instructs him in virtue, valor, and violence, and guides him in the way of men. Surely it can't be accidental that the knights-to-be in so many of these stories are boys without fathers?

It would be heretical, I suppose, to call Jesus fatherless, but might we admit that, as dads go, God was a little *remote*? Jesus was lucky to have Joseph, described and sanctified as a good man and a stand-up stepdad.

Patron saint of surrogate dads, Joseph might have given his little stepson piggyback rides or showed him how to use an awl or wield a hammer. Jesus learned to "suffer the children to come unto me" from somebody: why not Joseph? But Joseph goes missing early in Jesus's story (Christian tradition generally presumes he died). After Joseph, young Jesus found a mentor in John the Baptist.

John was a wild and manly man who lived out in the desert and ate wild honey and either locusts (insects) or the fruit of the locust tree (carob beans). The latter is a more accurate translation, but eating bugs makes John sound a lot more macho than eating hippie chocolate, which may be why the mistranslation sticks. Did John the Baptist teach Jesus anything about valor and violence? Someone must have, since Jesus demonstrates his familiarity with these themes as an adult, and John seems a likely candidate for that kind of education. The ancient Jewish historian Josephus says that Herod suspected John the Baptist of ginning up a rebellion against him. Though King Herod was notoriously paranoid on this score (hence the Massacre of the Innocents), there's a hint here that maybe John wasn't just a mild-mannered sinner-washer but could kick butt, too.

Though he didn't live long enough to see his pupil's apotheosis, John the Baptist seemed pretty impressed with the man who would go on to make and use a weapon (a whip braided from cords) to drive the money changers out of the temple. Jesus admired John, too: "Among them that are born of women there has not arisen a greater than John the Baptist..." (Matthew 11:11). It's even possible that Jesus toyed with the idea of taking up arms against the government in a literal rather than spiritual way. *"I did not come to bring peace, but a sword,"* he says, in the Gospel of Matthew (10:34); and then, *"Let him who lacks a sword sell his garment, and buy one"* (Luke 22:36).

When Simon and I began dating, Zach was seventeen and already halfway out the door, psychologically at least. He liked Simon just fine and liked the son and daughter Simon brought along with him. Zach thoroughly approved of the new direction his family was taking, but he wasn't going to be along for the ride. He was going to boot camp. Sangster was the man who would get him there.

But Peter was fifteen, and the "father-like replacement" he had come to rely on—my erstwhile boyfriend—had left me (and therefore my children) for another woman (and her children). This, too, is one of the experiences I recognized in Barbara Dafoe Whitehead's lists of the collateral damage divorce can inflict on childhood. Whether divorced or widowed, newly single mothers and fathers, naturally in search of both intimacy and their own emotional wholeness, form new liaisons. When these don't work out, the stability of family life gets disrupted again, and a child experiences yet another loss and a concomitant diminution of his or her faith in the constancy of love. Indeed, in response to some maternal injunction to "grow up!" Peter once asked, "What sort of man should I grow up to be, Mom-Dude? The one who dies or the one who leaves?"

Thanks to Reverend Jenks and other intermittent father figures, my son seemed to be managing well enough, but when Simon came along Peter muckled onto him with an urgency that spoke poignantly of famine.

Muckled onto is exactly the right term, because what Peter really, really wanted from Simon—more than advice, lessons in car maintenance, or the loan of a necktie—was a wrestling match. He wanted to "fight" and—this was important—he needed Simon to win. Not that he actually said so. Instead, when Simon would come to visit, Peter would find reasons to barge into this man, punch him on the arm, slap his back, and rub the top of his head. It's called *roughhousing* or *grab-assing around*. Simon, bless him, knew all about grab-assing around. It wasn't just that he was the father of his own son. He had taught high school students for fifteen years, half of them boys and many of them just as needy as Peter.

When I would stop by to visit Simon's classroom, I could see this neediness in his male students: "Yo! Mr. V!" they'd say and bump into him, punch him, somehow contrive to muckle onto him like a life ring in the turbulence of their own, young lives.

Peter was a little old for play-fighting, but he needed the outlet so badly that Simon gave it to him anyway. Even before our two households were made one, there occurred what Simon's daughter, Ilona, dubbed "Family Violence Hour." Simon, Peter, and Cobus, with occasional assistance from Ilona and Woolie (Ellie, like me, tended to leave the room mumbling, "Someone's going to get hurt..."), would flail around the living room, play-punching, play-shrieking, play-boxing, play-kicking, while Woolie's dog, Chaos, barked hysterically from the sidelines. One night, Chaos's inner wolf emerged to defend his mistress and he nipped Cobus, after which Chaos was banned from the house during FVH, and had to content himself with barking threats through the kitchen window.

"I still win," Simon told me, having dragged himself to bed after a particularly prolonged and strenuous Family Violence Hour. "But it's getting harder to beat them without hurting them."

Was Peter the way he was because he was Peter, or did the absence of his father contribute to his need?

"I'm the bad one, too," Peter's new stepsister, Ilona, assured him gloomily. "Cobus is the good, smart one, and I'm difficult."

Ilona and Peter were indeed something of a matched set of red-haired, hot-tempered, delightful, and "difficult" second children who offset the responsible, thoughtful firsts.

I was a difficult second child, too, I told them, though I had neither their red hair nor their charm.

"Believe it or not, there are advantages!" I said encouragingly. "The expectations are lower for problematic, bad-tempered people like us. One day, you'll surprise and delight everybody by turning out to be a reasonably decent, successful adult. Trust me, Tootsie-Rolls, you've got nowhere to go but up."

In the meantime, though, Peter required high-intensity mothering from me and substitute fathering not just from Simon but also from anyone willing to provide it. (Ilona, of course, still had a perfectly good mother as well as a father; she needed only supplements, not surrogates). Thank God for the men—Father Jenks and others—who proved willing.

After Peter passed his driving test and got his license, he and I made a special visit to the police station. There I explained to a bemused Chief Kevin Haj that Peter would be driving my car on occasion. Because of this, his officers should be given to understand that they had carte blanche to stop and search the vehicle for any reason or none at all.

"Wow. Okay," said the chief, and turned to Peter. "Your mother is the strictest mother in Thomaston," he said.

"It takes a village," I explained grimly.
"She loves me, sir," sighed Peter.

Throughout human history, men have been more likely than women to be absent from the lives of their children. Premature death from all causes (other than childbirth) was and still is more common in men, as are parental abandonment, incarceration, and jobs that demand prolonged separation (fighting Canaanites, say, or Nazis). So it shouldn't surprise us that, one way and another, the lack of a dad is a fairly common feature of the human biography. The fathers of George Washington, Thomas Jefferson, James Monroe, and Andrew Jackson all died when their sons were young, and both Bill Clinton and Barack Obama experienced early father-absence.

Since father-absence is so common, and since so many people have been successful in spite of it, one could conclude that dads aren't actually all that necessary to the well-being and eventual thriving of a child.

This is not, however, the conclusion reached by the people of the ancient Near East. In the Hammurabi Code of ancient Sumer, in the instructions of Egypt's pharaoh Ramses III, and in the Hebrew Bible, fathers matter. These texts were probably written by men, and those men weren't too likely to declare themselves disposable. In addition to affirming the benefits of a father-present childhood, however, the Scriptures were clear: the quality of care extended to the fatherless had better be good if the chosen people wished to maintain a strong, life-giving relationship with their choosy God.

Words were not minced: in the book of Exodus (22: 22–24), God warns, "You shall not mistreat any widow or fatherless child. If you do mistreat them, and they cry out to me, I will surely hear their cry, and my wrath will burn, and I will kill you with the sword!"

When the Hebrew prophets list the causal factors for the decline of Israel's overall strength and vitality, "vexing the fatherless" is emphasized. Abandon vulnerable individuals, they seem to be saying, and the community as a whole will be rendered vulnerable if not to a divine sword then to the far more realistic threat of a Babylonian blitzkrieg.

My children taught me that children who don't have a father ache for one. It's not hard to see how this unrequited longing could make a fatherless child easy prey for gangs, cults, and other predators. One could therefore assume that throughout history, fatherless children have been more prone to the kinds of repeated trauma that would adversely impact the kind of adults they eventually would become, which would consequently impact the effect they would have on their community and, ultimately, on civilization.

Material support, while necessary, is insufficient: the Bible (among other experienced witnesses) tells us that a strong society is one that encourages dads to be dads and all men to be stand-ins, like Jesus's stepdad Joseph, or Barack's grandpa Stanley Dunham, or, for that matter, like Simon, who "dads" so many boys, including mine.

I know a State Trooper who had a very rough childhood. Abandoned by his father, he was beaten by his stepfather, and occasionally these assaults resulted in injuries sufficient to put the child in the hospital. On one occasion, when my friend was around nine, a State Trooper drove him to the emergency room in the back of a cruiser. My friend retained a vivid memory of lying on the back bench seat, watching the telephone lines loop past against the night sky, and considering his options:

I can be like my stepdad.

I can be a victim.

Or, he thought, looking up at the back of the trooper's close-cropped head, *I can be that guy.*

I am personally acquainted with the trooper my friend describes as rescuing him that night: his name is Malcolm, but he's known as Mack. What makes the story really interesting, from my point of view, is that he is not one of your enormous, stern, terrifying troopers. Maine has its share of those, God bless 'em, but Mack is on the small side as troopers go. Though I have heard that Mack can more than hold his own when it comes to a rumpus, it is his intelligence, his kindness, and the quiet modesty of his manner that has always impressed me most. Mack became the colonel of the Maine State Police before he retired a few years ago, but when my friend was a battered little boy, Mack was a new, young trooper with little kids of his own.

Now my friend is a new, young trooper.

I wonder what glimpses of manhood he offers to the boys

he encounters in his work, what possibilities, what hopes are sparked by him?

Zach, fatherless, was still only seventeen and too young to join the Marines without my permission. But he had read all the books, endured endless lectures and family conclaves about Afghanistan and Iraq, about the president, the Corps, the inadequacies of war movies, the convoluted and not-always-honorable history of American military interventions in the world. He had taken every opportunity that Sergeant Sangster provided to discover what the Marine Corps was really like.

"Why you?" I asked him, one more time. Zach's enlistment papers were sitting on the kitchen table in front of me. There was a blank space waiting for my signature, and he was holding out the pen.

The answer to the first question was simple—at least, Zach saw it simply.

"Why not me, Mom?" he asked. "Lots of other guys are going to Iraq and Afghanistan. What makes me any different from them?"

You're mine, I thought, but I didn't say it aloud. I knew that wasn't a good enough reason.

"If you don't sign his paperwork and support his decision," Simon had said after long thought and much discussion, "Zach will wait until his eighteenth birthday and enlist then."

"That's true."

"And," Simon continued, "in that case we would have exactly the same fears for Zach's safety, but we'd have missed the chance to support him in his choice."

"Yes."

"I'm not a military person. So I can't say I trust Sergeant Sangster or his Corps," Simon admitted. "But I do trust Zach."

So I signed. Zach turned eighteen, and in what seemed the blink of an eye, he was gone.

The moment of departure was quick and vivid. My bare feet felt the rough cedar decking of the back porch, and the sunlight shone through the poplar trees and laid broad stripes across the backyard. A few of Zach's friends had come over to see him off. They teased him about his short hair, but their eyes were awed and anxious.

Sangster, font of all Corps wisdom, had advised Zach to get a haircut. "Short," he specified. "But not too short." Zach's head would be shaved upon arrival at boot camp, but the drill instructors disapproved of do-it-yourselfers.

So Simon cut Zach's hair.

His big left hand braced the crown of my son's head. His right hand held the buzzing clippers, and the soft, shorn hair fell to the bathroom floor around their feet. Simon's expression was attentive, serious, and gentle. Zach cracked a joke I wasn't near enough to hear, and they both laughed. It was unbearably poignant, like some tender, lovely, preparatory ritual recognizable and yet far, far beyond my ken.

"*Join the club*," a billion mothers whispered, from around the world and across the centuries.

Sergeant Sangster's car pulled in and parked on the driveway beneath the basketball hoop, just as though he was showing up for his usual grilled cheese and grilling, but he didn't get out of the car. He turned in our direction, waved, and smiled. Peter, Ellie, Woolie, Zach's friends, and I smiled uncertainly back. Swiftly hugged and kissed, my boy got into the car and was driven away.

CHAPTER THIRTEEN

Anatomy is destiny: a born brachiator, our pet gibbon never did learn how to walk. If, as a child, I had somehow managed to teach him to walk upright on his hind limbs, what did I imagine he would then do with his little hands— type out the plays of the simian Shakespeare?

Eventually, maybe. If he were to recapitulate the path set out by the evolution of the human species, however, then just as soon as the trick of standing up was mastered the gibbon would reach his newly freed hands not for the pen but for the sword.

Provoked to violence, a gibbon ordinarily attacks with his mouth.

When the python in the Thai klong attacked our neighbor's gardener, it did so with its mouth. When Chaos mistakenly nipped Cobus, he did this with his mouth, too: gibbons, pythons, and dogs fight mostly with their faces. As I've admitted, one or two of my babies were biters, too, but we can put this down to phylogeny recapitulating ontogeny. They outgrew their biting phase because human beings are the only animals whose primary weapons system is not mounted in the face. We fight with our hands.

When we—or rather, our prehominid ancestors—came down from the trees, we stood up on our feet, picked up rocks in our hands, and threw them. Chimpanzees sometimes throw stuff (rocks and dirt when they want to scare a rival, feces when they want to freak out a zoo-goer), but they throw underhand and not well. Humans are nature's throwing pros.

Weapons and tools created from the Bronze Age onward are variations on the theme of throwing things. This is reflected in our language: the word ballistic (as in missile) comes from the Greek *ballein,* which means "to throw."

"Today, Zach and Dada went down to Port Clyde," Drew wrote in his son's baby book in the spring of 1988. "Zach got to play his favorite game—throw rocks in the water—for almost an hour."

When the kids got older, their favorite games involved throwing Nerf balls, Wiffle balls, and Frisbees. Sticks found in the yard became swords and spears to be used on imaginary enemies and—occasionally with dolorous effect—on each other. At the same time, of course, they were learning to fight with language, though the boys were never quite as good as their sisters at wielding the sharp, weaponized word.

After I read them the stories of Robin Hood, I was importuned into making hats out of green felt and bows and arrows out of backyard sticks and spare yarn. These worked a whole lot better than any of us expected (especially me), and I had to supervise their use or risk a child losing an eye.

Had my son been a warrior in the Stone Age, he would have learned to throw rocks with devastating accuracy. Later, he would've learned to use a spear that carried a modified bit of rock at its tip (the original, lethal, litho-payload) and slings, bows, and catapults that made the rocks fly farther, hit harder, and kill more efficiently. Now that Zach was headed off to the Marines and to boot camp, he would have an M16. His hands would be trained until he could take the rifle apart, clean it, put it back together, and load it, blindfolded, with pieces of modified galena ore (lead).

Simon, meanwhile, "throws" pots on a wheel. Having made the linguistic connection between *ballein*, ballistic, and ball, can we go ahead and note that the words "artist" and "artillery" share a common root? These terms extend back to the Indo-European that predates Greek, Latin, and Germanic sources: a two-letter snippet, *ar*, refers to fitting or joining together, so the jointed (and joining) upper limb in the human body is an *arm* with which *arms* are wielded and *artistry* accomplished. And yes, infant and infantry are also etymologically related. Somehow, it seems, we have always been willing to expose our children to our violence.

———∿∿∿———

Dear Simon,

Even etymology is depressing me these days. Zach is right: I see awful things.

Like that thirteen-year-old who shot his stepbrother by mistake. "I did it on accident," he said, using the same turn of phrase my own children use. I guess "on accident" strikes them as the logical opposite of "on purpose"? But I've seen young people do stupid things on purpose, too.

———∿∿∿———

Five bored college students decided to have a party in the woods. Preparations for the festivities consisted of draping an old, blue plastic tarp over a fallen tree to form a sort of tent, laying a small campfire, and illegally purchasing several large bottles of coffee brandy.

All might have gone well, or at least better, if they hadn't set up camp in the middle of winter. An old, blue tarp and a small campfire are insufficient to counteract the effects of temperatures that, with nightfall, drop well below zero. And a snootful of coffee brandy merely serves to dull awareness of incipient hypothermia.

In fact, had the party stayed friendly and the booze flowing, all five might have fallen asleep and frozen to death. As it was, two of the five got into a fight, which quickly escalated.

One boy pulled out a knife and stabbed the other boy who, though not badly wounded, decided that he wasn't enjoying the party anymore and left in a huff.

Eventually he turned up in the emergency room of the closest hospital and, since the doctors couldn't help but notice that a crime had been committed, they called the police. When the town cop arrived, it took her some time to worm the story out of the victim. (No one wants to be a rat, after all.)

Upon learning that the stabbing had not occurred within town limits, the local officer handed the matter over to the State Police. A trooper was able eventually to locate the house where the dispirited remnant of the party, having abandoned the blue tarp and the weak fire, had repaired to warm up and drink more.

More unnecessarily protracted interviews followed before the trooper at last ascertained that only four of the original five young people were by now accounted for. Pressed, the now more-or-less-sober young men and women admitted that when they had last seen their friend with the knife, he was some distance behind them, staggering rather than walking, and incoherent. They assumed it was the brandy: "He was fuckin' wasted," they agreed, and he was being a jerk.

"He was acting so weird!" one of the young women confided. "I mean, like, he was taking off his shirt and stuff..."

The Warden Service was called and an urgent search mounted. Within a half hour or so, a Warden Service K-9 team had located the missing young man, but by then he had died of hypothermia.

"When you realized that he hadn't come out with you, didn't it occur to you to call for help?" the warden asked the kids.

They gazed at him, slack-jawed. At last one explained, "We didn't want to get him in trouble."

———

Simon, I need to tell you about the ill-fated party in the woods and the strange, Cain-and-Abel tale of the boy who fired a perfect sniper shot through his stepbrother's brain stem by mistake. And about the guys who set out to cross a lake in winter to rob a convenience store on the other side.

You listen, soothe me, and feed me.

People ask, "Who takes care of the chaplain?"

The answer for me has so swiftly and firmly become you.

Oh my love. I begin to fear that you are taking in too much, that you will catch my contagious convictions about the ubiquity of mortal danger, the flimsiness of our defenses, and—especially given that we have sons—about the courage and stupidity of young men.

———

But Simon already knew about these things. In more than fifteen years of teaching high school, Simon had lost students to car accidents, hypothermia, and suicide, easily one or two a year on average, and those who were lost weren't strangers to him. They were kids he had coached, cared for, reprimanded, joshed with, counseled, and loved.

Had the party in the woods, the stabbing, and the death happened locally, Simon would have known every young person involved. He would have had the slack-jawed girl in his homeroom, the boy who froze to death would have learned how to turn a clay cup on a spinning wheel, and the boy with the knife would've been one of those who'd muckled onto Simon, pure need disguised as grab-assing aggression.

"When you were getting your teaching certification, did they tell you how much sorrow the profession brings with it?" I asked him once, and he shook his head.

"Teaching," he told me once, "is about love." And to love is—always—to risk pain. More love, more pain. That's just how it goes.

"I didn't know the frozen boy in the woods," I confessed. "But I loved him just enough to hurt for him."

Simon makes me soup, and while he chops and stirs I talk about art and artillery, about how the human hand coevolved with the human brain for the wielding of weapons and subsequently became capable together of making not just weaponry but beauty, too, and love. Hands outlined in powdered pigment wave to us from cave walls across ten thousand years of history: *Hey people! We're people, too!* But even without the handprints that identify them as our ancestors, we would have known them by the stick figures they sketched, wielding spears.

In the Gospels, Jesus's hand, the one that braided then raised a whip and drove the moneylenders from the temple, also touched and healed a blind man's eyes.

"Our lives are in our hands," says Simon. "Is that what you're saying?"

"My life may be in yours," I answer.

Chapter Fourteen

I bought Zach a bathrobe for Christmas," I informed Simon.

"Uh-huh," he said.

I'd had a clear picture of the bathrobe I would get him, spent weeks searching through catalogues and stores until I found it, saved up to buy it; and when, on Christmas Eve, to whet their anticipation for the morrow, family members were allowed to open one present, I placed this reverently wrapped gift in Zach's hands.

He didn't like it.

"In fact," I told Simon, "dislike doesn't begin to describe it: Zach was deeply, profoundly disappointed by this gift, so much so that he could barely bring himself to mutter an insincere and unconvincing thank you. I was devastated."

"And he was how old?"

"Four and a half."

Simon began to laugh. "I know," I said. "I know! Of course he was disappointed! What four-year-old child looks forward to receiving a bathrobe for Christmas? It was crazy... but I thought he'd be thrilled. I had been looking forward to giving him this thing for *months!*"

"What made the bathrobe so special?"

"Nothing!" I said. "Or at least, nothing anyone else would care about, least of all a little kid. It was a white bathrobe, the kind that wraps around and ties. It looked like the ones that hung on a hook in the guest bathroom at my grandmother's apartment in Manhattan, the one I got to wear when I visited her."

"Ah," said Simon. "I get it."

"Do you?" I said hopefully.

"Sure," he said. "To you, it meant whatever visiting your grandmother meant..."

"Skipping down Madison Avenue wearing new, patent-leather Mary Janes," I said. "And being taken out to supper at Trader Vic's, or to see Yul Brynner in *The King and I*."

A faraway, unhappy look came into my husband's eye. "When I was in elementary school in upstate New York," he said sadly, "for the first day of kindergarten, first grade, second grade...my mother made me dress like a little Dutch child. In her day, at least, the first day of school was an occasion for lederhosen."

"Lederhosen?"

"Those leather shorts with the suspenders."

"Oh my. Oh honey."

"Yes. Imagine showing up on the first day of second grade wearing *Sound of Music* lonely goatherd pants? By third grade, I was old enough to refuse."

"And your mother was probably heartbroken."

"Yes, she was," said Simon. "On the other hand, because she had three boys and maybe had hoped for a girl, I was so thoroughly feminized by the age of fifteen that I was thrilled when she gave me a tiger-striped sheet set for Christmas. Oh boy! Home décor! My only disappointment there was that she didn't include a nice set of drapes. Why are you crying?"

"Because Zach is at boot camp being screamed at by strangers," I sniffled. "And I wish I'd given him a better Christmas present when he was four."

Our first communication from Zach, apart from one extremely brief phone call, was a form letter.

It began, "Dear _____, I have arrived safely at Marine Corps Recruit Depot, Parris Island, and have been assigned to Platoon _____, _____ Company, _____ Recruit Training Battalion, which is comprised of _____ Recruits from various parts of the United States."

The blanks were filled in, in Zach's recognizable, messy handwriting, but, as Ellie pointed out, this message resembled nothing more than the paper game Mad Libs we used to play on long car trips. The game leader would shout "NOUN" or "ADJECTIVE" and when these were inserted into a pre-existing story, the result was supposed to be (and often was) hysterically funny. (Dear <u>Chicken,</u> I have arrived safely at

Marine Corps Recruit Depot, Parris Island, and have been assigned to Platoon <u>four million seventy-eight</u>, <u>daffodil</u> company, <u>purple</u> Recruit Training Battalion…) On the back of this form, Zach had written, "Mom. It's really fun here… love, Zach."

"What does that mean?" I asked Simon but, at this he, too, was flummoxed.

Never had being the mother of a son seemed quite so bewildering.

Eventually, Zach's platoon advanced to a stage where writing letters was both permitted and not eclipsed by sheer exhaustion, and we began to get a few more details about boot camp, though none made it sound "really fun," at least to me.

"I ran three miles in 23:30, did 92 crunches, and 8 pull-ups," he would write. "And tomorrow we start learning how to shoot the M16A2."

Though Zach didn't explain, Peter knew that the M16A2 was a gun.

"Sick!" he said. "Can I join the Marines?"

No.

The Marines were teaching Zach to handle weapons, but they also taught him to do just about everything else you can think of, because everything he did now had to be done the Marine way. There is a Marine way to stand, sit, speak, go through a door, pick up a spoon, and carry a suitcase. There is a Marine way to wear a hat, buckle a belt, put on trousers (one leg at a time, of course, but it has to be the left leg first), lace up your boots, and tie them. It sounds absurd, doesn't it?

Nitpicky, power-trippy, and isn't the result bound to be a bunch of guys with service-induced obsessive-compulsive disorder? What difference does it really make if you put your right boot on before your left, or carry your duffel bag over your right shoulder? The only thing Zach needed to know in the beginning was that these things, done this way, made a difference to the drill instructor.

From the moment Zach set foot on the sandy soil of Parris Island, every move he made, every task he performed was done specifically according to the instructions given, or else. Or else what? Well, there was yelling, which doesn't sound like all that much unless you have heard how thunderously and relentlessly a drill instructor can yell. And there were theatrical demonstrations of power which, when Zach described them, reminded me of a silverback gorilla's threat displays: The drill instructors would burst into a squad bay glaring and roaring; they'd tear the bunks apart and pitch the mattresses onto the floor. Seizing the recruits' duffel bags, they'd dump the contents and then madly fling the steel garbage cans across the room to make a mess and a deafening din (Zach assured us that the USMC shall never switch to Rubbermaid). All the while, the drill instructors would be barking important, unintelligible instructions at impossible speed. Perhaps most frightening of all, through all of this, the drill instructors' uniforms would remain sleekly, almost supernaturally "squared away."

After the first three days of this, exhausted and disoriented, Zach and his platoon of new recruits were herded into the communal shower for their first ablutions since their arrival. Quickly but shyly, the recruits stripped and, eyes carefully averted from one another's nearby nudity, began dabbing at themselves under the cold water dribbling from the spouts.

Suddenly, the tiled walls were booming and echoing: "WHO'S TALKING?" The drill instructor was standing, fully clothed, in the doorway. "WHO'S RUNNIN' THEIR DAMN SUCK?"

Evidently, some foolish recruit had forgotten himself and whispered a request for soap.

"I SAID, NO TALKING. NO TALKING. DO YOU UNDERSTAND ME?"

"SIR YES SIR."

"I WANT YOU TO PLACE YOUR LEFT HAND ON MY BULKHEAD RIGHT NOW. RIGHT NOW. RIGHT NOW."

"SIR YES SIR!"

Seventy shivering, wet left hands were placed against the nearest walls.

"NO!" The drill instructor, his eyes bulging with rage, raised his arm (his biceps resembling an Easter ham packed tightly into its immaculate shirtsleeve) and pointed.

"I WANT YOU ALL TO PLACE YOUR LEFT HANDS ON THAT BULKHEAD RIGHT NOW. RIGHT NOW. RIGHT NOW."

"SIR YES SIR!"

The recruits scuttled toward the wall indicated, which, as luck would have it, was the bulkhead Zach was standing beside. So, as he would later tell us with perfect good humor, my special boy found himself crouched down and squashed against the cold tiles while the naked, soggy, dangly-wanglies of sixty-nine other boys flapped helplessly before his eyes. His still-civilian mind squeaked useless alarums: *Oh dear! Oh dear! My personal space-bubble!*

"I definitely don't want to be a Marine," said Ellie when she heard about this.

"I bet the girl Marines are in a different shower," said Woolie.

The two considered this. "Even so," said Ellie, and Woolie nodded in agreement.

If the Parris Island shower scene sounds like a tale from some creepy British upper-class Do-the-Boys Hall, get a load of this: When the platoon had been found guilty of a collective infraction, the drill instructors would line them all up, sternum to spine, and each recruit would stick his hands into the front pockets of the guy in front of him. Once they were all linked together in this way, they would have to rock back and forth.

"Um, Zach," I asked Zach, when we finally had a chance to talk in person. "Doesn't this strike you as slightly…well… homoerotic?"

"Slightly?" Zach retorted, and roared with laughter.

"Ours is not to question why," Peter intoned, when I asked him why he thought the Marine Corps would include this peculiar ritual in the repertoire of punishments.

"Mine is definitely to question why," I said, but Peter shrugged.

"It's tradition, Mom."

It's always been done, and always will be done: is that it? Or maybe—giving the Marine Corps some credit for sophisticated psychology here—the humpy-humpy lineup, along with the group-shower scenario, is specifically designed to get everyone over the gay thing and past the ordinary civilian male's inhibitions about seeing and touching other men's bodies?

At any rate, nothing in Zach's letters or, later, in his phone calls, indicated he minded the extravagant "consequences" meted out to him at Parris Island. "I figured it was theater, Mom," he explained. "I knew that the drill instructors were acting, and the point of the act was to teach me something. So I tried to just do my part and learn."

But there were those unhygienic push-up-till-you-puke sessions in the sandbox and, even if Zach didn't puke (he did), the chances were excellent that someone else already had, so olfactory insult was added to calisthenic injury. Though I distinctly remembered being assured that drill instructors don't hit recruits, Zach wrote about the day one threw a full breakfast tray at him accurately, and hard, when Zach was caught talking in line at the chow hall.

"Didn't that hurt?" Ellie asked, when I retailed the story to her.

Not much, evidently. "Mostly it was just hard to keep from laughing," was Zach's reassuring conclusion.

To this day, Zach has to put his pants on left leg first, and his belts have to point to the left, and the buckle must align with the zipper of his pants.

"I spend a lot of time fiddling compulsively with my belt area," Zach confesses. "Even if I'm not wearing a belt. It's a Marine thing: we all walk around adjusting imaginary uniforms. Oh, and when I wear a hat, the brim must sit two fingers above the bridge of my nose."

The impeccable uniforms, like the preternatural fitness of the drill instructors, spoke eloquently of power, and not just physical or even institutional power, but the personal power acquired through self-discipline and self-control. Even as they assumed near-total control of a recruit's every moment and motion, the drill instructors were modeling the end result: *This is what you are going to be.*

As the sixteen weeks of basic training crawled by, the drill instructors began, ever so slowly, to signal approval and acceptance of their charges. With one exception, Zach genuinely believed the DIs liked the recruits and truly wanted them to succeed.

By graduation day, the recruits were fit and spiffy in their neatly creased uniforms and spit-shined shoes (donned left foot first), their hat brims seated exactly two fingers up from the bridge of the nose.

As a State Police recruit, Drew also had to learn to do old things in a new way, and the applied didactic theory similarly emphasized shouting and push-ups, though I don't remember anyone throwing dinner at him. When I expressed a scornful opinion of the academy's teaching methods, Drew earnestly pointed out that his safety and the safety of others would depend on his having his equipment organized and instantly available for use should the need arise. "They don't want me to be fumbling around, trying to remember where I put my bullets or where I stuck my flashlight. They know how dangerous those fumbled seconds can be. I have to know the most efficient way to do something, and then practice doing it that way every time, until I can do it without having to think about it."

"Yeah, but your underpants?" I asked skeptically.

We used to do his week's laundry together on Saturday mornings at the Laundromat. Baby Zach lay on a stack of towels beside us, busily perfecting the essential nervous-system function of tracking hand movements that would later form the basis for tool use, though we just thought he was waving. During those sessions, I learned to fold Drew's tighty-whities according to the dictates of the Maine Criminal Justice Academy.

"You have to admit, it's the neatest way to fold them," Drew pointed out. It was, but I rolled my eyes anyway.

Through relentless instruction and practice, Drew learned to carry his bag and just about everything else, too — coffee cups, sandwiches, books — in his left hand. The mantra of the warrior, doubtless grunted from caveman to cavechild, generation after generation until at last it reached the ears of a new State Trooper (and his boy, a U.S. Marine), is: "Keep your gun hand free." On the last day of his life, I can be sure he carried his cereal bowl to the sink in his left hand, so as to keep his right hand — his gun hand — free.

To this day, my hands fold men's underpants (those belonging to Simon and Cobus, as well as to Peter and Zach) the State Police way.

As Sergeant Sangster had promised, the Marine Corps was teaching Zach how to work, something many of my friends loudly wished their own sons would learn. More enviably still, Zach had entered a far more controlled and structured environment than any American institution of higher learning can provide and thus, paradoxically, Zach was actually safer at boot camp than his brothers were when they went off to college.

No cutting classes, frat parties, date rape, or drunk driving. No cell phones, no MP3 players, no alcohol or tobacco, and no welcoming bowl of gaily wrapped prophylactics in the student lounge (no lounge!). Up by dawn, in bed and sound asleep by 2100, and kept active and working for all the hours in between, Zach and his fellow recruits were clean, safe, fit, and sober in every sense of the word.

That can sound pretty good to a parent. And heading off for a stint in an organization that teaches and rewards self-discipline, self-sacrifice, teamwork, and courage sounds pretty good to a lot of good kids. Add in a paycheck, college tuition benefits, and the opportunity to blow stuff up: "It sounds awesome!" said Peter, and even Cobus, who had been preparing for a college career since he was a zygote in utero, found himself strangely tempted.

"My boys would love it," said my friend Monica wistfully, of her three sons. "And if it weren't for the death and killing, so would I."

Zach's letters did not reflect any diminution either of his instincts for kindness nor of his sense of humor. Between sanguine descriptions of what were, to me at least, hair-raising incidents, his letters consistently expressed an endearing appreciation for all the things of home: everything from lighting candles at church to eating fruit that hadn't come from a can.

"I'm looking forward to family day more than I've looked forward to any day in my entire life," he wrote. "I smile just thinking about getting to see you all again."

Chapter Fifteen

Zach graduated from Parris Island skinnier but, to my relief, still recognizably himself: as kind, thoughtful, and just as funny as before—though he did now know how to work.

During the next phase of training, Zach developed cellulitis between his toes. This is a bacterial infection, and it is very painful. It can also be serious.

"The doctor said that if it doesn't start to improve, they might have to amputate my toe," Zach wrote, and I was—get this!—*happy.* This was the sort of strange, shameful thought we Proud Parents sometimes confessed to in those online chat rooms; I confessed the strange, shameful thought to Simon, too.

"I get it," he said. "If they amputate Zach's toe, that will mean he can't go to Iraq." He put his arms around me. "Oh Kate."

Zach kept his toe and he told us, "It wouldn't have changed anything anyway. As long as I can march and fight, they'll deploy me."

"Well, in that case, honey, I'm glad you're in one piece." (When he came home on leave, I'd count his toes and make sure.)

The prospect of a minor disability serving as an excuse from self-sacrifice appears more than once in human scriptures, though it seldom actually gets those afflicted off the hook. Having sustained a "sports injury" during his wrestling match with the Angel of the Lord, the Hebrew patriarch Jacob limped, but God didn't relieve him of his sacred task. Jacob still had to address his family's dysfunctions and then gimp off to Canaan. Called by God to lead the Jews from the flesh-pots of Egypt, the young Moses tried to beg off, saying, "Please, Lord, I'm not eloquent. I talk too slowly and I have a speech impediment." God wasn't sympathetic, and Moses had to learn to stutter his message ("Let my people go!") persuasively.

According to Islamic tradition, when the impeccable, steel-spined angel Gabriel commanded Muhammad to recite, Muhammad did not respond with a crisp, "*Sir, yes sir!*"

"I can't," he said.

"In the name of the Lord and Cherisher, who created man out of a clot of congealed blood," Gabriel boomed, the illiterate Muhammad needed to stop whining, pick up a pen, and write a Koran.

Zach seemed to take the toe-thing in stride (so to speak), but it was a revelation to me, albeit of an obvious truth: Now earning his own paycheck and holding his own health insurance, my son could sign away a whole body part without the permission (or even the support and comfort) of his mom. Rather than being dependent upon and responsible to his childhood family, Zach was now responsible for himself, to God, and to other adults because he was one, now, too.

As Zach's Marine Corps career proceeded, his younger brothers were considering their own next steps toward manhood. Balked of the chance to follow in his brother's footsteps, Peter planned to study music. Exposure to his stepbrother's uniforms and guns also prompted Cobus to consider military service (though he prudently concealed the idea from his parents until much later), but he had been planning his college career since the day he was born. Unlike his stepmother, this kid is, as they say, "very goal oriented." What we have in common is a liking for arguments and sugar. We were probably devouring a jar of intensely sweet organic maple spread the day Cobus told me about the thought experiment posed in his ethics class.

"Imagine you're in the basket of a hot-air balloon, and there are five other people in the basket with you. The balloon is overloaded, and if someone isn't tossed overboard, the balloon will crash and all six people will be killed."

"Sometimes it's an overloaded life raft," said Stepmama Know-It-All, taking another spoonful of maple spread. "Or a space capsule with limited oxygen."

"We have to figure out who would be the most logical person to throw overboard to lighten the load. There's a physician in the basket who knows the cure for cancer, there's an elderly person, a fine musician, a pregnant mother, a mentally retarded person…"

"No need to debate," I said, licking my spoon. "I know what the answer is."

Cobus frowned. "Really?"

"Yup," I said. "Easy. I jump."

"What do you mean?"

"I jump. Out of the basket. Problem solved."

"That's stupid. What if you're the doctor with the cure for cancer?"

"I was assuming I was me," I said. "And besides, in real life there isn't just one doctor who can cure cancer. No individual is really indispensable, except the pregnant lady, of course, because she's a twofer."

"The exercise is more of a metaphor, Kate," said Cobus patiently. "It isn't about anything that actually happens to six human beings in real life. It's about how to allocate resources in society."

In my head, I flashed back to 1984, and a college class entitled An Introduction to Medical Ethics. I took it because I was considering going into medicine, but I liked medical ethics then for the same reason I like law enforcement ethics now: because these ethical matters are by definition concrete— they shall be applied. No one is actually going to have to fling a musician out of an overloaded hot-air balloon, but life-saving drugs will either be given or withheld, living wills honored or ignored, the respirator will either be left on or switched off. Should we allocate more resources to prolonging the lives of old people or to saving and enhancing the lives of young people? I was exasperated by fellow students who answered, "But all lives matter equally to God!"

"All very well for God," I would snap. "God's resources are infinite. Ours are not."

Is it an early sign of senescence that I am now the one arguing for God's view of human worth? It's not as if I'm arguing that God would want us to let the overloaded balloon crash. It just seems reasonable to bring up and discuss the ethics of *self*-sacrifice before we ask students to weigh the relative utilitarian merits of artists, oncologists, and persons with special needs. Especially since, in real life, our shining ethical examples have always been people who are willing to *sacrifice themselves.*

Here is a real-life thought experiment that I posed to Peter and Cobus, and later to their sisters when they got old enough to party:

> You are a guest at a gathering well stocked with friends, acquaintances, and persons of the gender you are attracted to. A friend arrives, and it is obvious he is drunk. After a few minutes and a few more drinks, he departs. You know that he drove himself to the party in a car, and though you did not see him leave, you are sure he has also driven himself away. What do you do?

All of the kids arrived at the right answer for themselves but they didn't like it one bit. Dangerous unselfishness is hard: calling the cops on a drunk-driving peer risks sacrificing social standing, and instinctively, a teenager (and, frankly, many adults) would rather die than do that.

There are so many ways for a child to sacrifice his life, and so many lousy reasons for him to do it. He's drunk, high, angry, or depressed, has an undiagnosed mental illness, or a bunch of buddies standing around waiting to be impressed by his derring-do.

"Watch this!" he says.

I touch the bodies of so many sons, smooth their hair, clean the mud from their lips, and tuck them into the body bags so I can tell their mothers later that I did these small, forgiving things on their behalf and on God's.

By the time I'm called, some of these sons and their families have already sacrificed so much. Time, patience, attention, and small fortunes that might have paid for a sibling's education or funded a more comfortable retirement have gone instead to bail, rehab, bail, defense attorneys, and more rehab.

As soon as I had a son at Parris Island, I began to see the words "boot camp" all over. The local YMCA began to offer "Boot Camp" exercise classes, a shoe store advertised a Boot/Camp Sale, and there were articles in the news about the debate in legal and corrections circles about the ethics and efficacy of "correctional boot camps" for wayward youth.

The "change-is-forever" that Sergeant Sangster had promised so unnecessarily for Zach might sound great to out-of-shape Y-members, and like salvation to the parents of a troubled, drug-addicted or alcoholic kid.

During the Vietnam War, being conscripted and packed off to actual boot camp was used by criminal courts as an alternative sentence for young male offenders. No doubt this was in part because of the need for boots on the ground, but perhaps the courts hoped that military discipline and *esprit de corps* really could turn a delinquent's life around.

Once Zach began describing the Parris Island program, I couldn't help but wonder what the result of all that high-stress, high-volume storming around has been on anyone whose home life was filled with similar—and less safely theatrical—displays.

"It's hard to believe it would be positive," said Tonya.

"No," I said. "But so what?"

Tonya was shocked. "The Marine Corps has no business stacking more psychological trauma on kids who've already had all the tough love they can handle!" she retorted.

Presumably, weeding out pretraumatized kids was the point of those questions on Zach's application form, such as, "Have you ever been arrested?" and "Have you ever been under a psychiatrist's care?"

In stark contrast to those creepy youth camps hidden away in the Dominican Republic, the situation at Parris Island is, if nothing else, absolutely transparent. When we were there for Zach's graduation, platoons of recruits who were still in the beginning of the process could be seen marching or jogging around, their efforts attended by drill instructors yelling for all the world to see.

The real contrast between boot camp and the boot-campy programs intended to rehabilitate the young is that the goal at Parris Island is not the well-being of the recruits being trained there. *It is to train Marines to fight our country's wars.* It is so easy to forget this as you peruse those shiny pamphlets about travel, adventure, skill building, and paying for college!

If one believes that the United States should never engage in warfare for any reason, then it's a waste of time to argue about Marine Corps pedagogy, or even about who should serve in the military and how. For the true pacifist, the role of women or the service of gays and lesbians, for example, are logically nonissues.

If, on the other hand, you believe that there are or could be situations in which all other options have been precluded and the United States must use force to defend itself and its vital or moral interests, then there are two debates that every citizen has the right (indeed, the duty) to enter into.

The first relates to whether a given problem (Germany and France both claim Alsace-Lorraine, Japan has bombed Pearl Harbor, Saddam Hussein is an intransigent sadistic bastard) can be resolved by war. The answer is not always obvious, the stakes are very high, and even the best-case scenario will probably involve lots and lots of needless pain and death.

The second debate has to do with whether the military is set up the way it should be for maximum effectiveness when executing its mission and purpose.

The mission and purpose of the United States military is not to provide job training or career opportunities for young people. It is not to ensure employment for workers in defense-related industries. It is not to foster social bonds between a diverse set of Americans, nor is it the purpose and mission of the nation's military to serve as a vehicle for desirable social change—even if it has at times done all these things.

The mission and purpose of the military is to fight and win wars.

All other goals and priorities, however worthy in themselves, can only be attended to provided they augment or do not interfere with the primary mission. After all, any war our country needs to fight should be, by definition, a war we need to win. The most powerful argument against military policies that discriminate against a given group of Americans is that these result in a ridiculous waste of valuable human resources as when, for example, seven Army intelligence officers fluent in Arabic were dismissed for being openly gay at a time when there was a desperate need for Arabic interpreters.

That the pursuit of military effectiveness and the pursuit of human rights eventually arrived at the same conclusion—sexual preference does not interfere with one's ability to serve—should not obscure a fundamental truth: the service of gays and lesbians is not about gays and lesbians. *It's about the service.*

Since Zach was born, various persons or organizations were entrusted with his care, beginning with the nurses in the maternity ward and from there, all the pediatricians, dentists, babysitters, daycare providers, teachers, therapists, youth ministers, camp counselors, and coaches. All these people explicitly made my child's well-being their business and their highest priority (or at least they made a credible pretense of doing so).

Had Zach, like his brothers, gone on to college, the college would have claimed a similar, sympathetic focus.

But Zach joined an organization whose highest priority was not Zach. His interests ("I want you to teach me to work") and the interests of the Marine Corps could be said to intersect, but they were not identical.

If our sons had come of age in the 1930s and '40s rather than at the start of the twenty-first century, Peter and Cobus would have been drafted to serve in the Second World War. Dick and Donald—the young men who attempted robbery by canoe—would have been called up, too. The boy who froze in the woods could have frozen at the Battle of the Bulge instead, and it would have been a telegram from the War Office that regretfully informed his mom rather than a Warden Service chaplain.

Washington Post reporter Tom Ricks once told me that it was during the Vietnam War that the word *wasted* came to mean "killed."

"That was how it seemed to the grunts," he said. "That

their friends were dying for nothing. Not sacrificed for a purpose. Just wasted."

I wonder how long it took for this word to follow other bellicose verbs (*stoned, hammered, smashed*) back to what the soldiers called "the world" to be co-opted by their peers. "Wasted" is how the frozen college boy's friends described him, long before they knew that he was dead.

Chapter Sixteen

When compared with other stories from the vast human tradition, the stories in the Bible are hardly unique in their calm acceptance of the notion that God, like Stalin, had to crack a few eggs to make an omelet. Given human nature, it would be surprising indeed if any scripture sacred to those days (or, sadly, our own) didn't involve bloodshed. The really remarkable thing is that the Bible tells stories whose heroes aren't particularly heroic by the shining-armor standard.

Take Jacob: He would eventually be a hero and a patriarch but, unlike Jesus, he wasn't born virtuous. Born (literally) on the heels of a better brother, he would steal his dying father's blessing and the birthright from his twin, Esau. Greed, covetousness, deceit, and treachery are Jacob's first defining traits, but there was some courage in him, too. When Esau, still resentful, assembled an army to catch and kill him, Jacob sent his wives, slaves, sheep, and children to safety, then lay down alone in the desert to sleep. He was in the middle of a dream about a stairway to heaven, angels climbing up and down it, singing, when—sudden and scary as a Parris Island drill instructor—a big, strong seraph appeared on the sand beside Jacob, ready to pop his personal space-bubble. *Oy!* And Jacob has to wrestle this angel of God, who might actually be God.

Jacob was a thinker, a dreamer (some might say a schemer), but he wasn't a killer. Jacob would manage to live out his normal-for-the-Bible life span of 147 years without a single recorded homicide to his credit.

It is the vigor and stubbornness of his struggle with God, not its violence, which distinguishes this wrestling match. We are told that Jacob limps ever afterward, and I imagine God limping, too, as, post–Family Violence Hour, he heads at last to bed. ("It's getting harder and harder to win without hurting 'em," he says to Mrs. God.)

If the lesson of Jericho appears to be *kill 'em all and let God sort 'em out*, the lesson of Jacob's bout of physical/metaphysical violence would seem to be that there is more than one way to be a hero.

As our younger children began, one by one, to graduate from high school and go off to college, so did the children of our friends, and we all felt the bittersweet pang of separation, though Simon and I, comparing college with Parris Island, weren't quite as maudlin about it as we might otherwise have been.

True differentiation between child and adult gets muddled and delayed by the extended financial and emotional dependence of college students. Unlike in Marine Corps boot camp, college life is not one long stress test. But the tests our young ones sometimes devise for themselves are not just hazardous, they are meaninglessly so.

Even if we assume that—unlike the boy who got drunk and died of hypothermia in the woods—most survive such tests, how many college sophomores emerge from a weekend of binge drinking, wipe the vomit from their chins, and proudly declare, "If I can do that, I can do anything"?

The problem isn't that college is dangerous, it's that college students are, like Dick and Donald, and Sergeant Sangster's recruits, young persons at the personal and statistical apogee of developmental human brainlessness. At your average four-year institution of higher education, students have neither adult supervision nor the threat of adult consequences to compensate.

Take my own representatives of this particular demographic. "I could be a sperm donor!" exclaimed Peter, a gleam of witless avarice in his eye, when I told him about my companion on the plane to Mobile.

"You can be a sperm donor when you're thirty-five and have children of your own," I said. "So you'll know what you're giving away."

"It's my sperm."

"It's not the sperm I'm thinking of, sweet pea, it's the

babies. Those little doodlebugs would be my grandchildren. What if they got into trouble? I wouldn't know them, or be able to help them if they needed it."

"My sperm, my decision. I'm a grown-up."

Dourly, I informed Peter that, should he leave school to devote himself full-time to rock and roll, as was his present plan, he would become, at best, a donor to moms-to-be on a budget. "There aren't a lot of childless women prepared to pay top dollar for the semen of homeless drummers."

"Homeless?"

"You can drop out of school if you want to, but you won't be moving back in here with us."

"Mom!"

"You're a grown-up," I said affectionately. "Remember?"

I'm not sure I would recommend having six kids, no matter how you conceive or acquire them. There are disadvantages.

First of all, they eat. A lot. The philoprogenitive should refrain from introducing their young'uns little palates to exotic foods, however beneficial the stimulation might be for little brains. Like dummies, Simon and I reared kids who are expensively enthusiastic about sushi and scampi: if yours will only eat Happy Meals and Yoplait, count yourselves fortunate. After all, having six kids means saving for six college educations.

It's fiscally impossible. Scratch that. What you are really saving for is the trip to Paris you're going to take with your spouse (assuming your minds, bodies, and marriage have survived) when the last child matriculates on his own dime (or debt).

On the plus side, having six children gives parents ample opportunity to compare, contrast, and come to the astonishing conclusion that *every child is different.*

Oh, not in everything. There are basic ways in which all children are pretty much the same. Since human beings are bipedal, for example, human children walk, absent specific disability.

Most begin around the age of one, give or take a couple of months, though it is often difficult for the first-time parent to really believe the first steps will ever happen. I started giving Zach walking lessons when he was ten months, but he ignored me and walked at a (normal) year. A friend took her child to a specialist because the kid was crawling, pulling herself up on the furniture, and "cruising" but not actually walking at fourteen months (normal). Meanwhile, my (normal) fourth and youngest child, whose development in this as in so many areas I disregarded, walked at nine months.

Drew's theory was that Woolie didn't want to be left behind by a mother who might have forgotten she existed (okay, it could happen), but for all I know, early walking is actually an indication of some wondrous *enfant* precocity. What it meant in practice was that, because Woolie hadn't done a full, twelve-month reconnaissance of the spatial features and properties of her environment, she tended to walk off edges and smack into walls.

There are many human societies (most of them, in fact, if you're counting historically) that never invented written language, so writing and reading can't be called "natural" the way walking is. Still, most youngsters in literate societies learn to read at around the age at which they are taught to do so—at four or five in England, six or seven in the United States. And intelligence, defined as the ability to learn new facts and skills, is a human characteristic even if literacy per se is not—a Yanomamo baby brought up in Sweden would learn to read Swedish, just as the Swedish baby she was swapped for would learn the properties and utility of thousands of rainforest species.

Humans are intelligent, so it is reason rather than maternal fondness that leads me to conclude that all six of my children are smart, possessed of an innate, human ability to learn facts and skills, process data into usable information, and discover and create new facts and skills. What they do with this ability varies.

Yes, some of the variation comes from gender. Little girls really do learn to talk earlier than their brothers. Admit that aloud in a room full of women, and they will respond with knowing, superior smirks, but beware, sisters! A superior smirk goeth before a fall: Lincoln, Churchill, King, and Obama probably toddled around, pointing and grunting, even as their female peers uttered complete sentences with multiple modifiers and subordinate clauses, and yet the last shall be first, the first shall be last, and boys catch up.

In fact, there's a general principle I wish I'd posted on my fridge or maybe tattooed on my forearm: Becoming a fully developed human being isn't one job, it's a thousand jobs. All the jobs are crucial, they all take time, and multitasking just makes for confusion and inefficiency.

If your little boy doesn't seem to be getting around to learning to talk, it probably means his brain is busy elsewhere, maybe knitting up his synapses into the peculiar neural network that allows males to be unendingly amused by flatus or to distinguish a passing Nissan from a Bimmer in the dark, at highway speed.

The development of a child takes place in broad strokes (children walk at a year) and fine, idiosyncratic detail (this one collects light bulbs, that one has to take his shoes off before he can poop).

Pick two children—Son A and Son B—and compare them side by side. You'll discern characteristics in common.

They're both boys. They both walked at about twelve months of age and learned to talk a little later than their sisters.

Son A earns good grades and tests well on standardized tests, and so does Son B—which is to say, Son B gets good grades in subjects he is interested in, and does better than he has any right to on the tests he never bothers to study for.

Son A and Son B have particular gifts and talents, and these present them with some concomitant challenges. One of Son A's gifts, for example, is that he is good at identifying a long-range goal, determining which of various paths lead to that goal, getting himself onto the best path, and then, with diligence and self-discipline, moving steadily along it. Elite universities are filled with kids who share Son A's gift, so it's not hard to see the advantage it offers.

The challenge for Son A makes itself known in situations in which there is no path, no recognized or even recognizable "right way" to do something. Oh, but watch that superior smirk, Son B! A challenge is not an inability. When it's necessary, Son A can think outside the box even if, in general, he's an in-the-box guy.

Son B's gift is the polar opposite: Push him into a prescribed track and he will want to jump the curb. Give him a wide-open field of tangled possibilities, unscripted and uncharted, and he will happily scythe, stomp, or weed-whack his own path. It might not look like a path, and it's possible it will end at a brick wall, at which point Son B will have to change direction and create yet another whole new path.

The challenge here is scarily obvious, at least to Son B's harried parents: there are important, worthy, universal goals that can only be reached by prescribed paths or discovered inside the box.

From a parent's point of view, Son A's career is likely to be, if not completely predictable, at least agreeably recognizable. Son B's parents will spend years worried their boy is going nowhere. I would worry a lot about my own Son B if it weren't for the fact that I was a Daughter B.

Sons A and B would squawk to hear me describe them this way. "Typologically!" Son A would say, and Son B would chime in indignantly: both he and his brother are far more flexible and nuanced in their ways and means than I've made them sound. This is, in a way, the point.

If you were a customer at a sperm bank browsing among the vials or a parent seeking to mold a child according to a set of desired outcomes—attendance at selective schools, high earning power, the best chances for physical or social security— you would choose Son A.

Everyone chooses Son A. (At least, everyone willing to skip that pesky height requirement: my own Son A is only 5′9″, a fine height for any purpose other than, apparently, impregnating strangers via FedEx.)

But if you were a young woman inclined by a biological imperative toward falling in love with and getting married to an actual human man, who knows? While you are batting your eyelashes, or discussing the second law of thermodynamics, your brain might be evaluating your date on an evolutionary level that is ancient, experienced, and much more broad-minded and discerning than our conscious minds could ever be.

By means and criteria unavailable to conscious cognition, you'll be checking out his teeth, gait, muscle tone, the timbre of his voice, and, for all I know, the pheromones in his armpits that signal enhanced resistance to viruses or the ability to ingest, unharmed, a wider range of organic toxins.

Ellie informed me, the other day, that the darkness and width of the ring around a woman's iris signals fertility. When Drew gazed deeply into my eyes, was he making measurements?

Romantic love—so often mistaken for the highest and holiest—may be furthest removed from the true, essential, unselfish love known and named in the great spiritual traditions (*hesed, agape, maitri*), but even romance is more willing than commerce to resist immediate self-interest and jump past present prejudices.

"What do you mean, commerce?" Peter demanded.

"Didn't you just say you wanted to sell your sperm?"

"I could use the money! Besides, it's not as if all babies can be born to people who love each other. Tons of babies get conceived because women want to trap a man into marriage..."

"*Tons?*" I said. "Seriously?"

"...or because men are rapists."

"I don't approve of mantraps or rapists," I said.

"And lots of kids are raised by people they aren't biologically related to. Adoption, Mom: you do approve of that."

"A child is put up for adoption when the alternative is believed to be worse."

"Isn't nonexistence worse than existence?" said Peter. "Wouldn't you want all your donor-baby grandchildren to get a chance to live, even if you didn't get to know them or help them or whatever? I mean, God, Mom, think about it! What if you were dead?"

I thought about it.

Drew's grandson will be rattling around in the world and Drew will not know or be able to help him, but this isn't a good thing. It isn't even a neutral thing: it's one of the sorrows that make his death as a young man tragic.

But I didn't want to play the dead-dad card with my son — it wouldn't be fair.

"Peter," I said. "I'm not dead. And, as you say, you're a grown man. You have the right to sell your vials to anyone willing to pay for 'em. I'm just saying that there are thorny issues involved, ones that, as of today at least, you won't be able to claim you didn't know about."

Peter stared at me. "You are," he said at length, "*brutal.*"

Dear Zach,

You and your siblings occasionally came down with illnesses in which a high fever was combined with nausea, and you couldn't keep medicine down long enough to affect your temperature. Whether pitching or catching, everyone loathes a suppository. Having admitted as much, might I nonetheless recommend keeping a box of Tylenol suppositories in your refrigerator just in case my grandson is ever similarly afflicted?

Love, Mom

CHAPTER SEVENTEEN

It was probably from my stepson, Cobus, that I first heard about experiments done in the 1970s by Stanley Milgram to determine the degree to which a man (all Milgram's test subjects were male) would be willing to obey an order to hurt another.

Subjects were asked by a scientist (fake) to deliver increasingly painful electric shocks (fake) to (fake) victims, supposedly in the service of some unrelated scientific research goal. Two-thirds of Milgram's subjects went on obediently shocking their victims to the point of (fake) mortal injury, though, for what it's worth, no one actually seemed to *enjoy* doing it.

Among the conclusions Milgram drew was that obedience in such circumstances is more likely to be secured if the test subject is offered an implicit or explicit ethically defensible justification—e.g., "scientific research is important"—for the act.

This likely comes as no surprise to anyone interested in starting a war: American leaders from the president on down asserted that invading Iraq, for example, was crucial in order to defend the nation from terrorism. The perpetrators of abuse at Abu Ghraib would go on citing the defense of Americans from terrorists as justification for their own violence long after they had been discredited.

Naturally, I thought (and fretted) about what dishonorable and soul-destroying orders Zach might be asked to obey in the cause of freedom, but I reconsidered Stanley Milgram and his electric shocks when my stepdaughter announced that she wanted to go to nursing school.

High school graduation loomed, and the stressors associated with it inevitably brought out Ilona's "difficult" side. One day she accompanied an apology for rudeness with a worried lament: "Maybe I wouldn't be a very good nurse. I'm such a bitch!"

Ordinarily, I would've responded to this bit of self-abnegation with the reassuring denials Ilona was doubtless fishing for, but I had Milgram on my mind.

"Actually," I said thoughtfully, "being a bitch might make you a better nurse. Not that you're actually a bitch," I amended hastily, since Ilona was beginning to look both hurt and inclined to be "difficult" again. "It's just that you aren't especially empathetic... how shall I put this? Being tuned in to other people's feelings isn't one of your natural strengths..."

Nettled, Ilona retorted, "That sounds like the definition of a bitch."

"No, no... Ilona, as a nurse you'll have to do all sorts of painful, humiliating things to people, right? You'll have to give children cholera shots, administer nauseating chemotherapy, manually disimpact the miserably constipated, and, if you work in obstetrics, you'll have to endure the cries of women in labor. Sheesh, during the Civil War, nurses had to help surgeons saw off wounded soldiers' limbs without anesthetic. We don't think of those women as sadistic. Maybe a nurse who identifies too much with the feelings of other people has a kind of handicap. If you can't bring yourself to inflict pain when inflicting pain is the route to healing, *then* you won't be a very good nurse."

"Uh-huh," said Ilona, unconvinced.

Not long afterward, as luck would have it, I had occasion to demonstrate the principle: I cut off my thumb.

Okay, that's a small exaggeration. In a foolish food-prep accident, I lacerated the top of my left thumb, all the way to the bone. Sadly, this wasn't even the first time I had done so.

The first near-amputation was inflicted by Simon's mandoline food slicer, an evil implement that crouches in our knife drawer, its razor-sharp blade concealed within a toy-like, mint-green plastic body. After I had accidentally seasoned a nice *gratin* of paper-thin potato slices and Gruyère with a good half-cup of my left thumb's blood, Simon forbade me from using or even touching the mandoline. Then I did the same thing to my right thumb with an ordinary paring knife, so now I am only allowed to cook and serve whole things (potatoes, chickens, unsliced bread).

Anyway, having examined the wound with a soon-to-be expert eye, Ilona drove me to the ER. The doctor agreed that she could remain with me and witness the repair. This was the same doctor who had fixed my first thumb, so he performed the procedure with raised eyebrows and exasperated sighs, but he was nice about explaining everything to Ilona. She watched eagerly, her nose mere inches away, as he inserted the hypodermic needle loaded with novocaine directly into the open wound. At the same time, she was making soothing noises and letting me squeeze her fingers with my uninjured hand.

"See?" I said, as she drove me home. "You'll be a *fabulous* nurse!"

The moral life would be so much easier to sustain if things were just a tad clearer: if, for example, inflicting pain was always an expression of sadism or craven obedience, always the Devil's work. But America's doctors and nurses, not just her soldiers and prison guards, are drawn from the two-thirds of us Milgram suggests are capable of at least some indifference to suffering.

And they aren't the only ones: Warden Chris Dyer, instructing recruits in defensive tactics at the Maine Criminal Justice Academy, likewise has good reason to hurt people. A blow from his knee to a colleague's subscapular nerve demonstrates for his students how effectively pain can "change the channel" in a suspect's brain, and allow him to be taken into custody (deprived of liberty, a painful matter in itself) without permanent injury. And Chris and his colleagues might also squirt pepper spray into recruits' eyes or use a Taser on them, so they, in their turn, won't be too casual when it comes to using less-than-lethal weapons on human beings.

And what about parents? Even if you leave aside the "violence" of the time-out chair, didn't I have to deafen myself to my children's protests when I allowed them to be immunized, washed their skinned knees, or extracted their splinters?

"Not to mention the suppositories," Peter said, shuddering, when I brought the subject up with him. "Those were awful."

"Thank you," said the young wife of a game warden, the mother of toddlers and a new baby. "But I already have this recipe."

It was "my" recipe for what my children called Play-Go. "Really?" I said.

"Everyone has it," she explained. "It's on the Web."

Oh.

"But we adore the little hat. Did you knit it?"

When I was the mother of very young children, recipes for homemade Play-Go and bubble soap and advice on suppositories, laundry soap, and other mysteries were passed around like Soviet-era samizdat, but we didn't have the Internet. Now, everything is there, writ large on a hundred blogs and websites, all the advice new parents will ever need is available 24/7 and continuously updated.

Since my grandson will be living in southern California, a colorful, hand-knit wool hat will only make the poor kid sweat. Maybe I'll buy the kid a bathrobe.

Dear Ilona and Cobus,

I can't promise to love you.

Don't get me wrong: you are lovable people, and even if there exists a woman incapable of recognizing so obvious a truth, she isn't a person your father would marry. He's not stupid and since I'm not, either, I find you both delightful.

Though you will always be part of my family, you will only be part of my household for a few more years. After that, you'll be off, making your own homes and your own lives. My own kids have biology and habit on their side, but however much affection I might feel for you on the day of the wedding, affection is variable in a way that honor, at least among the honorable, is not. It seems to me that the most appropriate commitment I can make has to be one I can honorably keep whether or not we actually like each other all that much at any given moment.

Therefore to you, Ilona and Cobus, it shall be on my honor that I vow to support and encourage your father in his fathering, to be with him and stand by him as he protects, encourages, nourishes, and nurtures you. And I will do my best to be with you and stand by you as a steadfast guide and champion, bearing loving witness as you, Cobus, and you, Ilona, grow to strong, independent, and honorable adulthood.

CHAPTER EIGHTEEN

When it came to our wedding, the first question Simon and I had to answer was, "Which church?" Simon is a mostly lapsed Catholic and functional communicant of the United Church of Christ, and I am an ordained Unitarian Universalist, and inaugurating a mixed marriage always requires some delicacy. Admittedly, we are not that far apart either theologically or in terms of practice, and compromise was possible, but to insist on a Unitarian Universalist officiant and/or a Unitarian Universalist church when I am a Unitarian Universalist minister made for a lot of UU (or "me me"). So we asked Simon's minister to perform the service in her little local church—she was not only an old friend of Simon's, but also a seminary classmate of mine.

With fine collegiality, Pastor Susan invited me to help craft the service. But the only part I was really concerned about was the vows—not mine to Simon or Simon's to me, but the ones we each would make to the kids.

What could Simon promise Zach, Peter, Ellie, and Woolie? What could I promise Ilona and Cobus?

"And what would you want the children to say in return?" Pastor Susan asked, after we'd hammered out a matched set of vows for Simon and me to say during the service.

"Nothing," I said. "They're *children*."

During the ceremony, when the time came to turn toward our children and speak to them, Simon and I both did so weeping. Neither of us could resist adding "I love you" to the otherwise restrained and rather formal phrases. The kids said "I love you" back, too, but that wasn't a vow, really, just grace.

Upon completing basic training, Zach was sent to Advanced Combat Training and thence to Fort Meade, Maryland, where he began to learn the skills required for his specific Military Occupation Specialty, or MOS (following in his *morfar*'s footsteps, he was to be a correspondent for military publications).

He lived with other newly minted Marines in a barracks presided over by a very large, muscular African-American man who would become familiar to us through Zach's stories. Sergeant Purcell taught his charges to run faster and fight harder. He inspected their uniforms and meted out punishments, but I was surprised to learn that it was he who took Zach's temperature when he was ill and made sure Zach flossed his teeth. One day, Zach called to tell us he'd run twelve miles in record time. "When it was over, I was on my knees, puking. Sergeant Purcell was standing over me hollering, 'That's what I call a quality effort, Devil-Dawg!'"

The pride in Zach's voice brought tears to my eyes.

Not long after this, Zach called to tell us the barracks had held a talent show. I tried to imagine what talents young Marines might be able to conjure for such an occasion. My bigoted, maternal mind pictured armpit-farts and karaoke.

"Sergeant Purcell recited love poems of his own composition," Zach said. "And you know, I realized I hadn't written a poem since I was in high school."

"Wait, did you say Sergeant Purcell *recited love poems?*"

"Yeah. It was inspiring. So anyway, since then, I've been writing a lot of poetry."

Revelation always seems to reveal what I should have known already. "Your dad wrote poetry," I said.

"I know, Mom," Zach answered gently.

Periodically, over the coming months and years, the United States Marine Corps would make plans to send my son to Afghanistan or Iraq. At least once Zach called to say he had volunteered for the next available posting to Baghdad, but to my imperfectly concealed relief, the nation's needs always altered, and Zach would be sent instead on some humanitarian mission.

It turns out that when there are hurricanes in Honduras, mudslides in the Philippines, a tsunami (and a damaged nuclear reactor) in Japan, America sends Marines. Zach seemed to be spending most of his time zipping around the Pacific Rim helping people.

"I had no idea!" Simon marveled. "Trust Zach to get a Peace Corps experience out of the Marine Corps!"

He came home on leave from Okinawa to attend our wedding. In his elegant, full-dress uniform, he walked his mother down the aisle.

Zach brought a girl home with him.

"Are you sure?" I asked, when he called to let me know what his travel arrangements would be. "Bringing a…ahem…friend to a family event is kind of a big deal. It's a commitment."

"I know what I'm doing," Zach said.

Erin had been described to us as a Southerner, a Marine who had actually outranked Zach when they first met, and as the owner of a Harley-Davidson motorcycle. I was picturing, well, okay, not a leather-clad behemoth but, anyway, a person built on slightly more substantial lines than the slender, delicate, blue-eyed flower Zach introduced to us.

Erin was adorable and authoritative, holding her own in a crowd of siblings, stepsiblings, and assorted relations (all of them in fierce and friendly competition for the Big Personality prize). She was witty and—most endearing of all—she clearly thought the sun shone out of Zach's eyes.

"And Mom, get this," Zach told me, in an after-the-rehearsal-dinner aside. "Erin is *good at math!*"

To Erin, he told the story of the time that I had lifted him off the floor by the front of his sweatshirt and pinned him against the wall. "And Mom told me, 'Zach, if you ever hit any woman, ever, I will kill you.'"

"Zach!" I squeaked. "Are you crazy? Why are you bringing that up?"

"Why not?" asked Erin.

Sadly, I confessed, "It's not a moment in my motherhood that I am proud of. In fact, I feel sick with guilt every time I think about it."

"You're kidding," said Zach.

"No."

"Mom, I think it was awesome!"

"You do?"

"Sure," said Zach merrily. "I was being a little jerk. You did what you had to do to keep me in line."

"Ooh-rah!" said Erin.

Oh.

Dear Ellie,

Your Great-Aunt Harriet had no grandchildren and thus had no reason to keep toys at her house, but when you were very small, she used to entertain you with playthings she invented. For instance, she would take a Ziploc freezer bag and squirt mustard in one corner and ketchup in the other. Or it might be lumps of coconut oil, some ice cubes, or the Jell-O I wouldn't let you eat. But anyway, once the bag was zipped shut, you could mash the contents around for a happy hour, making a colorful, disgusting, but completely contained mess. (I suppose if you had managed to open the bag, or break it, the contents would have been icky but nontoxic.)

Later on, of course, for the delectation of your dolls, you made mud pies and mud soup garnished with grass. These childhood play-cooking activities are time-honored in a way that mixing condiments with ice cubes in a plastic bag definitely is not. Still, I was thinking you could keep the mustard-and-ketchup Ziploc trick in mind for when your nephew comes to visit?

"Oh yeah," said Warden Bruce Loring. "My wife did that with our kids... I think she got it off a website."

Chapter Nineteen

Among my second (right-on-time) husband's many virtues was that he liked to cook, and did it well. This was much appreciated by all of my children, who enjoyed eating, and by Ellie in particular, as she now, at long last, had someone to nurture her own culinary interests. No longer alone in the kitchen, inventing recipes that would, at best, receive mixed reviews ("Remember the cucumbers with hot sauce?" Zach wrote to her from Fort Meade. "Believe it or not, I wish I were eating those now..."), Ellie spent her evenings cooking with Simon.

"We're making *erwtensoep*," she informed me, when I asked. "It's Dutch for split pea soup."

From the living room couch where I sat knitting, I could hear Ellie and her stepfather talking and laughing together as comforting, nourishing smells wafted forth, promising a family meal worthy of a few thankful prayers.

Together, my eldest daughter and her stepdad rinsed and

picked over the split peas and put them into the stockpot together with water, chicken broth, and pork hocks. They brought this to a boil, and Simon showed Ellie how to skim the foam from the surface. The soup would simmer for an hour while they chopped garlic, onion, potatoes, celery, carrots, and leeks to add, then the soup would simmer, covered, for another hour or so, until vegetables could be pierced with a knife. Pork hocks removed, the soup would be pureed, seasoned with salt and pepper, garnished with the remaining ham and parsley, and placed before the family.

"Beautiful soup!" I said, and Ellie grinned proudly.

"Simon could make gravel delicious."

"He's a good cook," I agreed.

"He's a good dad," said Ellie, matter-of-factly. "Seriously, how many men can buy tampons at Rite Aid and not get embarrassed?"

In a household now boasting four female members, this was no small matter. "I really prefer living with men," Ilona announced one day, in a remark that could so easily have been taken for an insult. The three other people present in the room at the time were, after all, the very persons whose arrival on the scene meant she was no longer living according to this preference, namely, Ilona's stepmother and two stepsisters.

As the glow of a glorious wedding wore off, we were all engaged in the complex and sometimes fractious effort of combining two households into one. In a summerlong, prewedding building binge, Simon had more than doubled the available "biomass storage capacity" of his house. Nevertheless, each of the children still living at home felt the need to assert and defend his or her right to space, time, and parental attention, sometimes loudly. So Ilona's remark could have sparked a quarrel—it may even have been intended to do so—but I decided to take it at face value.

"Hey! Me, too!"

"Thanks a lot, Mom," Woolie snapped.

"At least, I seem to like *working* in a virtually all-male environment. Law enforcement. The Warden Service. Y'know."

"It's because you're kind of butch," said Woolie.

"I'm not butch!" I said. "I'm just…assertive."

"Hey! Me, too!" said Ilona. "My kindergarten teacher used to call me The Steamroller."

Ellie considered. "It's more comfortable to be a steamroller if the room is full of heavy equipment…"

"Dump trucks," added Woolie dryly.

"Front-end loaders," I suggested, leering, which made Woolie shriek and fake-gag. At twelve, she was offended whenever I uttered smutty double entendres, though she still felt comfortable talking to her Aunt Mary about sex.

By this time, Zach and Peter were gone and Cobus was going. Ellie and Ilona were finishing up their secondary education and eagerly anticipating next moves.

Meanwhile, with a prescience born of having seen her elder siblings depart childhood never to return, Woolie had clearly concluded there would be plenty of time to be a teen, let alone a grown-up. Time she might otherwise have spent perusing *CosmoGirl* and fretting about her weight was devoted to making forts in the woods and painting portraits of the dog. Woolie was fortunate enough to have a few friends who shared her distaste for what they'd seen of teen culture. So, while many of their classmates were downsizing from underpants to thongs and upscaling nascent breasts with padded bras, Woolie and her buddy Madeline slept overnight in a graveyard (no ghosts, lots of mosquitoes) and took a Huck Finn–style trip down the Mill River on a homemade raft. (No, they did not wear life jackets, and yes, I had a fit when I heard about it.)

At the start of her freshman year of high school, Woolie set up a tent in the yard and spent every night out there until well after the first snow had fallen, but camping out didn't keep her a kid. She was a teenager. Everything was dumb and sucked, and she didn't see why she couldn't quit school or get a tattoo or a ferret or something.

Woolie didn't even get the satisfaction of an outraged reaction to her querulous complaints. Simon and I, veterans of five previous adolescences not counting our own, smiled sympathetically and said, "This too shall pass," a remark which was no less irritating for being so obviously true.

She had her first period at school, and her teacher greeted the arrival of her menses with what Woolie regarded as unwarranted enthusiasm.

"Miss Agnew said it was a beautiful thing," Woolie reported. "She said it means I can one day have babies."

"You'll get used to it. Have a napkin," I said. Then I tried to cheer her up with stories from my own painful adolescence, like the one where I accidentally bled on the bleacher where my scary gym teacher was about to lay her new, white sweater and how, when Ms. Zappacosta yelled at me, instead of doing something sensible like bursting into tears, I corrected her pronunciation ("It's menstruation, not menestration…").

And what did Woolie have to say about all of this? "I don't want to have babies. I want to be a high school dropout with tattoos. And an artist."

"Adolescence is the time in a person's life when a young mind opens," my friend Tonya commented, "and the brains fall out."

She was referring to her own children, of course, but I could sympathize. My children did things during their teenage years that were stupid. Luckily for them, my memories of my own youth remain clear enough for me to regard stupidity as a normal and generally transient feature of adolescence. In fact, even the worst of my own kids' misbehavior—yes, even Peter firebombing the backyard—didn't come close to the idiotic, rotten things I did when I was young.

When Woolie, at fourteen, was arrested for shoplifting, I wasn't happy but I wasn't shocked. When the misbehavior occurred, both Simon and I were away from home, so the arresting officer, Sergeant Hall of the Camden Police Department, hadn't been able to serve my minor child with the summons for her crime. He released her into the care of a friend and instructed her to have me call to arrange a meeting.

"She was very polite," Sergeant Hall told me over the phone.

"Good to know," I said briskly. "Now, Sergeant, there are some things we need to discuss."

Sergeant Hall, who was also very polite, responded warily, bracing himself, he later told me, for the parental response he was accustomed to.

How dare you arrest my child! She stole a seven-dollar bottle of hair dye. Do you know how much we probably spend at Rite Aid every year? Do you have any idea who I am in this community? Sergeant Hall, my adorable daughter is up in her room weeping. She's experiencing shame—do you know how toxic shame is? Can you even imagine what this has done to her self-esteem? If she has a criminal record, it might affect her chances of getting into the college of her choice. Did you think of that? We will certainly be meeting with you tomorrow, and I suggest you have your supervisor present, since we will have our lawyers with us.

Woolie was indeed in her room, weeping copiously. I had no doubt she felt ashamed of herself and that her self-esteem had taken a pretty good whack.

"Listen," I said to Sergeant Hall. "I'm sorry my daughter has done this. We'll be at the PD tomorrow at eleven, and this is what Woolie is going to be doing between now and then…"

In this situation, if in no other, Woolie was lucky to have me as a mother, though she might not have thought so at that moment. As mentioned, I had been a truly awful kid. And luckily for Woolie, as an adult I belonged to the law enforcement community.

When I was young, I stole from our local drugstore all the time. At least once a week I'd walk in with a quarter, buy a pack of gum, and leave with my pockets bulging with candy bars, comic books, fountain pens, and trinkets. In case you're wondering, I think my kleptomania was indeed a result of low self-esteem. Unfortunately, it was also a *cause* of low self-esteem, for on what can a thief base her good opinion of herself? No matter how often my parents might have assured me of my lovability, the girl in the mirror knew the truth.

At Woolie's age, I also stole hair dye, eyeliner, lipsticks, and a bottle of Jean Naté perfume. Unlike Woolie, I was never caught, let alone arrested. Thirty years later, the smell of Jean Naté still calls forth in my conscience a deep and distinctly unpleasant residual shame.

I reformed eventually. I grew up and became the strictest mother in Maine. So I was not displeased that Woolie was ashamed of herself for the time being. This was the healthy sign of a functioning conscience. On the other hand, I did not want my beloved daughter to still feel ashamed thirty years down the road. I was indeed determined to protect her self-esteem from the toxic effects of shame. This meant that I was going to have to let Woolie be made even more unhappy in the short term so that in the long run she would know herself and trust herself to be a genuinely good person.

Woolie had already experienced punitive consequences

for her action. She had been arrested and taken to the police station. Hadn't she suffered enough?

Um, no.

Because I work with law enforcement officers, I was aware that Sergeant Hall had no power—none—to mete out real consequences to my daughter. The most he could do had already been done: he could place Woolie under arrest and put her in handcuffs (though because she had been so polite, he hadn't done so); he could file a report and he could serve her with a summons in the presence of a parent. That was it.

While it seems obvious, you'd be surprised at how many people expect the police to be surrogate moms and (especially) dads. But a police officer does not serve *in loco parentis*. The officer called to deal with an "out of control" six-year-old (this really happens) can't put her on the time-out chair, can't even touch her unless it is to protect the child from imminent harm. Sergeant Hall couldn't ground Woolie or take away her allowance. Nor could he reassure her, tell her she was a good person, say he loved her. Only Woolie's parent could do these things.

Parents also frequently assume that the sight of a police officer will be enough to intimidate, even terrify, a teen. Baby boomers remember the Chicago police riots of 1968, the movie *Serpico*, and the videotapes of the Rodney King episode, and these associations arise subconsciously when a beloved child runs afoul of the law. If I lack this automatic defensiveness, it is in large part because I know so many law enforcement officers very well. Not only am I familiar with the limitations of their role, but it is also easy for me to regard them as human beings: essentially decent, well-meaning men and women who share my hope that all the children in our community will grow up safely and become decent, well-meaning, productive, and happy adults.

So, although I hadn't been personally acquainted with Sergeant Hall prior to Woolie's arrest, I approached our initial telephone conversation with the confidence that he was my ally, not my enemy. Once Sergeant Hall was convinced the same was true about me, we were able to make a plan based on the fact that both of us sincerely wanted Woolie's first crime to be her last.

The next morning, promptly at eleven A.M., Woolie and I presented ourselves at the Camden Police Department and were ushered into the sergeant's office. For a man with a rather sweet face, Sergeant Hall was doing a splendid job of looking dour and uncompromising.

"Well, Woolie," he began. "What are we going to do about this?"

Woolie took a deep breath and told him what she had done so far. "I made a list of everyone who had been disappointed and hurt by my behavior. Then I wrote a letter to the manager of the Rite Aid and one to each of the clerks there, saying how sorry I am for stealing from them. And I used the word *stealing*," she explained. "Mom wouldn't let me use *shoplifting*."

"I see," said Sergeant Hall gravely. "So you've already mailed these letters?"

"Mom wouldn't let me mail them. She says if you do the crime in person, you can apologize in person."

"Ah."

"So this morning, Mom and I went to the store and gave out the letters, which was really...uh..."

Woolie's voice shook slightly at the memory. For twenty long minutes, she had dithered miserably on the sidewalk before finding the courage to go into the store.

"Yes?"

"They were nice about it, sir," Woolie assured him earnestly. "I just felt bad. I told the manager that I wouldn't come into the store without a grown-up for a whole year. At the end of the year, I will ask his permission to be a customer again."

Sergeant Hall caught my eye and coughed.

"I offered to do something for the store, like clean up or something," Woolie continued, "but the manager said they couldn't let me do that because of insurance rules. So I'll volunteer at the hospital for a year instead."

The corners of the sergeant's mouth twitched upward. Faced with this gawky vision of adolescent contrition, Sergeant Hall's mask was beginning to slip.

"And what else, Woolie?" I prompted hastily.

"Well," said Woolie, "I told him, too, that of course I would plead guilty if there is a trial. Is there going to be a trial?"

"Um...probably not."

"Which is not the issue, Woolie," I interrupted. "Remember? This is about making things right with your community.

This is about taking responsibility and repairing the damage you have caused. The law will do whatever it has to do. You are going to do the right thing."

Woolie nodded. "Oh. Yes. The thing is, I told the manager I wouldn't lie about what happened, in court or wherever. And Mom said I should give you this." Woolie produced a letter from her pocket. "It says how sorry I am for putting you in a position where you had to arrest me, and for doing something stupid. I'm really sorry, Sergeant Hall."

"Thank you very much," said Sergeant Hall, gazing down at his letter. I could see he was getting mushy on me. Time to wrap things up.

"Woolie, why don't you go out to the waiting room, so the sergeant and I can discuss...your fate?"

Woolie gulped and went out.

"Omigod, what a great kid!" Sergeant Hall burst out as soon as the door was closed.

I didn't argue with him: I was her mom. Of course I thought Woolie was a great kid and one unlikely to be destined for a life of crime, no matter what Sergeant Hall and I did or didn't do.

Still, Woolie and I have since agreed that the episode was an extraordinarily educational experience. My daughter learned that stealing wasn't about the value of what was stolen, but about the injury done to relationships with the people of her community. She realized that stealing "from a store" was really stealing trust and goodwill from her neighbors. Most useful of all, Woolie now knew how to rectify her errors.

By taking responsibility, offering recompense, performing service, and apologizing fully, truthfully, and personally, Woolie not only restored the original relationships but also strengthened and expanded them.

Woolie would grow out of brainless adolescence as her parents and siblings had done before her. She remained in touch with Sergeant Hall, and to this day, I can't pop into Rite Aid to buy panty hose without the employees asking after my daughter.

"Such a nice girl!" the manager says.

Woolie also remains on friendly terms, via Facebook, with her probation officer, to whose minimal supervision she was indeed remanded for a period of a few months.

"Your daughter did a lot more reparation than I could have asked for," he told me.

"You're not her mom," I replied.

Sometimes, Dr. Milgram, it's love and only love that overcomes a parent's instinct to protect the young from pain.

Dear Woolie,

To be happy, you need three things.

Well, technically, you need four things. The first
and most important thing is that you have to love and
be loved. But if we take that as read, there are three
more that might not be as obvious.

First, because you like to eat and (intermittently)
have a roof over your head, you'll need to earn money.
Second, you'll have to match your skills and talents
with people who want what you've got—writers need
readers, lawyers need clients, nurses need patients, and
so on. And third, you'll need to be of service to the
community and/or the world.

Some people can combine all three in a single job.
As a State Trooper, your father earned a living for
himself and his family, his skills and talents were
necessary and useful, and he helped people. Ditto for
Simon, your stepfather, a teacher.

Your mother, on the other hand, has to combine a
couple of jobs—writer plus chaplain to the Warden
Service—in order to cover all the bases.

Chapter Twenty

"Come here, you dreadful child," my mother used to say. Or maybe "horrible" or "hideous."

Once old enough to compare and contrast parenting styles, I asked my mother why my friends' parents could express their affection without the hair-raising vituperation that Mom seemed to find necessary.

"They believe in kinder gods," Mom explained. "If I were to call attention to your perfection, the gods might just decide they have a use for you."

In photos, I am a pasty pudding of a child with little raisin-eyes and a disgruntled expression. My father said that as an infant I looked just like Winston Churchill (but then, as the great man himself declared, babies do). No gods worth fearing would take a second look at me, but perhaps Darwinian evolution gives the edge to parents who can't see their own baby as just another Winston look-alike among the teeming millions.

My firstborn, Zachary, on the other hand, really was different. When my pregnancy with him had advanced sufficiently to be noticed, our local homeless man, taking his daily drunken stagger around the park, caught sight of my bulging stomach. Pointing, he cawed: "Lady, that child is special! He will be sacred to God!"

I said "thank you," went home, took my prenatal vitamins, elevated my swollen ankles, and pondered this message in my heart.

Then a neighbor appeared, bearing a bag of hand-me-downs from her own child. Tiny-footed jammies, little fuzzy socks, and endless cotton caps to protect a small, bald head from cold drafts or hot sun, all nearly new. Only the undershirts—the kind that overlap and snap in front—showed any sign of wear. Grayish-white, stained around the neckline and down the front with baby puke, these might be useful as cleaning rags, I thought. Fortunately, I didn't say so out loud. As the original owner toddled around the apartment, mumbling gibberish ("I have nothing to offer but blood, toil, tears, and sweat...") and looking for trachea-sized objects to put in her mouth, her mother spread the T-shirts reverently across her lap. Moist-eyed, she caressed the spit-up stains that marked the fronts as if these were the stains of the stigmata on the Shroud of Turin.

"You have no idea," she said, "how much you are going to love your baby."

Ah, I said to myself. *I get it.*

If, as was probably the case, that homeless man prophesied the same to every pregnant woman he encountered, each would hear and ponder as if his message were exclusively for her.

Of ordinary babies like my mother's and mine, the educator Sophia Lyon Fahs wrote: "No angels herald their beginnings. No prophets predict their future courses. No wise men see a star to show where to find the babe that will save humankind."

The conclusion that might be drawn is that there is no such babe in the offing, but Fahs swings the other way: "Each night a child is born is a holy night."

Every child is special, every child is sacred, but by middle school, my child (and his siblings) could've told the homeless man, and Sophia Fahs, too, that "special" isn't so good. It's the adjective that, when applied to ordinary words (needs, education, Olympics) concretizes a pregnant parent's most potent fears. Still, if "special" is worrisome, my mother would point out that "sacred" is even worse. From Buddha to the prophet Samuel, from Isaac to Jesus, those whom divine messengers (whether radiant and winged or drunk and smelly) single out may be destined for great things, but not necessarily for safety, happiness, or prosperity.

No wonder so many sacred children are said to have been conceived by a miracle, often through an infertile mother's bargain with the divine. *Just let me have a baby, God, and you may do with him as you will.*

We are meant to see such prayers as evidence of simple faith, not abject desperation, and the resulting pregnancy a sign of God's compassion and mercy, never mind that the baby and his mom seem doomed from the get-go to one awful experience after another.

Siddhartha's mother died within twelve days of the future Buddha's birth. The Hebrew matriarch Hannah wanted a child so badly she agreed in advance to an arrangement whereby her son, Samuel, was handed over to the custody of the temple just as soon as he was weaned. Abraham's strange, conflicted marriage to Sarah resulted in some collateral damage when Ishmael and his mother, Hagar, got dumped out in the desert for Yahweh to look after, while the legitimate "special boy" Isaac was tied up and threatened with death before his dad was served with a divine protection-from-abuse order. Is being the progenitor of a people as numerous as stars worth a bad case of PTSD? No wonder adult prophets from Moses to Mohammad, upon being promoted by God, do their best to duck the honor.

"The most excellent jihad is the uttering of truth in the presence of an unjust ruler," says the Hadith of Tirmidhi. Right—and such a jihad tends to be bloody, brief, and painful. Why would anyone sign themselves—let alone their kids—up for that?

"Thanks but no thanks," I whispered, tucking my own "horrible, hideous" offspring safely into bed.

Long ago, before I was married or had children, I volunteered in the geriatric ward of a hospital in Washington, DC. I read aloud (loudly) to those whose eyes and ears were failing, chatted with the lonesome, and gave backrubs to those who ached for touch. Washington is a diverse city, with substantial numbers of immigrants and expatriates from all over the world. So it was not unusual for a patient's accent to serve as our conversation starter. One day, as I was massaging Keri lotion into her shoulders, an elderly woman began to reminisce about her happy childhood in Germany, her school days, and her time preparing for a career in scientific research at the University of Potsdam. She matriculated in 1939, she said, and her parents were very proud.

She was seated in a chair, her back turned toward me, the ties of her hospital gown untied. To this day I remember the pattern of freckles on her back, the wisps of gray hair escaping from the crocheted cap she always wore, and the smell of Keri. The woman's skin suddenly felt different to me, and perhaps my hands felt different to her, too, for she hurriedly began to speak of the cruel Allied bombings, the end of her dreams of being a scientist, the rapine and plunder Germans endured at the hands of the Red Army.

"With only the belongings we could stuff into our car, my family fled to the American zone before the Russians reached our city. We were not Nazis," she assured me. "Ordinary Germans suffered very much during the war. No one thinks about people like us."

So I thought about ordinary Germans. Specifically, I thought about this woman's parents, bringing up their daughter in the 1920s and '30s, doting as she learned to toddle and talk. They took their child to the pediatrician, to the park, to church, and enrolled her in school. Anxiously, they perused report cards with comments like "Her handwriting is much improved" or "She needs to practice her times tables." They sponged her sweet little face, combed and braided her soft hair, read stories out loud, and sang lullabies.

Their family life had been part of the bland, bourgeois backdrop to the collapse of the Weimar Republic and Hitler's ascent to power. He brought welcome prosperity, pride, and order, if at the price of the persecution of my patient's Jewish neighbors, the Nuremberg Laws and Kristallnacht and then the Holocaust.

There are probably snapshots of my patient on her first day at university, September 1939, with her parents beaming beside her.

"All we want for our little girl is that she will be healthy and happy," my patient's mom and dad might have said.

If so, they would only have been expressing the common and indeed definitive desire of the good parent. I wanted health and happiness for my children, too. But if my darling child was not an American college student in the year 2014, but instead had matriculated at a German university in 1939, would I tell her to keep her head down, work the system, maybe even join the Nazi Party, so that she might live and prosper?

Or would I encourage her to resist, and risk herself?

"What could we do?" the patient asked rhetorically, while the candy striper toweled the Keri lotion off her hands, tied up the ties of the patient's hospital gown, and pressed the button that would summon a nurse to put the patient back to bed.

Like my patient, Sophie Scholl was a university student in Germany in the Nazi period. Having discerned enough of the shape and shame of the Holocaust from the evidence available at the time, Sophie, her brother Hans, and a number of like-minded friends founded the resistance group The White Rose. The organization's mission was to inform ordinary Germans about the horror that was unfolding, and rouse them to resistance against the Nazis.

In photos, Sophie Scholl has a serious, determined little face that breaks into a puckish smile. Did an angel herald this girl's beginnings, or a prophet predict her future back when she was, to any reasonable eye, just another pasty, Churchillian infant? And if such prophesies had been made, would Sophie's parents have humbly acceded, like the Virgin Mary ("Let it be done according to Your word"), or would they, like Siddhartha's dad, have vowed instead to thwart divine design by any means necessary?

Not without trepidation should parents hope for, let alone instill, moral discernment, civil courage, and spiritual strength in their child. The path of the child who follows the will of God is hazardous. Even when it doesn't lead toward destruction, it almost certainly will lead away from the prosperity and social position that any parent may be forgiven for equating with both success and safety. Success and safety, not self-sacrifice, are what any parent wants for her child.

Having been caught delivering anti-Nazi leaflets, Sophie was condemned to death by a Nazi court. Her last words were: "Such a fine, sunny day, and I have to go, but what does my death matter, if through us, thousands of people are awakened and stirred to action?"

She was beheaded. She was nineteen.

"Why not me, Mom?" Zach had asked me, reasonably, and I could not bring myself to reply, *Because you're special. Because you're mine.*

What was I afraid would happen to Zach? In his wars, even beheading wasn't beyond the realm of possibility.

Zach was my baby, the first one who, clad in a hand-me-down onesie, had looked up at me with his little raisin-eyes and smiled that first toothless, radiant, heart-stopping infant smile.

"Oh, you dreadful little baby," I'd breathed. "You horrid boy!" Just in case the gods were paying attention.

Chapter Twenty-One

Here's a question for the modern childcare expert: should a loving parent bring an eight-year-old to a political protest that is likely to end in violence?

On March 7, 1965, when six hundred civil rights marchers set off to walk from Selma, Alabama, to the state capital, Montgomery, as a peaceful protest against black Americans' effective disenfranchisement, children as young as eight marched beside their parents. Is love of freedom sufficient justification for exposing a child to the risk of violence?

Out of the mouths of babes and Sophie Scholl: "How can we expect righteousness to prevail when there is hardly anyone willing to give himself up individually to a righteous cause?"

I spend a lot of time in the car, so a lot of my "reading" takes the form of listening to audiobooks. One of my better discoveries was historian Taylor Branch's magisterial trilogy about Martin Luther King, Jr., and the American civil rights movement. In three fat volumes (*Parting the Waters, Pillar of Fire,* and *At Canaan's Edge*), Branch's gripping tale is good for about thirty-six hours of listening, or the equivalent of five round trips between Kittery and Fort Kent.

I was listening to the second book, somewhere on the Maine Turnpike, when the question about the connection between love and risk arose.

It is not a secret that a number of white Alabamans were more than willing to injure and kill black citizens who attempted to vote. Beatings of civil rights workers were frequent and savage, and murders were not uncommon. And still the marchers—men and women from eight to eighty and virtually all African-American, led by civil rights workers Bob Mants, Albert Turner, John Lewis, and Hosea Williams—formed up and started walking.

Soon they were marching, four abreast, up Selma's arched Edmund Pettus Bridge. Upon reaching the peak, marchers caught a dispiriting view of fifty State Troopers in riot gear massed on the other side. Behind them, dozens of local police officers were joined and mingled with a mob of extremely angry whites who screamed obscenities and brandished baseball bats.

And yet—get this—*the marchers marched on!* When the leaders arrived at the foot of the bridge, the major in charge of the troopers stepped forward to meet them. Governor Wallace, he informed them, had declared this peaceful protest march a hazard to public safety.

Hosea Williams countered that the courts had already ruled the march a legitimate expression of a U.S. citizen's First Amendment right to freedom of speech and assembly. The major said that, nonetheless, he was ordering the marchers to disperse. Williams requested a moment to kneel in prayer, and this was granted.

As soon as he and the other marchers rose from their knees, the State Troopers attacked. Firing canisters of tear gas and breaking bones and heads with their nightsticks, the police officers, in concert with the mob, drove the marchers back from the bridge in a frenzy of violence that would later be known as Bloody Sunday. More than fifty were hospitalized, and the only reason the number wasn't higher was that most hospitals in Selma did not accept black patients.

Fifty law enforcement officers—fifty troopers?!!—attacked and injured unarmed civilians. For me, whose feelings toward law enforcement officers tend toward the warm and fuzzy, it was an appalling image.

I was about three when it happened, too little to retain a memory of Bloody Sunday, but Branch describes the scene so powerfully that, nearly fifty years later, I actually had to shut off the car's CD player and recover before I could think about proceeding to the next chapter.

So I was driving along in shocked silence when, suddenly, there in the sky above the Maine Turnpike, I spied a number of large, ominous black objects.

What the heck...?

In a moment, I'd identified them as helicopters. These were big military ones, like the Hueys my father flew around in back when he was reporting on the war in Vietnam. *Whup-whup-whup.*

They were flying low over the highway ("nap of the earth," as my dad would say) as if seeking to avoid enemy fire.

Something bad has happened! I thought. *There's some kind of major emergency going on, and because I wasn't listening to the radio, I missed the alert.*

Cell phone in hand, I was already speed-dialing the number for the dispatcher in Augusta to find out where I should "deploy." The helicopters were thundering right over my head when the light went on.

Of course! It's the president.

Obama was making an official trip to Maine.

He and I were both about three on Bloody Sunday, and about six in 1968, when Martin Luther King, Jr., was assassinated. My family lived in Washington, DC, then, and King's murder provoked widespread riots there. My mother told me I couldn't go outside to play. "The city government has imposed a curfew," she said.

"Why?"

"It's because of the tear gas," said my mother.

She, and all the grown-ups in my house, had been crying all day.

People on television were crying, too. I figured tear gas must be made from tears, so I hung out of my upstairs bedroom window all evening, listening to the sirens and trying to catch a whiff of the gas that arises from sadness.

Decades later, in recognition of Martin Luther King Day, I was leading a Sunday service in a church located at the lily-white center of one of the least racially diverse states in the union—it was the same Sunday on which I would preach about the 1943 October Miracle, and the rescue of the Danish Jews; but first, out of curiosity, I asked a question of the congregation.

"Show of hands: how many of you have a family member of a different race or ethnic group from your own?"

Astonishingly, about a third of this all-white congregation raised a hand, but (and this is equally astonishing) all had to stop and think about it. Some parishioners actually needed to be reminded by a neighbor in the pew: *Isn't your grandson adopted from Vietnam?*

Because my nephew was adopted from West Africa, I could raise my own hand to the question. So could Maine's then-governor, Angus King, and America's then-president, George W. Bush. Then-senator Barack Obama could raise his hand to the question, since his mom was white. Tea Party conservative and Maine governor Paul LePage, can raise his hand, since he has an adopted African-American son.

Ten percent of American marriages are interracial these days, a statistic that doesn't even take into account the number of people who have moved in with folk their grandparents would not have shared a drinking fountain with. If you think about it, that is astounding.

Don't bother trying to astound the young'uns. The election of an African-American as president of the United States and leader of the free world was a miracle my kids could grasp, but only intellectually: they hadn't smelled the tear gas.

Simon and I took as many offspring as could be mustered to Washington for Obama's first inauguration. There, we joined thousands of other families pretty much like ours, all of us waving flags and singing "My Country, 'Tis of Thee" along with Aretha Franklin. No matter what color(s) everybody was, the generational divide was drawn in tears: the under-forties were smiling, but their parents and grandparents were weeping for joy. As Senator John McCain, Republican presidential candidate and the adoptive father of a Bangladeshi orphan, said in his concession speech, "America today is a world away from the cruel and prideful bigotry of [the past]. There is no better evidence of this than the election of an African American to the presidency of the United States. Let there be no reason now for any American to fail to cherish their citizenship in this, the greatest nation on Earth."

It seems less than ennobling to say so, but war has played a big role in the miraculous (if still incomplete) achievement of racial justice in the United States—and I don't just mean the Civil War. Uneasy Southern colonists weren't happy about it at the time, and preferred to forget about it afterward, but five thousand African-Americans fought for liberty in the

Revolutionary War. Throughout the next two centuries, military service was a powerful way black American men affirmed both their mature masculinity and their citizenship. Over a million African-American men and women served their country in the Second World War (though the military wasn't integrated at the platoon level until the Battle of the Bulge), and it was hoped—even optimistically expected—that victory abroad would be swiftly followed by victory against racism and discrimination at home.

This optimism was doubtless fed by the common battlefield experience of racial concord, though the unity found in combat did not necessarily translate back to civilian life. Hosea Williams (later set upon by troopers at the Edmund Pettus Bridge) fought courageously in World War II alongside white soldiers and was badly wounded in France. But upon his return home, Williams made the mistake of drinking from a bus station water fountain marked "Whites Only." A group of angry whites beat him so badly that they actually thought they'd killed him. Fortunately, the driver of the "Blacks Only" hearse noticed that the corpse he had been called to transport to the morgue was breathing. He drove Williams to a veterans hospital, where Williams spent a month recovering from his injuries.

While bus stations, drinking fountains, and lunch counters would continue to be legally segregated in the South for another two decades, a mere three years would pass before President Truman signed an order for the racial integration of the armed forces. Executive Order 9981 was in effect in time for my father to fight in Korea alongside black troops, even if during his four years at Yale my father met only one black student.

After Vietnam, the military began to offer its leaders seminars on improving race relations while providing programs in basic skills and management training to incoming minority troops, as well as setting overall goals for affirmative action. It's probably not surprising that, as the first federal body in the United States to be officially desegregated, the military to this day has a much higher percentage of nonwhite generals and admirals than large corporations have nonwhite executives.

Sergeant Sangster was white, but the drill instructor who gave Zach his first homeopathic dose of Marine Corps calisthenics back at the VFW was black. The instructors, coaches, and supervisors I met at Zach's graduation from his course at Fort Meade came in every human skin tone. Zach didn't think anything about this. It was his liberal, politically correct, middle-aged mother who found herself mentally contrasting the Corps' panhierarchical diversity with the monochrome professors and administrators I met when Peter and Cobus, and later Ilona, Ellie, and Woolie, took us along on their college tours. The resounding, celebratory "oooh-rah!" roar with which Marines conclude a graduation ceremony made me jump out of my (white) skin, but the patriot in me was gratified to know that, if my boy now counted himself a man among men, at least he was a man

232

among *all* men (and, as it turned out, some pretty impressive women, too).

That Zach and his siblings have grown up in a world where it is normal for families as well as platoons to come in rainbow packs and the election of an African-American president is "cool" but not "FREAKIN' INCREDIBLE," well, isn't this just the miracle Martin Luther King, Jr., Hosea Williams, and all those heroes from eight to eighty prayed and worked and died for?

Bible-type miracles are characterized, even defined, by two features: they are *impossible*, and they *happen quickly*. Whatever conditions the miracle worker seeks to alter—the solidity of Jericho's walls or water's inability to support a sauntering human—that condition must be seemingly unalterable. The miracle worker changes what cannot be changed, and he does it fast: the televangelist lays his hands on the woman in the wheelchair, importunes the Holy Spirit to grant healing, and WHAM! A permanently paralyzed woman stands up and hollers, "Praise the Lord!"

Real miracles are the opposite. They aren't just possible, they are *inevitable*. Even the miracles that appeared to have happened quickly have been a long time in the making.

The single most common phrase we middle-aged and old folks uttered to one another there on the National Mall in 2008 was this one: *I never thought this would happen in my lifetime.*

To which God could only reply: "Well, but it's *been* happening in your lifetime: Remember Shirley Chisholm? Jesse

Jackson? Colin Powell and Condi Rice? Alan Keyes? Sooner or later, y'all were bound to elect an African-American president, because all men and women really are created equal. They really are endowed by their Creator with certain inalienable rights among them: life, liberty, and the pursuit of happiness. That wasn't just a passionate activist's wild idea, you silly sinners. It was simply true. And in the end, what is true is love, and what is love wins."

Chapter Twenty-Two

I am sure the firearms instructors enjoy teaching wardens how to shoot as much as Warden Chris Dyer enjoys teaching them how to fight...but there were few jokes and no giggles during firearms training, and not just because it was pouring rain.

With gun belts and body armor strapped on over our raingear, we were gathered at an outdoor firing range about the size of a soccer pitch near the city of Augusta. At one end, "downrange," a number of plywood stands had been set in front of a hill made of mounded scree and topped with a couple of determined alder saplings. Some of the wardens got busy staple-gunning paper targets printed with what looked like big bowling pins onto the stands. Later, when the lessons to be imparted were more arcane, these would be swapped for targets illustrated with internal human anatomy, the skeleton, that is, and major blood vessels and organs all outlined in shades of gray. On these, the instructor could point out alternative areas to target should a dangerous subject emulate James Holmes, the man who opened fire on patrons in an Aurora, Colorado, movie theater, and wear body armor to the massacre.

I joined the rest of the students under a temporary awning set up to shelter two of the day's ancillary but vital activities—loading weapons and assembling lunch. Warden Cody Lounder showed me how to force-feed bullets into the maw of a thirty-round magazine, how to line them up, rounded end foremost, then press them down with my thumb against the internal spring. Having been in the military before applying to the Warden Service, Cody could do this very quickly. He easily and efficiently filled three or four magazines while I, laboriously, filled one.

As a chaplain, I am unarmed. This is not as self-evident as it might seem: there are law enforcement chaplains who carry weapons, either because they do double duty in their departments as sworn officers, or because, for whatever reason, they think it's a good idea.

I don't think it's a good idea.

Since I'm not sworn, not trained, and not useful in situations involving the discharge of firearms, I am not called to or even permitted at scenes where such has been predicted. If I happen to be riding along with a game warden, and a call comes over the radio requesting his or her assistance at, for example, an "active shooter" event, I would expect to be unceremoniously dumped at the nearest gas station or if necessary right there by the side of the road, to remain until the situation has been resolved (I always bring along my knitting, just in case).

Even if I don't use guns, however, they are abundantly present in what we might call my "work environment." It seems worthwhile to possess at least some basic knowledge of their function and safe handling, so when seven new game wardens were undergoing their firearms training, I requested permission to join them.

If nothing else, it was an opportunity to wear my spiffy new ballistic vest.

On the theory that a situation might arise where, in the performance of my legitimate chaplainesque duties, I found myself involved in a tense situation with an armed person — e.g., giving death notification to a distraught duck hunter — I am issued body armor. For the first ten years this was a hand-me-down vest that had once belonged to Warden Cheryl Bardon. She and I are more or less the same size, and when she left the Warden Service, I inherited a lot of her old gear (I still wear Cheryl's extrawarm fleece long johns in the winter, for example).

When body armor was first becoming standard issue, many law enforcement officers objected to it because a bulletproof vest is heavy, hot, and uncomfortable. For me, there's an additional problem: Have you ever tried to hug someone wearing body armor? I have, and let me tell you, however tender the emotion, it's like hugging an oak. Cheryl's vest, like all the older-model wardens' vests, was designed to be worn under clothing. To put it on, I'd first need to strip from the waist up, clerical collar and all, and the Maine outdoors doesn't offer a lot of handy ladies' rooms for changing in. So for a decade the vest remained at the bottom of one of the gear bins in the back of my car.

Then the new "external carrier" body armor was issued to the wardens. This is worn on the outside and, while it is still heavy, hot, and uncomfortable (and is distinctly "military" in appearance), getting the thing on and off is comparatively easy. Not only can wardens remove it when they are in a safe environment—stopping off at home for lunch, or pausing at headquarters to fill out paperwork—it can be jettisoned in the event that the warden falls or is pushed out of his patrol boat into deep water. That's a lifesaving improvement on the old model, and more than worth the military vibe.

The chances are extremely high that I will never have cause to wear it in the field, but on the shooting range body armor is *de rigueur*, along with some accessories: ear protection, safety goggles, a hat with a visor (to prevent ejected bullet casings from whacking me in the forehead), and a gun belt holding a spare handgun and two extra clips of ammunition. On top of all that, there's a fiddly webbing harness designed to keep the AR-15 patrol rifle dangling between my legs while not in use, like a particularly repulsive marital aid.

The first day of training was spent indoors learning how

to dismantle, clean, and reassemble the firearms issued to Maine's game wardens. These were the SIG-Sauer 226 hand-gun, the AR-15, and a Mossberg 590A shotgun, for those who are interested.

It turns out that I like cleaning guns. I like the 3-D puzzle dimension of the task, and enjoy going after deposits of crud in the nooks and crannies with a toothbrush. I take pleasure during the reassembly when, with a crisp, metallic click, some biddable doodad locks itself into the right slot. By the time all the weapons assigned to my care were gleaming clean inside and out, my hands were impressively grimy and my clothing reeked agreeably of gun oil.

Warden Service firearms instructors take the danger of firing these newly clean weapons extremely seriously. On the range, their directions were given with the obvious expectation that these would be followed to the letter. The instructors never took their eyes off anyone with a weapon during the firing exercises.

To qualify—that is, to be authorized to carry and use firearms while in law enforcement service to the State of Maine—game wardens are required to demonstrate compe-tence in shooting all weapons issued to them. They must be able to shoot with reasonable accuracy from a standing posi-tion, while walking forward, walking backward, lying on their tummies, or from behind various kinds of cover and from various distances.

We spent the morning practicing these skills.

I didn't much like the actual shooting. Even after an honest attempt to enjoy it, if only to please the wardens who were so touchingly eager to share their shooting pleasures with me, actually firing a gun seems merely loud and dangerous.

During lunch, a local granddad and his little grandson arrived and asked permission to gather up the brass shell casings.

"A five-gallon bucketful will fetch fifty bucks these days," the granddad told me proudly, "and that's my cigarette money!"

Swallowing the last of my sandwich, I went to help the little boy pluck treasure from the sodden turf.

Yup, those guys are police . . . that is, they're law enforcement officers. They're game wardens. Ooh, there's a casing, right next to your foot . . . see it?

They shoot at those bowling-pin pictures that guy is attaching to the stands. What? Oh. Well, it's not likely.

Okay, yes, if they really had to do it, they would shoot a bad guy. But they don't want to hurt anyone. No, even if the guy was really, really bad, they would hope they could take him to jail instead of hurting him.

The child gave me a pitying look and, terminating what had obviously become, from his point of view, an unexciting tête-à-tête, he picked up his bucket and followed his grandpa back to their car.

"Hey Kate!" one of the instructors called. "While the rest of these guys finish eating, let's see what you can do."

Standing, as directed, square to the target with my feet

planted shoulder-width apart, tush thrust out, knees slightly bent and elbows tucked in, I drew and fired the 9mm pistol a few times, demonstrating to my own satisfaction that I could do some serious damage to a bowling pin provided it was no more than nine feet away.

"That's the CQB distance," the instructor assured me.

"Say what?"

"It stands for *close quarters battle*—most deadly-force encounters take place within three yards of the target," he explained. "You'd do fine."

Deciding this was enough success for the day, I retired to watch the young wardens go through their firing drills. It's always fun to watch people do what they are good at, especially when, having tried it yourself, you know they are making something difficult look easy.

Standing behind the firing line brought me, irresistibly, back to the time I spent pacing the edge of a sports field waiting for my sons' soccer practice to be over. There was the same smell of damp feet and rain-soaked grass, the same male voices raised in guidance or encouragement, plus the mild intragroup competitiveness that invariably provokes within my middle-aged female breast a certain condescension: *Oh for God's sake, boys, it's only a game.*

Until, that is, the wardens began the exercise in which, weapons holstered, hands empty, they walked toward the target. Behind them, the instructor bellowed: "THREAT!"

Hurriedly drawing their weapons and raising these to

ready position, right hands clasping the gun butts, index fingers extended alongside (*not* through) the trigger guards, the wardens simultaneously chorused: "POLICE! DON'T MOVE!"

Then the instructor bawled, "GUN!" and the wardens—still moving forward in unison toward their targets—began firing: *bam-bam-bam-bam.*

We were no longer on the soccer pitch, the ball field, not even the hunting ground. This wasn't sport.

In 2012, the year Jason, Josh, and I went to Police Week in Washington, forty-eight out of the ninety-six officers killed in the line of duty were murdered, and forty-four of those were killed with firearms.

It was hard not to think of these game wardens as boys, since they were right around the age of my own sons. They were training for the possibility that someone would point a gun at them with lethal intent; at Kyle, with his big brown eyes, at Josh, who shoots so well and blushes when he's complimented, at Chad, with his Roman nose and slightly sorrowful expression, or Corey, who stopped loading magazines long enough to show me photos of his brand-new, redheaded baby.

I walked downrange with the firearms instructor to examine the targets. From three yards away—CQB!—I was close enough to see the grin begin around the edges of the instructor's stern mouth and pleat crow's feet around his blue eyes. "Check this out, Kate," he said.

Even while moving and shouting, Josh had somehow been able to punch tight clusters of holes through the "head" and "center mass" of the paper bowling pin.

"Wow, honey-bunny!" I squeaked, and Josh's ears turned pink.

Once all the targets had been studied, the bullet holes marked with a Sharpie to distinguish them from the next set of holes, the instructor called his students back to twenty-five yards where he re-formed the line.

"Ears and eyes?" he barked, and all the young men pulled their ear protectors over their ears and adjusted their shooting glasses. On command, the wardens started walking forward.

"THREAT!" came the shout, and all I wanted to do was fling myself out there, put my middle-aged self between these young ones and whatever threat the instructor might be shouting about.

This would not be helpful. In fact, it occurred to me, as my eyes stung and I wrapped my arms across the stiff, unyielding front of my vest, that this was really why I was there, at firearms practice. I was learning to stay the hell out of the way.

Not long afterward, Bruce called to tell me that the ice was out: it was time to go back to Masquinongy Pond to look for Donald.

It was spring at last, and the land was humming with the urgent routines of a fast and fertile season. Male goldfinches traded in their olive drab winter uniforms for the most fetching shades of lemon and posed amid the delicately tinted blooms of poplars and sugar maples. By now the owl's nest down in the dead tree at the edge of our bog might boast a few hatchlings, peering and peeting indignantly at the lingering chill from beneath their absurd toupees of white fluff.

"They have to hatch and fledge early in the spring," Bruce told me. "So they'll be ready to learn to hunt by late summer, when there'll be plenty of small animals around for them to practice on."

Other birds can safely postpone laying their eggs but not for too much longer. Already, phoebes were skimming the dark, damp spreading patches of bare ground, along with the heavy-bodied queen bees, both species searching out good nesting sites amid the patches of remnant snow.

One of the divers owned a hunting camp about a half-hour's drive from where Dick and Donald had overturned their canoe. The camp would grant the search team close but convivial rustic accommodation for the duration of the dive operation.

There was a slumber party feeling about the hunting camp the night before the first diving day. Upon arrival, the wardens took off their field uniforms and donned soft sweatpants and T-shirts, cranked up some of the country music beloved by the team's leaders (though not, it should be said, by everyone else), and cooked a whole lot of meat for supper.

A little river, fat with snowmelt and spring rain, rushed by outside. Rain fell during the night and the river sounds increased in tempo and volume. At dawn, a bird began its tender come-hither love song, that to human ear shrilled like a querulous demand: *Tina! Tina! Teee-nah!*

In the morning, Bruce fried eggs for breakfast while we yawned and dressed. "You can ride with me, Kate, and keep an eye out for moose."

He was being kind: while driving, Bruce had to direct my gaze or I would have missed seeing the big male turkey promenading under the trees, his chest feathers puffed, his glossy tail fanned as he strutted. The females, apparently impervious, went on scratching at the leaf mold with their big pink feet.

Bruce had to point out small things like the pair of little kestrels hunting together from their perch on a telephone wire, but also a creature as large as the doe that dithered witlessly on the verge as our truck drew near. Only when we were almost upon her did she — *oh, what the hell!* — make a dash for it, cantering past the front bumper and into the woods, her white tail flashing amid the shreds of mist that lingered as though snagged on the budding twigs.

And then there was the young cow moose, drawn from the woods by the leftover road salt many creatures consider a seasonal delicacy. At its best, *Alces alces* is a weird-looking creature, and a moose is never at her best in spring. The thick coat so necessary for warmth through winter's blizzards sheds in clumps, leaving leprous patches of naked, sooty skin, and this particular specimen looked, in Bruce's words, "as if she'd been napalmed."

When Bruce stopped the truck to grant me a better view, the moose gazed dismally back at us from beneath the clump of shedding hair that flapped foolishly from her eyebrow. Then she blundered off on her long legs, banging one knobbly knee on a rock along the way.

Bruce waited until she had disappeared before turning the key in the truck's ignition. "In a few weeks, she'll be back on the roadside, trying to escape the black flies," he said sympathetically.

Nothing is easy for moose, we agreed. They like standing in swamps, but get stuck in them sometimes. They are prone to brainworm, which makes them psycho. Swarms of spring black flies inflict relentless misery, and in summer vampiric colonies of fat ticks form along the tender edges of their eyelids.

Some years back, a hunter came across the bodies of two large male moose lying in a clearing. Evidently the two had gotten into a pre-mating joust, clattering and clashing their enormous, palmate antlers together so fiercely they became accidentally but inextricably locked together. No doubt both moose did their best to free themselves. Since rutting moose have plenty of rampant power, even before frustration and then desperation add oomph, it must have been a hellish scene.

Eventually both animals succumbed to exhaustion, starvation, and despair. Resurrected by a taxidermist, the former adversaries shall spend eternity locked together and on display at the LL Bean store in Freeport, Maine.

I seldom take comfort from taxidermy but I do find the locked moose comforting, if only as evidence that humans aren't the only animals that screw up, make mistakes, do what they ought not, and leave undone that which God would have them do.

"It's okay, Donald. We've got you."

Bruce is accustomed to overhearing my attempts to comfort the dead, and also to correcting my lapses in proper procedure. "Gloves," he said, and handed me a pair, Barney the Dinosaur violet and surreally festive. I wriggled my hands into them.

Having lifted Donald's body off the bottom of the lake, divers Tony Gray and Rick Oulette had borne him over to the side of the dive boat, handed him off, and then swum to the chase boat to haul out, so it was Bruce and I who dragged the body on board. Searching through his pockets, we found a couple of bottle caps, a still-wrapped Trojan, eighty-four cents, and a wallet containing his driver's license — confirmation, should any be required, that we had plucked the right body from the depths of Masquinongy.

Now Bruce and I were performing the clumsy physical labor of getting Donald's body into a white plastic body bag that was laid out on the steel deck.

"Now that I'm a dive team leader, I don't actually get to dive," Bruce was saying sadly, as he tucked Donald's sodden boots into the bottom of the bag.

"Yeah," said Warden Scott Thrasher, at the wheel of the

dive boat and piloting us toward shore. "And the ones who do the diving don't have to smell the body."

A person doesn't spend months on the bottom of a lake without getting a little whiffy, and Donald stank. There was a deep laceration under the floppy wet hair pasted to the right side of his yellow-white forehead, perhaps from having struck the side of the canoe as he went over. His expression was one of mild surprise, his eyebrows slightly raised above his closed, long-lashed eyes.

Warden Scott Thrasher's brow was puckered with his characteristic slight frown, as if his mind was preoccupied with a weighty matter unrelated to the task at hand. This is, in fact, often the case: Scott frets about things like the deficit or the expansion of the Earned Income Tax Credit. (Once, he and I were standing together by a dawn-lit lake watching an osprey dive for breakfast in the pale water, and Scott suddenly declared: "Here's what I want to know: how are we going to *pay* for Obamacare?")

"So what's with the mom's boyfriend?" Scott asked now. "The guy breathes like a landed trout. Is he going to have a heart attack or what?"

I was kneeling down to peer more closely at Donald's face. "He carries an inhaler in his shirt pocket," I said.

"Asthma," said Bruce.

"Oh. Well, that's all right, then. The paramedics are standing by anyway, but I'd want to give them a heads-up if there was a specific issue."

"Poor guy," said Bruce, meaning the boyfriend (I think). "Would you like some help with that, Chaplain?"

"Uh, maybe. Yeah." I'd been trying to turn Donald's body onto its side and he was a large man. "His mom wanted me to look for a tattoo on the back of his neck."

"She wants you to make sure we haven't brought up the wrong guy?" asked Scott, and Bruce gave an understanding grunt. We all knew that in such situations a sticky, still-seductive hope lingers to torment the mourner. *The wardens could be wrong, the body might be someone else's, the chaplain could be lying, or the whole community conspiring against our family in a cruel charade.*

The tattoo was there: a name and dates in flowing turquoise script, commemorating an uncle who died in a motorcycle accident, was inscribed at the base of his neck. Under the name, an old rugged cross headed down Donald's spine, though most of it was hidden under the sodden collar of his coat. The bit that was visible was inked in blue with "R.I.P." carved on an elaborately wood-grained horizontal beam.

"You know, I think Donald's father—his biological father, that is—is going to be on shore when we get there," I said.

"I thought he was in prison."

"He just got out." Bruce and I allowed the body to sag back ("Here you go, Donald"). The outermost layers of the skin of his hand, which had been loose, fell away with the motion, and lay on the deck like a discarded white glove. The underlying skin was pearly and smooth, like a child's.

Bruce picked up the skin and, shrugging, tucked it down by Donald's feet.

"The hand looks pretty good, anyway," I said. I zipped up the body bag, careful to position the zipper pulls just above that hand, in case Barbie might be satisfied with seeing only this.

The medical examiner called to say that, since Donald's was in effect an unattended death, she wanted to do an autopsy. Donald's body would have to be taken to Augusta. Scott explained that the victim's mother was waiting on shore and wanted to view the body. After some back-and-forth, the M.E. agreed that Barbie could have her time with Donald first.

"The M.E. would like one of us to stay right with her for that, though," said Scott, when the call was concluded. "The doctor wants to confirm that this is a straightforward drowning, wants to have a look at that wound on his head. So if the family wants to see him, she says to make sure there's no chance anything could be changed or removed..."

"Does she want us to restrict the visit to just Barbie?" I asked, and Scott considered my question.

"We'll just keep an eye on 'em," he said.

As if eager to discharge its sorrowful cargo, the boat raced for the town landing, the bow throwing up great shining wings of spray. I seated myself by the gunwale, closest to Donald's body. "To keep him company," I explained when Bruce raised his eyebrows at me, and he smiled and shook his head indulgently.

Closer to shore, amid the foam churned up by the boat's motor, were roses, red as lipsticked mouths. They danced, swirled, and shed bright petals.

"What the hell?"

"It's his birthday," I explained. "Barbie and her family threw them into the water this morning."

Chapter Twenty-Three

Germany, like the rest of Christian Europe, had a long history of anti-Semitism, and this had occasionally been expressed in violence. Still, most historians seem to agree that the Germans were actually more accommodating toward Jews than some of the country's neighbors—Poland, for example. This helps explain both why Germany had a relatively large and long-standing Jewish population, and why so many German Jews remained even after the Nazis had taken power and the persecution had begun. In fact, in one of the manifold tragic ironies of the period, Christian Germans who showed ordinary kindness to their Jewish neighbors, commiserated with Jewish friends and family members, and deplored the disgusting "un-German" violence of the storm troopers may have encouraged Jews to trust in a "real" Germany and maintain their own natural but illusory conviction that staying patiently put was a sensible strategy.

Pondering this among the myriad tragic ironies of the

period with Jason and Josh back at the Holocaust Museum, I thought about love and un-love, and how one can masquerade as the other, cruelly. And, because I went to a Christian seminary and therefore think in parables, I thought about Judas's kiss.

On the morning he was to be captured, Jesus was in the middle of a conversation with his disciples when Judas arrived. Judas had a posse with him, deputized by the chief priests and scribes, and armed with swords and clubs. Evidently, these didn't know Jesus well enough to recognize him. Rather than point him out and, perhaps, make too plain his collaboration, Judas, as arranged, went up to Jesus, said "Rabbi!" and kissed him, and Jesus was seized and taken away.

No wonder this story resonates: what a crummy thing to do!

Kissing is so naturally innocent. Smacking your mouth against someone else's mouth or face: there's no practical or even reproductive value to it. It's just a strange, funny, endearing little human gesture and so purely affectionate. Couldn't Judas have identified Jesus by...I don't know, giving him a guy-punch in the biceps, or a noogie or something?

"Would you betray me with a kiss?" Jesus asks. *Really?*

In the original, Koine Greek version of Mark's Gospel story, what Judas gives Jesus is *kataphilein,* a word that suggests no mere, insincere air kiss but a real, firm, intense, even passionate smoocheroo.

In our culture—simultaneously puritanical and prurient—the word "kiss," by itself, is more than enough to bump our minds into the gutter, and so a quick survey of the Web will demonstrate that when the title "Judas's Kiss" is applied to anything other than a biblical illustration, it's attached to something explicitly sexual and generally homoerotic.

In ancient Near Eastern culture, on the other hand, a kiss was a normal way for buddies, pals, and homeboys to greet one another. Arab men still meet with embraces and drape their arms around each other's waists or shoulders while walking or sitting together. When King Abdullah Al-Saud of Saudi Arabia came to America in 2005, he greeted the president of the United States with a tender kiss on the mouth, after which Abdullah and George W. were photographed strolling hand in hand through the Texas bluebonnets.

Americans were a little freaked out, according to the media, not because George was literally kissing up to a representative of an oil-rich but freedom-poor country, but because they were both guys. Like, *kissing*.

Frankly, it would be much easier to talk about Judas's kiss this way. Bringing sex into a theological discourse always adds a little *frisson*, and anyway, I could draw brilliant connections between Judas's lethal lips and Eve's; between the original labial sin and all the varied, icky troubles God's libidinous children have gotten into, up to, and beyond the Gospels' bromance-gone-wrong.

But no. *Kataphilein* contains the root *philos*, meaning "brotherly love," and the context makes it clear: this was a kiss of connection, kinship, and human love turned inside out into treachery. In all four of the Gospels, moreover, that perfidious kiss is framed by additional failures of brotherly love.

The night before his arrest, knowing what was coming, Jesus was distressed and agitated. The disciples weren't asked to be sensitive, or work this out for themselves: *Jesus told them.*

"Guys, I am deeply grieved," he said. "Grieved even unto death...stay and keep awake for me?"

Mark tells us that the disciples "did not know what to say to him," and anyway, they were tired and superstressed, they still had kind of a buzz on from the wine at the Last Supper. You know how it is. So Jesus returned from his anguished prayers to find that his friends had walled themselves away from him behind their blameless sleep.

After Judas kissed and identified Jesus, after Jesus was arrested and taken away to be interrogated and beaten, Peter—the Rock—was given a chance to step up, show some backbone or at least a little faith:

"You were with Jesus, the man from Nazareth," a servant girl said to him. "You're one of them." But Peter chickened out before the rooster crowed; he denied even knowing Jesus, let alone loving him.

"All of them deserted him and fled," the Gospel reports. Even if Jesus hadn't predicted it, we wouldn't be all that surprised, would we? *Love one another,* the commandment says, but aren't these the most common forms of our failure to obey it? Not with aggression, vituperation, or violence; no, we just avoid the friend whose pain and grief we'd rather not have to deal with.

"I wouldn't know what to say," we mumble.

When a neighbor is in trouble, we distance ourselves.

"I really don't know her that well," we explain. "I don't know her. Really." (*Cock-a-doodle-do.*)

So when German Jews who survived the Holocaust looked back at life in Germany, their most haunting, nauseating stories aren't the ones in which they were openly insulted, beaten by the Brownshirts, tormented by people who made no secret of their hatred.

Rather, the easiest stories to identify with and the hardest to hear are those in which a Jewish German meets an old friend in the street, and watches his face go carefully blank as he turns away... it's the colleague's silence when an announcement was made that Jews could no longer work at the company... it's the neighbor, known for years, who closed her curtains and softly shut her door when the soldiers arrived to take everyone away...

It takes a nation to murder millions, a few to do the actual killing and the rest to betray, desert, deny, stand by, or run away.

Judas's kiss, the spineless slumber of the disciples, Peter's denials: the bad news in the Bible is always so recognizable! It's the good news that comes as a shock.

The Holocaust Museum isn't like the National Gallery of Art, which, as Jason, Josh, and I discovered, boasts any number of doors through which a visitor may enter and explore the collection...or politely exit if, for example, the visitor is a game warden whose interest in art is not quite as keen as that of his chaplain.

Visitors to the Holocaust Museum begin at the top—prewar Nazi Germany—and descend, floor by floor, through increasingly hellish exhibits until, at long last, the Hall of the Rescuers is reached. Here, the wardens and I breathed a sigh of sheer, blessed relief.

There's an actual Danish fishing boat in the wood-and-paint flesh, bearing a strong resemblance to a Maine lobster boat; there's a photo of a young and puckish Sophie Scholl; and on one wall is inscribed a poem by Hannah Senesh, the heroic Jewish partisan eventually captured and killed by the Germans. "Blessed is the heart with strength to stop its beating for honor's sake..."

In his two-volume history of the Jews in Nazi Germany, historian Saul Friedländer expressed the concern about the dangers of normalizing the atrocities of the Holocaust through historical contextualization or overexposure. But the more I've learned and read, the more painful, bizarre, and ultimately inexplicable the facts become. Like the wardens who sighed with relief when we at last reached the exhibit on the rescuers, I cling to stories about human decency, moments of redemptive embrace. I told Jason and Josh two such stories on the day we went to the Holocaust Museum, both of which, as it happens, are—like Judas kissing Jesus—man-on-man.

The first was, of course, from Germany during the Nazi period, but the second came closer to home.

* * *

Prisoner Coen Rood was 5'8" tall and skinny to begin with: he weighed 143 pounds when he arrived at Bergen Belsen, and by the time the camp was liberated, he weighed less than half of that.

At sixty pounds, Coen was desperately sick and starving. Indeed, he was dying. Unable even to move, he lay on the dirt floor within the rough hut in which he and a number of other prisoners had taken shelter.

As Rood describes it in a book by veteran and journalist Michael Hirsch called *The Liberators,* "Suddenly, I heard my friend Maupy. I heard him talking English, saying [to someone] 'go in there. My friend is dying. He should know that he is free before he dies.' [The doorway] got dark, then it opened up and there was an American soldier [standing] there...I was laying in the dark, in the dirt, and he told me 'come, comrade. You're free now.' And then I start crying. I try to get to him...I was...crawling over the ground, trying to get to the door. And then he picked me up...and he was holding me in his arms.

"I remember [thinking] 'Man, is this guy strong!' And he looked so clean and well-taken care of, and he was full of weapons...he told me 'you are free now. It's over.'"

And as dirty and skinny and sick as Coen Rood was, that American soldier kissed him. "And I kissed him back. And he cried, too."

The Liberators details the stories, impressions, and reactions of American soldiers who came across the concentration camps as they raced to engage the German army during the final battles of the war. Hirsch pauses in the narrative to emphasize an important point. Credit for "liberating" a concentration camp is generally awarded to the military unit that first arrived on the scene and broke open the gates, whether or not they met with German resistance there or, indeed, whether or not they remained to look after the sick, starved people they found within. Often they paused just long enough to register horror and utter incomprehension...then soldiered onward, leaving the camps to the care of the units that came afterward. Thus their role, while important, should not obscure the fact that the liberation of the concentration camps was in fact a collective effort, the work and achievement of every single Allied soldier, sailor, and airman who fought so long and hard to defeat Nazism.

The Second World War in Europe was not ultimately about who gets to claim the Sudetenland, not about Schleswig-Holstein or the Rhine Valley, not even about which country would dominate the politics and economy of Europe. It was about worldviews, and this is what makes World War II the rare war that just about everyone agrees had to be fought. Mere geography can be discussed, argued about, compromised over ("Okay, you take Alsace-Lorraine and let me have the Saarland...") but worldviews can admit no compromise.

One of the two clashing worldviews was perhaps a little muddled, imperfectly applied, and articulated only over time in a sort of chorus of disparate and occasionally cacophonous voices ranging from the prophet Hosea to Thomas Jefferson, Lincoln, and Gandhi.

What Hitler called his *Weltanschauung,* on the other hand, was clear, consistent, and virtually devoid of hypocrisy. As he told attendees at the Nuremberg Rallies in 1933, the whole point of conquering Europe was to re-create it according to the Nazis' racial principles. "Europe is not a geographic entity, it is a racial entity."

Central to this worldview was a definition of human that declared innocent men, women, and children to be *Untermenschen,* and Jews in particular as unworthy of moral consideration or even pity, subject to merciless persecution and systematic slaughter. As the distinguished and oft-quoted German philosopher Carl Schmitt declared, "Not every being with a human face is human."

The Nazis had done everything possible to make their prisoner Coen Rood look as little like a human being as possible. Starved, stripped, shaved, degraded, and sick, he was literally crawling in the dirt when liberation came.

And still, that unnamed American soldier lifted Coen up in his arms. He knew just what to say: "You're free." The kiss he offered was *kataphilein,* firm, passionate, and the very opposite of betrayal, the undoing of Judas.

I know you. You are my brother. I am with you.

I have no personal experience of genocide (for which I'm grateful), so if I want to recall what it actually feels like to be abandoned and betrayed, the worst memories I can come up with are from middle school. However unpleasant those memories may be, they're hardly worth comparing with biblical or historical dramas. Still, I would like to propose that it isn't just Nazis, or seventh-grade mean girls: any of us might find ourselves behaving as if we, too, believed that "not every being with a human face is human." Oh, we might not be actively unkind (let alone murderous), but just as India had its untouchables, we all have our unkissables.

I am an ordained minister and a certified good person, so by definition no one is unkissable to me. Still, I'll admit there are a few folk I don't pucker up to that easily.

Usually these are people who have a history of harming or neglecting children. Frankly, it was hard to be as moved as I should have been by the tears of the parents who let their kids play with a loaded gun. And there was a certain dad who had just gotten out of prison on the day his son's drowned body was recovered: it was hard to warm up to him, especially since it was the third time he'd been convicted and imprisoned for badly beating people, including his son's mother.

Barbie, that is, the mother of Donald.

When the dive boat bearing Donald's body arrived at the town landing and I went ashore, I was met by a little crowd. Barbie was there, of course, along with Donald's current girlfriend, his former girlfriend (each with small children in tow), Barbie's boyfriend (emitting his strange, strenuous sighs), half a dozen cousins, and Donald's friend Dick. And

Donald's biological father was en route "to be there for Donald," Barbie told me.

The local police chief approached Barbie. "Now ma'am, I know you don't have any protection orders or anything, but we do want you to feel safe. I can take steps to keep your ex-husband away if that is what you'd like me to do…"

"Yes, keep him away, Barbie honey," Donald's ex-girlfriend agreed. "He'll just make trouble for you."

Barbie considered. "No," she said at last. "No, let him come."

"Are you sure, ma'am?"

"Yes. Our boy's death is bigger than any problem I have with him."

The chief and I looked at each other and I would guess that we were both thinking the same thing: that the "problem" Barbie had with her ex-husband was that he had broken two ribs and her jaw.

Barbie did not look like a saint. She was, as mentioned, covered with tattoos, and had taken up chain-smoking over the winter, besides which when quoting her here I've deleted the expletives that punctuated every single sentence…and yet Barbie was a freakin' saint.

Donald's father arrived. He also had tattoos and the cigarettes and profanity, plus that long, ugly record of violence. Barbie might be a saint but her ex was a thug.

The police chief had plenty of experience with guys like him. The chief had been in law enforcement a long time, long enough to get cynical about a lot of things, but especially about the possibilities for reforming or redeeming violent offenders.

Before he was a police officer, the chief had been a United States Marine. He was strong, clean, full of weapons, and definitely intimidating. In a private consultation we decided that he would stand by, vigilant and ready to rock, should things get ugly with Dad.

"Now, Barbie and I are going to board the dive boat in a few minutes so that she can spend some time with Donald's body before it goes to the medical examiner's office."

The chief scowled. "I've never seen that happen."

"The Warden Service does it all the time," I assured him.

"Well, does the convicted felon get to see him, too?"

"Let's leave that up to Barbie," I said…but Barbie had already decided. She and her ex-husband would both go aboard the dive boat, to see, touch, and grieve for their son together.

Having tied up at the dock, the wardens tactfully withdrew. I accompanied Barbie and her ex down the ramp onto the dock and helped them climb aboard the boat. The chief stood by. I unzipped the body bag.

I won't go into what Mom and Dad did on the boat. They did what any parents would do in such circumstances. After some time—perhaps twenty minutes—they were finished. I closed the body bag. We climbed back onto the dock. Barbie walked beside me, up the ramp, and into the embrace of her friends.

Donald's father, the thug, the three-time loser and convicted wife-beater, walked up the ramp alone. It was the police chief, not the chaplain, who met him on the shore, who put his arms around him, held him close, and let him freely be a grieving dad.

How is it that I learn so much of love from armed men?

Oh God, may I and my children and their children all be good kissers.

May every kiss we give, every embrace, be the undoing of Judas, true *kataphilein*, firm, passionate, and the very opposite of betrayal. With the words and the kisses of our mouths, may we say again and again:

I know you by your human face. You are my brother. You are my sister. I am with you.

CHAPTER TWENTY-FOUR

Imagine a landing craft full of soldiers grinding forward toward Omaha Beach on D-Day. Bullets are flying, there are bodies everywhere, guys getting hung up in the barbed wire obstacles, or mowed down by strafing German airplanes.

The landing craft gets as far up the beach as it can, bullets ping-ping-pinging off the steel sides, and then the high steel tailgate flops down. The soldiers are given the order to jump out into the surf and charge the beach.

They do. Isn't that crazy?

Why do they obey?

Veterans will tell you that in combat, a soldier isn't actually charging out of the landing craft, or storming up Heartbreak Hill, for his country. He isn't even doing it because he's been ordered to, by an authority figure who represents a higher purpose. He is there for the guy beside him. I heard my father say this, and I didn't disbelieve him. But I can't say I really understood.

Though it did represent a somewhat dramatic departure

from normal, middle-aged ladies' experience, assisting in the recovery of Donald's decomposing corpse was hardly the Battle of Gallipoli. But because Scott and Bruce were hauling the body out of the water, grunting with effort, gagging at the smell, I would not retreat upwind to the bow and leave them to it. I had to be with them.

Which makes me think that if Scott and Bruce had to charge up Omaha Beach under withering fire, I might go with them then, too. Not because I love my country (though I do) but because I love them.

What do you want for your son?

I want him to know the love that sponsors courage.

"I think my dad would have liked to see me doing this," Zach wrote from Fort Meade. "And I hope I can work as hard at protecting those in need as he did."

Okay, that moved me.

This is what I've learned so far about how to be a parent to an adult child. It's in chart form, suitable for refrigerator-posting:

WHAT IS MINE, WHAT IS NOT MINE:
AN OWNERSHIP CLARIFICATION CHART

MINE (Parent's):	NOT-MINE (Adult Progeny's):
My body	His/her body (including eating and exercise habits, weight, toothbrushing...)
My continuing education	His/her continuing education (including "none")

MINE (Parent's):	NOT-MINE (Adult Progeny's):
My work	His/her work (including "none")
The decision as to whom I will share my dwelling with, have as a guest in my home (including animals), or serve at my table	Whom he/she lives or associates with, including animals
How I want my own home to look, sound, and smell, and how clean and tidy I want it to be, what foods I eat and serve	His/her housekeeping choices and habits
My choice of friends, sexual partner(s), and/or spouse and whose babies (if any) I will take care of	His/her choice of friends, sexual partner(s), or spouse
My financial and legal obligations	His/her debts, lawyers, tuition, parking tickets, bail money, and fines, and overall relationship with various institutions, e.g., colleges, law enforcement, credit agencies, welfare agencies, the department of motor vehicles…
My projects	Whether he/she has a baby
My decision as to what kinds of projects I will support with my time and/or resources	
My religion, politics, or aesthetics (including fashion)	His/her religion, politics, or aesthetics (including fashion)

What was once a virtually all-encompassing and multi-faceted parental power and responsibility is, by the time the child is an adult, whittled down to one, essentially binary choice: contribute enthusiasm, practical assistance, and/or money to your child's proposed project...or don't.

Simon and I were coming up to our first wedding anniversary when Zach called to tell us he had made two decisions on matters that are unquestionably in the province of the "adult": he was reenlisting, and he intended to marry Erin.

Distrust of America's leaders had intensified throughout the first years of Zach's enlistment, even as General Petraeus advocated a "surge" in American troop levels in Iraq. Soldiers and Marines who had expected to leave the military at the conclusion of a four-year hitch (inspired, for many, by the events of 9/11) found themselves involuntarily retained by stop-loss orders, while those who had already departed were being recalled as so-called ready reserves.

Zach's decision to reenlist was met with voluble parental dubiety until Zach — when he could get a word in edgewise — explained how likely it was he'd be recalled anyway and that voluntary reenlistment came with a nice monetary bonus while recall or stop-loss did not.

At which point Simon and I said, "Oh, okay," as if it were up to us.

When Zach told me he planned to propose to Erin, I said "Oh, okay!" right away and with a lot more enthusiasm, then instantly — and I mean, I might not even have paused long enough to hang up the phone — began making a baby bootie.

Let's be clear: Zach had not called to tell me he "had to" marry Erin. No outraged *paterfamilias* with a shotgun loomed in the background. They were merely madly in love. A wedding was all they were expecting.

Naturally, I had already knit things for Erin, my future daughter-in-law, not that there was much point. She, too, was a Marine, stationed in the Pacific, where the need for warm wooly clothing seldom, if ever, arises. But I was knitting this girl into my family the only way I knew how. Upon her arrival in Maine, she was offered a heap of hand-knit hats and scarves.

"Wow," she said. "You'll have to teach me how to do this."

I showed her how to cast on.

Which only makes the bootie thing crazier: by the time Zach and Erin had children, she would be able to knit whatever booties were required. Zach was only twenty-one, after all, and I was forty-six. Plenty of friends of my own age still had their own young kids at home, and at least one had recently given birth for the first time. It wasn't as if the grandchildren I was already anticipating were overdue.

I tucked my creations carefully away in a box with a lavender sachet, telling myself that it was just as well to have a head start. With six children altogether, there would eventually be lots of grandchildren.

At the local bike shop, while waiting for Ellie's bicycle to be repaired, I began to eye a shiny, tiny, kid-sized bike helmet. Would they still be making red helmets by the time the grandchildren were old enough to ride bikes? "I didn't actually buy the thing," I said defensively to Simon...but it was close. And there was a really sweet little baby-sized personal floatation device, too.

Simon understood, at least a little: when we were combining households and donating excess possessions to the Salvation Army, he carefully set aside the Brio train set, toy sailboat, and building blocks. He'd been looking forward to grandchildren, too.

I spent two decades doing my best to keep my children alive and in one piece. I breast-fed them, took them to the doctor when they were sick, made them sit in a child car seat until four years and forty pounds (the standard of the day), put a helmet on each little head for the very first bike-riding lesson, and on the day each learned to ski.

After Drew died, I bristled when a well-meaning acquaintance told Zach he would have to be the little man of the house. "No," I said flatly. "Zach is a child, and I am his parent." I meant it, though my children—Zach, especially—did take on responsibilities that their peers would avoid for years. Even Woolie could make herself a grilled cheese by the age of seven.

Inspired by an NPR interview with a security expert, I had my kids practice choosing the safest adults out of a crowd of strangers. On visits to malls, museums, and unfamiliar cities, I let them approach strangers with questions like "What time is it?" and "Excuse me, but if I walk in this direction, will I get to Madison Avenue?" The kids got pretty good at this sort of thing. I never saw them choose a helper I wouldn't have chosen for them, and everyone they asked for help gave it, and was kind.

Paranoia is an endemic, occupational condition for law enforcement officers, and their chaplains are prone to it, too. Seeing is believing when it comes to our perceptions of risk and safety. I know, for example, that thousands of Mainers ride snowmobiles all winter long, having fun, without ending their lives in some blood-bright, snowy cataclysm. But because I see the cataclysms, a snowmobile is simply a death machine to me. I wouldn't dream of allowing my children to go near one. Meanwhile, since they flew to visit relatives at least a couple of times a year on their own, and nothing bad ever happened, I trusted them to the stranger-laden departure lounge at O'Hare without batting an eye.

In the car on the way to the airport, I'd lead Socratic dialogues on such topics as "What will you do if you get separated from your siblings at the airport?" and "What will you do if you realize you're on the wrong plane?" I'd write all relevant phone numbers onto each child's left forearm with a Magic Marker.

Simon and his wife were teaching the same sorts of lessons to Cobus and Ilona, as they, too, traveled, in their case between Holland and Maine or later between Maine and Pennsylvania.

My friend Tonya, a State Police "A-unit" (spouse) and thus subject to vicarious paranoia, was politely dismayed: her Michael and Meghan not only did not travel anywhere without Mom or Dad, they also weren't even permitted to spend the night at another child's house unless the parents were close family friends (and had passed a criminal background check). Especially Meghan.

Tonya's husband, Tom, a State Trooper with much experience, would take no chances on that score, though Meghan was allowed to go out in a canoe, which *my* experience tells me is hideously hazardous.

"Hey, Mom, guess what I'm good at?" a reenlisted Zach called to inquire.

"I can't imagine."

"Extracting myself from a helicopter that has crashed into the sea," Zach said triumphantly.

No, he hadn't survived an accident: Zach had just finished up a week's worth of training in Helicopter Emergency Egress.

"Um…do helicopters frequently fall into the sea?" I inquired in what I hoped was a casual tone.

"Pretty often," he said. "They figured out that a lot of the guys who die in these crashes could've escaped. They just didn't know what to do, and they panicked. With this training, more of us will be able to survive."

Oh.

As Zach described it, the training involves dropping a simulated helicopter loaded with Marines into an enormous swimming pool, in the dark. The "helicopter" then flips upside down, as a real one would in such circumstances, and begins to fill with water. Since the Marines are strapped in, their heads go underwater first.

"How interesting!" I said, turning the kettle on and scrabbling in the cupboard for the Tension Tamer tea.

"So what we have to do is unsnap ourselves from the seat harness and swim to the exit before the helicopter sinks," Zach explained.

"What happens if you don't?"

"We had some guys freak out and start flailing."

Aha.

"Since it's training, there were divers in the pool who would swim in and fish those guys out," Zach went on happily.

Between gasps into the paper bag now firmly placed over my mouth and nose I asked, "And you were, um, able to get out?"

"Oh yeah," said Zach. "That's what I wanted to tell you, Mom. I got out the first time with no trouble at all. So then the instructors started giving me extra problems to solve. Like, my harness won't unfasten, or the first exit I try is blocked, or there's a wounded guy I have to bring with me..."

"Oh Zackie!" I said.

"Isn't that cool?"

I took a deep breath, forcing my cringing rib cage to expand. "Yes, my darling," I said. "It's really cool."

Once, at a dinner, the colonel of the Connecticut game wardens told me he'd figured out how to cut the rate of accidental drowning down to nothing.

"Really?"

"Yeah. Don't let males swim." He laughed at my expression. "Think about it: how many female accidental drowning victims have you recovered?"

I had to admit I couldn't think of one.

Young male victims far outnumber female ones when it comes to virtually all accidents, homicides, and suicides I've responded to. Out of curiosity, I looked up the statistics, and, according to Census data, male Americans are *much* more likely than female ones to die prematurely from any cause.

The top three leading causes of death for Americans between the ages of fifteen and twenty-four are accidents, homicide, and suicide, in that order (for Americans as a whole, the top killers are heart disease, cancer, and stroke, with accidents coming in fourth), but young men are nearly three times as likely to die in an accident (twice as likely in auto accidents, specifically) and more than five times as likely as women to be murdered. Young men are seven times as likely to commit suicide. Yet, when a friend who works at a domestic violence shelter became pregnant, she unhappily confessed that though she counted herself a feminist, she was hoping to have a boy, if only because being female is so very, very dangerous.

Behavioral scientists assert that none of us are much good at accurately assessing risk. My priorities when it came to protecting my children are probably as irrational as anyone else's. For instance, when my children flew across the country as unaccompanied minors, I put my faith in the sheer, statistical rarity of stranger-kidnappers. Back in Maine, I was positive only a meticulous concern for life jackets and helmets could keep my kids undrowned, their skulls intact. And now, it seems, the government plans to strap my precious firstborn into a helicopter and let him fall into the fathomless sea.

Not long after my first husband died, I read that a significant loss experienced early shortens a human life by an average of five years. If this statistic is true—and it certainly could be, given all the ominous cellular damage prolonged stress inflicts on the human body—it's a gyp! Wasn't it enough that the kids would have to grow up deprived of Drew? Would they have to have shorter lives as well?

Our culture is of two minds about the spiritual significance of emotional trauma. On one hand, we are convinced that, in the absence of professional attention, permanent damage will be the inevitable result of bad experiences ranging from being given a stupid name by your parents to losing friends before your eyes at Fallujah. On the other hand is the idea that trauma, and its attendant sufferings, confer strength, perspective, and even a kind of wise nobility.

A trauma can't simultaneously make you stronger and weaker, can it? These seem to be mutually exclusive ideas, not that mutual exclusivity is an insuperable impediment to the religious mind.

My father's wartime experience inarguably granted him skills and insights that made him a better reporter and historian. On the other hand, his body sustained damage over and above the multiple wounds that, because they were inflicted by a hand grenade, were honored with a Purple Heart. The body is injured by psychological stress. If the stress is severe or prolonged, the injury will be significant enough to impair normal functioning and leave a lasting mark, at which point we can describe it as *traumatic*. Diseases associated with traumatic stress — post-traumatic stress disorder but also clinical depression, anxiety disorder, kidney disease, heart disease, and stroke — are likely to arise in the human body when stress has been prolonged and/or when the experience is not only miserable but also meaningless.

When the Maine Warden Service first began offering the services of a chaplain to its officers, and mandating peer-debriefing sessions after what are known as "critical incidents," some veteran wardens grumbled that the services amounted to mollycoddling: in their day, they'd been told to "suck it up" and keep going, and you didn't see anyone complaining about stress or taking pills. I pointed out that in their day it was common to smoke a pack a day, drink a lot, and die within five years of retirement.

To be fair, some of the resistance came from wardens' previous experiences with well-intentioned but unhelpful group therapy sessions led by therapists with no understanding of law enforcement culture and a therapeutic model that emphasized emotional catharsis. While many people are reasonably comfortable weeping and caviling in front of others, as a rule law enforcement officers are far more likely to express themselves in dark jokes — a tendency they share with doctors, nurses, firefighters, and others constantly exposed to human vulnerability, suffering, and death.

"Let's not hide our feelings behind humor," a social worker reportedly said to a group of State Troopers and wardens, a remark so memorably offensive that I heard about it from three guys on three separate occasions as an explanation for why they didn't want to attend debriefings ever again.

There are "psycho-educational group intervention models" developed by and for emergency service providers, and here in Maine, we have found these most helpful for game wardens and other law enforcement officers. Ours is a humble formula, in which trained peers respectfully facilitate a conversation between intelligent, essentially healthy adult men and women. We offer user-friendly information about how the body is affected by stress, and how to care for our bodies (and with our bodies, our minds and spirits) so as to recover and return to normal functioning as swiftly and completely as possible.

Traumatic stress is not new and, in some ways, neither is psycho-educational group intervention. In the passion narratives of the New Testament, for example, Jesus's death is presented, very clearly, as a miserable, traumatic experience for his followers. They watched their friend and teacher being tortured to death, with none of the miraculous reprieve they had come to expect while in his company, and then had to survive the attentions of hostile authorities. In the immediate aftermath of the crucifixion, the disciples are torn asunder with grief, shaken by terror and its concomitant urge to fight or flee.

Fifty days later, the disciples are functioning as an effective team, pulling together and forming a fledgling church. That weenie Peter, who thrice denied even knowing Jesus, now preaches His word fearlessly before the crowds in Jerusalem. Doubting Thomas has become a born-again convincer. Even Jesus's brother James, formerly a skeptic, is on board. What happened?

Jesus was resurrected and returned to them, but this has never struck me as a wholly satisfactory explanation for the disciples' resilience. The bereaved take what we can get, of course, so even a partial, brief, and hallucinatory visitation from the dear departed will be clutched at when the alternative is nevermore. But in my experience, even without resurrection, without even the sure and certain hope of such a thing, mourners do recover. Knocked down and buried by grief, we stay close to one another, as the disciples did. We cry and talk, tell the life story over and over, and slowly dig ourselves out from under our mourning.

I don't mean this in a dismissive, time-heals-all-wounds way. We never go back to who we were before the death. Instead, we struggle, flail, tell the story, and then struggle and flail and tell it again until at last we achieve a truce with loss that allows us to summon the courage to love again, and more.

Every time I see this happen, it strikes me as a miracle more glorious, ennobling, and encouraging than any vacant tomb. Somehow, we have in us the capacity to creatively fuse what is lost with what remains and make meaning rise out of emptiness.

Donald's funeral was held in the memorial parlor of a funeral home a few days after his body was recovered, and the place was packed with weeping people. I was struck, not for the first time, by how much devotion a person could command from a family that, by all accounts, had been ill-used. Of course, Donald was not the only repeat offender in the family. It wasn't just his father, who, having violated the terms of his parole in the mere days that passed between the recovery and the service, was back in jail. Two or three of the cousins tearfully accepting condolences from the game wardens were well known to local law enforcement owing to their unfortunate tendency to make life hazardous and unpleasant for others.

When Barbie asked me, after the service was concluded, whether Donald, a well-documented sinner, really was in Heaven, I pointed out that for all his faults, he had been well loved on Earth. Looking into her tear-filled eyes, I said, "You went on loving him even when he screwed up. If you can still care for him so bravely, after all he's put you through, surely God can, too."

In his eulogy, Dick had just described their final conversation, out there in the black, winter water.

"Donald! Hang on! I'll come get you!" Dick had cried.

"No, dude . . . just go. Tell everyone I'm sorry."

So I, too, had tears in my eyes. "God has room for Donald," I said to Barbara.

"I'm spiritual but I'm not really religious," Barbie confessed. Most of the guests had departed, but the coffin was still there, with Donald and a six-pack inside.

The coffin rested on a wheeled cart concealed and disguised as a marble catafalque by a cover complete with buxom trompe l'oeil caryatids, and Barbie, the roots of her hair freshly dyed manilla-ochre, was posed beside it.

"Say 'cheese,'" said her boyfriend, and Barbie did.

He was taking photos. Presumably, the idea was to seize a rare opportunity to document best clothes and best behavior, but whatever the reason, Donald's family and close friends had been asked to remain behind after the service for pictures. Barbie had asked if I would mind being in one or two of these, so I stayed, too, together with a pair of wardens disinclined to depart until they had seen their chaplain safely headed homeward.

Barbie named and then arranged various familial subgroups around the coffin while Barbie's boyfriend, the designated photographer, juggled cell phones and disposable Fun Cameras, and Donald's ex-girlfriend began posting the "cute ones" on Facebook. When my turn came, I posed with Barbie and the coffin. Taking my cue from her, I obeyed instructions and said, "Cheese."

"Barbie and I, and all of us, we're all Christians," Barbie's boyfriend assured me, when all the pictures had been taken, tweeted, and uploaded. "We believe in, you know...Jesus and stuff."

Barbie said, "And I was thinking that maybe, Kate, you could, like, say one more prayer for us?"

We put the cameras and cell phones down and held hands in a ring around Donald.

O God whose name and being is love, we thank you for the gift of Donald. We ask you to release him from his weaknesses, and to help us to forgive him, mourn him, and remember him with love. God bless him and bring him into the safety and comfort of Heaven.

Her eyes still closed, Barbie lifted our clasped hands toward the funeral home's acoustic-tile ceiling and the sky. Her hand was warm, her tattooed arm, upraised beside my face, smelled faintly of fresh-mown grass.

"Thank you, Jesus," she said. "Thank you for Donald. And thank you for the wardens who got him back for us," and the assembled all said, *"Amen,"* except for Barbie's boyfriend, who just wheezed reverently.

In his dark suit and shiny shoes, the funeral director, with practiced ceremony, stripped the cart's faux-marble cover from its Velcro anchors, folded it solemnly, and handed it to his assistant as if it were a flag. Then he wheeled the coffin down the hall and into the elevator that would carry it down to the basement to await cremation. Raising one hand in benediction, he pushed the button, and the doors closed. We watched and waited until the floor indicator lit up, revealing a red, digital "B."

"That's that," Barbie sighed, but it still wasn't. Out in the parking lot, the family continued to linger. Barbie was holding my hand as if she weren't ready to release not me but the moment.

Donald's ex-girlfriend sidled up and requested that I keep Donald's little daughter in my prayers.

Bruce and Scott were standing by their trucks, waiting tactfully for me to depart. Diffidently, Donald's friend Dick approached them.

"So," he began. "I was just kind of wondering. How does a person become a game warden?"

Scott explained that employment opportunities and information could be found on the department's website. Taking a leaf from his notebook, he wrote down the Web address, as well as the phone number of the warden in charge of recruiting.

"I felt like I was lying to the guy," Scott admitted afterward. "Maybe I should have said: *Hey pal, the Warden Service doesn't hire druggies, wife beaters, or thieves.*"

"You answered the question Dick asked you," I pointed out.

"Yeah. I did." Scott frowned, unconvinced.

I tried to picture Scott as he might look to Dick, or to anyone who didn't know him personally. With State of Maine patches bright on his uniformed shoulders, he stood sturdy and competent, the badge on his chest lit by the pale, heroic light of a still-tender spring afternoon.

"You and I know it's unlikely that Dick could ever become a game warden and he probably knows it, too," I suggested. "But he could be something more and better than he is right now, couldn't he?"

Scott made a noise somewhere between a snort and a laugh. "Anything would be an improvement."

"Exactly. And I think he wants to redeem his friend's death, to give it meaning, by making a change. Maybe you and the other wardens have given him a glimpse of a way he could do that. Not just a better job, I mean, but a better way to be a man."

"Huh," said Scott. He pondered, Scott-like, then shrugged. "I hope he makes it."

I see awful things, but I see good things, too: kindness, courage, forgiveness, generosity, strange beauty. I see roses in lake water and the way gratitude can be mingled with the deepest grief in a human countenance.

For the whole of the summer after Donald's body was found, whenever I saw a river birch—a tree whose bark sloughs off continuously in irregular, pinky-white strips—I flashed back to Donald, his hand, and his mom.

Deciding to take advantage of this classic symptom of post-traumatic stress, I let it be a reminder for me to pray for Donald's daughter. *Grow and go forth, little woman. Be blessed and a blessing, little one.*

Chapter Twenty-Five

I am more or less conversant with the principles of basic first aid, and I carry certain items in my car that can be useful in a crisis—flares, ropes, body armor, Band-Aids. But I am a chaplain, not a police officer or a paramedic, so I don't presume to leap into action unless there isn't anyone around who might leap with more practical effect.

The accident was a bad one, with two cars askew and smashed across both lanes amid a lavish scattering of glass and shredded metal; and, in the field beside the road, there were huddled figures draped in blankets, at least one of whom was prone. Other passersby had stopped, and there were folks directing traffic while others appeared to be performing the calm fox-trot (slow, slow, quick-quick) of competent first aid, so the question I had to ask myself as I pulled onto the verge and examined the scene was: *Does it look as if anyone here might be in need of my particular expertise?*

That is to say: might anyone here be, well, dead?

There was that one body, lying down, with someone huddled over it as if weeping. Stepping out of my car, I headed toward the material center of this storm, the body in the field. I was calm, yet the soles of my feet felt the cold clods of churned mud through my shoes; and, glancing down to gauge the footing, I saw with vivid precision the funnel-shaped web of a grass spider spangled around the opening with three droplets of dew. An autumnal crimson was just beginning to seep along the edges of green leaves in — whoops! watch it! — a stand of poison ivy.

If I approached the scene of sudden death with confidence, that confidence was coupled with and might even have been dependent upon humility. In the middle of a maelstrom I have learned that I can, at most, set myself as a provisional anchor and only to the degree that a new mourner will accept me as an embodied promise of all who are not yet there to hold her — her own family, her own friends, her own minister, her own integration of this loss into a new and deeper understanding of God.

Confidently, humbly, I made my way to where the body lay, and as I drew near, I heard a wondrous sound. It was the groan — oh, beautiful, musical groan! — that people make when something *hurts*.

No one else in that field was smiling. A young woman who had witnessed the accident from her nearby house stood, pale and trembling, clutching a second blanket in her arms to add, if necessary, to the one with which she had covered the injured woman. En route to work at the Pen Bay hospital, a nurse had stopped when he saw the cars and it was he who knelt beside the victim, his knees set on either side of her head so as to stabilize her neck.

Another passing motorist had taken it upon herself to direct traffic; belatedly, I recognized her as Stacy, the superb local caterer who had, as it happened, made the meal for Simon's and my wedding celebration. Neither the witness with the blanket, the nurse, nor the caterer gave any evidence of feeling celebratory, and of course the victim wasn't too happy, but I was. Really, truly happy: "I'm a chaplain," I said jubilantly.

The woman on the ground stopped groaning and eyed me doubtfully. "Oh yes?"

I introduced myself. "But guess what? You don't need me."

"All I really needed was paper towels and lettuce," the woman said confusedly. "Everything else I could have done without. I was going to Shop 'n Save. Now this man thinks I've broken my collarbone and maybe dislocated my shoulder."

"Ouch!" I said sympathetically.

"It hurts. Who did you say you are?"

"A chaplain," I said, "for the Maine Warden Service."

I saw the question on her face and answered it: "Game wardens, not prison wardens."

The woman closed her eyes. "Lord, what a day," she said.

We heard sirens. The nurse breathed, "Here they come," and looked, if not jubilant, at least relieved.

I was able to persuade the young woman who witnessed

the accident to go indoors and get herself a jacket. Stacy the caterer was yielding her place in the middle of the road to a firefighter in a tangerine raincoat; she caught my eye and waved good-bye. *She has mouths to feed*, I thought. A wedding, perhaps?

And I had a warden's baby to bless! Dashing back to my car, I passed a couple of local police officers.

"Hey Kate! What are you doing here?"

"Nothing at all!" I told them. "Isn't that fabulous?" They grinned back. They knew enough to be happy, too.

The grenade thrown at him by a North Korean or Chinese soldier exploded in my father's foxhole and injured him badly. Patched together by a Navy corpsman, he was lugged down the mountainside on a litter by six South Koreans who, though they probably couldn't have translated what my father was saying word for word, probably knew from his tone that he was screaming curses at them. The stretcher bearers met up with a truck marked with a red cross and equipped with racks for the wounded. Dad was in a lower rack beneath a man who was bleeding so heavily his blood dripped down onto my father. When they extracted Dad from the vehicle at the field hospital, the chaplain took one look at him, covered with his own and the other man's blood, and began to give him last rites. (Dad apparently objected so strenuously to this procedure that both the chaplain and the doctors were persuaded that he might live after all.)

Back in the United States, on the other hand, my father was dead.

His parents—my *farfar* and *farmor*—had received an official visit from two Marines in dress blues. "We regret to inform you..." they said.

Three days later, my grandfather and grandmother received a second deputation. Presumably with some appropriately apologetic preamble, the second pair of visitors admitted that Lieutenant Peter Braestrup, USMC, was in fact alive and on a hospital ship somewhere in the South China Sea.

While I was growing up, that story was part of a legend that began with Dad swiping his medical records from the Marine Corps recruiter, and ended with the grenade and the two notifications. Sometimes Dad would add another bit— agreeably disgusting—about the moment when, years later, he felt a tickle in his throat and coughed up a shard of shrapnel in the middle of lunch.

It wasn't until I was an adult with my own bereavements available for reference that I really thought about the three days that passed between the visit of the first pair of Marines and the follow-up visit from the second.

Three days is a *long* time. Within three days of my first husband's death, hundreds of relatives and friends had been notified, the date and time of the funeral had been set and pallbearers chosen, while people who lived in other states had made travel and hotel reservations, sent flowers, and mailed letters and cards. Three days had filled my kitchen with food prepared by my neighbors, and with friends determined to hold my children and me through our grief. Within three days our minister, having prayed for understanding, had already written the homily she hoped might set this death into a comforting cosmic context.

Even without the presence of a body to bury, three days would be more than enough time for so terrible a loss to fully register in any family: *Our boy, our Peter, is dead.*

And then...he wasn't. For my father it was a close shave, but for his parents it was a resurrection.

A church near my house greeted Ash Wednesday with the following message, carefully installed letter by vinyl letter on its curbside marquee: GOD HUNG THE KEY TO HEAVEN ON A NAIL.

For Easter, the marquee offered this:

CHRIST WAS BORN!
CHRIST IS RESIN!

And I was charmed by what struck me as an accidental verity.

Dead as the doornail on which God hung him, the executed man's body was wrapped in a grave cloth and laid in a tomb. When his friends arrived to freshen his corpse with a bit more resin and spice (*Christ is resin, indeed!*), they found the tomb empty. The conclusion—later to be confirmed by mass sightings, one-to-one conversations, and even (ooogh!) a finger in the wound—was that Jesus was not resin but risen, and not dead.

Generally speaking, *not dead is good.* On this we can all agree.

During spring break, close to Easter, a seventeen-year-old boy was finishing up a ski weekend with his family at one of western Maine's resorts. He took a chairlift up to the top of the mountain for one last run and vanished. When he did not appear as expected to join his parents for an après-ski supper in the lodge, they sounded the alarm. The Maine Warden Service was called and, despite the high winds, falling snow, and bitter cold, wardens searched all that night and through the following day while the boy's family waited miserably, unable to do anything but entertain their fears. As the hours passed, the fear only intensified. Another night went by without result and the wardens had all but concluded that the boy was dead. So the chaplain was sent for, to sit with the family to be there when the bad news came.

"And the news is going to be bad," said the lieutenant flatly, rubbing his hair.

But then I got the second call: *Disregard!*

The boy lives!

"In fact, other than a little frostbite here and there, he's fine," said the lieutenant, and I could hear the wide smile in his voice even over a cell phone with a poor signal.

It turned out that on that late afternoon, wanting to take one last, delicious run through a newly opened glade, the boy had taken a wrong turn. As darkness fell, he realized that he was lost and—oh, splendid, clever boy!—instead of blundering around in the darkness trying to rescue himself and eventually succumbing to exhaustion and hypothermia, he dug himself a snow cave, crawled inside, and went to sleep.

When no one found him the next day, he stuck by his cave, spent another night, and then, the following morning, having done a bit of exploring, he came across a set of snowshoe tracks one of the wardens had made while searching, so he followed these out to the road and to safety.

The lieutenant, who was prepared to give the terrible news, got to deliver good news instead: *Your son lives.* And the lieutenant's eyes filled with tears.

For his parents, who had already begun to accept that their son was dead, this was resurrection, empty tomb and all. Hallelujah.

This, too, is resurrection: I got a phone call from Barbie.

"It's me," she said. "Donald's mom. You know…who drowned in Masquinongy?"

"Yes, of course!" I said. "Barbie, how nice of you to call. What are you up to?"

"I'm in school," she said. "I figured I'd, like, honor Donald's memory by getting my GED. I've been studying for that. And this lady at UMaine in Augusta has been helping me. Turns out they have this special program that's for people like me. She thinks she can get me into that, so I can start working on my college degree."

"Wow," I said.

As if she'd mistaken the awe in that monosyllable for skepticism, Barbie rushed on. "It'll take me some time. I know that. But the thing is, I thought I could become, like, a counselor. A grief counselor."

"Oh Barbie," I breathed.

"Well, because, like, I've been there, y'know?"

"Yes. Exactly."

"So maybe I could help people who were going through something kind of like what happened to me."

I don't know what I said to that. Something enthusiastic and encouraging, and I hope I didn't shout at her because the angels were singing pretty loudly in my ears.

She got a tattoo in Donald's honor, too—her son's dates of birth and death—inscribed in black cursive on the crossbeam of an old rugged cross. It runs down her spine from the nape of her pale neck.

I see awful things. And I see wonderful things.

At some point during what turned out to be his last summer of life, my father told me about how he had cursed the Korean guys who carried him down the mountainside and saved his life. He still felt badly about it.

With what I can only think of as a kind of stoic compassion, these men bore the cursing, groaning American down a mountain road in darkness toward the only resurrection a grieving family really wants. It's the one we pray for until, at last, we resign ourselves to the inevitable and start praying for the strength to go on alone.

Along with the prayers I still offer up for Donald's daughter, I say prayers for those Korean litter bearers. I hope they were granted long and happy lives, surrounded by loving families. I hope they got to dandle beautiful little grandchildren on their ancient knees and that when, at last, the time came for them to be gathered to their ancestors, their deaths were painless and peaceful. If there is a Heaven, I hope my father got to greet and thank them there. In my mind's eye, they are about ten feet tall. With wings.

Chapter Twenty-Six

Woolie says she can part the mists of memory enough to glimpse the time before cell phones were ubiquitous and people went to paper maps rather than Google to figure out how to get where they were going. But it is hard for her to believe that some more vivid memories—the ones in which her father hides in the darkened living room, ready to snatch her, shrieking and laughing, into his embrace—are also back in that misty temporal realm. Did her father really never text anyone or binge-watch reruns of "The Office" on Netflix?

Peter and I were having an idle conversation about a Ford Taurus station wagon we used to have, "back in the day," as he put it. It featured a rear-facing backseat that Peter remembers fondly. "I wish we still had that car," he said with more nostalgia than logic.

"We had that car when your dad was alive. That station wagon would be a decade old by now."

"No, Mom," said Peter. "Dad died in 1996. That's almost two decades ago."

"Holy cow," I said. "So it is!"

It doesn't seem that long ago that our family lost Drew. I don't mean that I've yet to "get over" the death of my first husband, whatever that means. It's that memories from before the day that sharp line was drawn in all our lives still actively inform my thinking and pop up as anecdotes that easily enter into and match the texture of everyday conversations with family and friends. They should feel outdated but, strangely, they don't.

"I remember it like it was yesterday," said the fifty-year-olds of my youth, and now I know what they mean. They could easily have been talking about the D-Day landings that took place less than twenty years before my birth—events no further removed from them in time than Peter is now from that Taurus wagon.

When I went off to college in 1980, brutal racial segregation could easily and vividly be recalled "like it was yesterday" by any American adult because it *was* yesterday: Martin Luther King, Jr., gave his "I Have a Dream" speech a mere twelve years before I arrived at my college dorm. I've been the Maine Warden Service chaplain longer than that, and yet it feels like no time at all. Time and memory do the fox-trot through our minds: fast-fast-slow, quick-quick. It seems like no time at all since Zach was a baby, asleep and trusting in my arms, but he has been in the Marine Corps forever.

*   *   *

As a reporter in Vietnam, my father interviewed a young man named John Balaban, a conscientious objector to the war. Balaban had become a Quaker at the age of sixteen. He was an enthusiastic member of his local Quaker meeting, so he was able to convince his local draft board that his objections were based in long-standing and deeply held beliefs and were as conscientious as anyone could ask for. The board granted him conscientious objector status and told him he was free to go.

But Balaban refused to be excused. Instead, he insisted that his draft board must somehow contrive to send him to Vietnam for humanitarian service.

He wound up working for the International Voluntary Service, first teaching—he was wounded when the Viet Cong blew up his classroom during the Tet Offensive—then organizing medical care for Vietnamese children who had been injured in the fighting.

Years later, when I was an undergraduate at Georgetown, John Balaban—who was also a poet—was invited to give a reading. When we were introduced, Balaban told me his story because he remembered my father.

"Oh yes," said Dad, when I asked him if he remembered interviewing a Quaker named John Balaban in Saigon. "Brave guy."

High praise!

Is the lunatic, self-risking courage that allowed young American men to charge young Vietnamese men in battle the same courage that sent John Balaban to help war-wounded children? I ask because I picture Balaban seated before the draft board with the same polite determination on his face that Dad demonstrated to his recruiter and Zach showed to Sergeant Sangster and, I don't doubt, Sophie Scholl showed to her executioners: *I will serve.*

How can any of us be sure our children won't end up like those boys in the movie I saw at the Holocaust Museum during Police Week—the handsome, smiling monsters who rode their motorcycle past the starving little ones?

Doctors Samuel and Pearl Oliner, a husband-wife team of social scientists, conducted a famous Holocaust study in which they attempted to answer this question, albeit with a more positive spin. The Oliners sought to understand the human quality of altruism using neither the victims nor the perpetrators but the *rescuers* of European Jews as their subjects. They asked excellent questions with their work: What was different about the people who risked their lives to save others? Why did they *rescue* while their neighbors either participated in the persecution or stood by and did nothing?

Here are the qualities that did not set the rescuers apart: The rescuers were not particularly tall, good-looking, or healthy. The rescuers were not, on the whole, better educated than the bystanders. In fact, none of the traits that the vast majority of us might look for when consciously selecting a sperm donor are associated in any way with the kind of brave love and moral courage that can make, and has made, the world a better place.

Incidentally, though it pains me to admit it, rescuers weren't any more or less religious than perpetrators and bystanders either. So-called Christian beliefs could motivate rescuers to rescue if they were using the What Would Jesus Do principle, but it could excuse bystanders and perpetrators because "the Jews killed Jesus." Lest we imagine that Christianity per se was the problem, it should be noted that alternative belief systems were around in those days: In 1944—in the middle of the war—Germany hosted an astrologer's convention. German women were exploring Goddess-worship and devoted Nazis tried hard to shift from celebrating Christmas to observing the winter solstice. One Dutch rescuer recalled a bystander earnestly informing her that she really needed to take a more "astral view of things," rather than fuss about the fate of the Jews.

So what did the rescuers have that the bystander didn't?

The Oliners' study identified three basic clusters of traits in the rescuers that, when combined, motivated these exemplary persons who proved capable of what Dr. King would call "dangerous selflessness." One cluster is what I think of as a cognitively based concern for justice, fairness, and equity in human relationships. Another is more heart-centered: an emotional concern for empathy, kindness, and caring for those in need. These two concerns—fairness and kindness—were accompanied in the rescuers by a strong sense of personal responsibility: not just "someone ought to do something" but "*I* must do something." These three characteristics were described by the rescuers as values they *learned at home,* values their parents emphasized and modeled.

A typical rescuer told the researchers, "My parents taught me to think logically, to be tolerant. They showed me how to love my neighbors, to help whoever needed it, and to consider all people my equals no matter what their nationality or religion."

As the Oliners said, "What is striking about a large percentage of rescuers is the consistently universalistic orientation, exemplified not only in the values they recall learning from their parents, but also in the reasons they give for rescuing Jews."

Or, as one of the rescuers was quoted as saying, "I found it incomprehensible and inadmissible that for religious reasons...Jews would be persecuted. It's like saving someone who is drowning. You don't ask them what God they pray to. You just go ahead and save them."

I read that quote, and the words "saving someone who is drowning" jumped out at me: *Good grief,* I thought. *The rescuers were game wardens!*

Or maybe what I meant was: *Game wardens are rescuers.*

Game wardens — Bruce and Scott, Jason and Josh, "my" game wardens, the men and women I am privileged to serve and serve beside — do indeed combine a cognitive, brain-based concern for justice, fairness, and equity in human relationships with a heart-centered concern for empathy, kindness, and care. For game wardens, as for rescuers, care is not a spectator sport. It is activated by a strong sense of personal responsibility: not just "someone ought to do something" but "I must do something." And so game wardens do.

They risk their safety, day after day, year after year, wading through snow, swimming under ice, pushing through dark woods, and climbing mountains in order to help people they know nothing about. Fifteen wardens from the Maine Warden Service have their names inscribed in the granite at Judiciary Square, more than any other law enforcement agency in our state. Like the rescuers interviewed in the Oliners' study, Maine's game wardens think they're ordinary. They don't even see themselves as particularly brave or heroic.

So I have found myself wishing I'd told that woman seated beside me on the plane to Mobile: listen, sister, what you really want to do is find a sperm bank in which all the donors are game wardens, even if they are short, bipolar college dropouts.

Being a rescuer not only means sacrificing things we take for granted in normal life, like a predictable schedule or a safe work environment, but it also means risking your life for the sake of love. I am so proud, so grateful, that I get to work with these "altruistic personalities," that I get to be a chaplain to rescuers, the chaplain of the Maine Warden Service. And I hope with all my heart that my children and grandchildren will receive from me and from the village that helped me raise them whatever they might need to be rescuers, too.

CHAPTER TWENTY-SEVEN

When I told Simon the story about Zach going to sixth grade with a rainbow patch sewn to his backpack, Simon replied, "You know, Kate, I'm not convinced that Zach needs the Marine Corps. But I think the Marine Corps might really need people like Zach."

"I'm proud of Zach," I said to Warden Bruce Loring. He had just pointed out a ruffed grouse I otherwise would have been blind to and I had just told him about my son's newly discovered, esoteric talent for extracting himself (and a "wounded comrade") from a crashed, submerged helicopter.

"I'll bet you are."

Well, and why not? If Zach were at college, I'd probably be proud of him for being good at lacrosse or *a cappella* singing or some other activity I wouldn't otherwise give thought to... Maybe not *quite* as proud, though. The "wounded comrade" part really hits me where I live.

No matter what direction Zach might have chosen to

take, I would like to think I'd have been able to recognize and honor the moment(s) when he took a further, substantive step toward bona fide adulthood, but it was Zach's enlistment that forced me to think about the essence of this transformation, since military service is a — and perhaps the — universal traditional indicator, at least of the boy-to-man version.

It is, like seemingly everything that matters, a paradox: Simon and I did not wish all our children to follow Zach's example and sign up to be warriors in a time of war. With our blessing, all the other kids entered adulthood by degrees, crawl-toddle-walk-run, and there is much to recommend this, even without considering the white gravestones at Arlington. And yet, we are proud of our boy. Like his *morfar* and his own dad, like the poet John Balaban and Bruce himself, he self-consciously assumed moral responsibility for himself and for the well-being of others within a complex, morally ambiguous, hazardous, and yet needy world.

"Of course you're proud of him," said Bruce comfortably. "Zach stepped up."

Zach was the first of our children to do it. But all six will eventually have to find their own ways to step up and respond to the call of love and service. There are so many ways, and there is The Way.

"Oh, and guess what else, Bruce?" I said. "I'm going to be a grandmother."

Zach had called to say that Erin was pregnant. Simon and I were, as I have mentioned, beside ourselves with delighted anticipation, but we didn't have to be. We could feel whatever we wanted to feel: approval, disapproval, a yen to contribute to this as to our progeny's previous projects (educational, occupational), but the project wasn't ours. Zach and Erin had their own home, their own work, their own paths to follow or forge through the world. The pregnancy, choice, and baby belonged to them.

Fortunately, they seemed disposed to share.

If the three stages of man are optimism, pessimism, and cynicism, I think I'm going through them in reverse order. I was more cynical when I was younger, and every year brings me closer to optimism.

It was easier to be cynical about men before I married one and had my sons.

It was easier to be cynical about American race relations before my brother adopted my darling African-American nephew, and my son received surrogate fathering from men of every hue.

It was easier to be cynical about crime and punishment before I worked with cops, easier to be cynical about war and peace before my son joined my father's Corps, and downright easy peasy to be cynical about the future before I had a grandson on his way into it.

These days, cynicism seems uncomfortably close to despair, and I no longer believe that the only alternative to despair is blind denial. Despair isn't realism, it is the apocalypticism of the clever unreligious and just as much an abdication of responsibility. Bad things happen but the world isn't ending. No bang, no whimper, no sudden fix, just this long, slow slog we're all taking together toward the next shining, inevitable miracle.

On a hot July day, I held a baby squirrel in my hand, its little forepaws clinging to my thumb with the faith of the defenseless, and I was the miracle the creature didn't even know enough to ask for, let alone expect. This, by itself, might have made it a fine summer, but there was more.

Maine is never really hot, not by the standards of Bangkok, and by August the weather had become what the Maine summer is famous for: a morning of fog and the mournful honking of foghorns yielding to days of blue skies and air sparkling like Prosecco. The coolness was especially delicious at night. I began to chill and cheer up, stopped wishing our offspring would leave, and began enjoying their stay.

Simon turned fifty and we conspired to throw him a party in the yard, with a little extra celebration on the side for Zach and Erin, who flew in from California for the event. Her stomach was enormous and her smile was beautiful. For the time being, Zach said he would continue to be stationed at Miramar near San Diego, with no prospect of being deployed: Baby Drew would be born in a couple of months and his dad would be home to hold him. Everyone was well and happy, full of plans, and I did, at least, have the sense to be truly, deeply grateful.

* * *

I've written a book about prayer, and I am a minister, so this is the question I am invariably asked: does prayer work?

Sometimes this happens on television, though I prefer radio interviews, since you don't have to wear makeup, and you can load the dishwasher while, say, chatting with Dr. Oz.

It will tell you something about my level of cultural awareness that I had never heard of Dr. Oz before he interviewed me, which was a little embarrassing. Luckily, most of the radio personalities who call are local celebrities, at best. My introductions to "Frank Harris, from WMAD, Madison Wis-*con*-sin!" or "Joel and Susan, bringing you the joy of Jesus…" are occasionally preceded by advertisements for acupuncture or for organizations devoted to the sanctity of marriage. Further clues to the interviewer's bent might be offered by the music, but by the time I'm listening to "Drop Kick Me, Jesus (Through the Goal Posts of Life)" or a chorus of whales, it's too late to adjust my message, even if I wanted to.

"Does prayer work?" asks Frank or Susan or Dr. Oz.

Sometimes the question is asked with happy confidence, sometimes with an irony bordering on sarcasm, but always, it seems, with the expectation that my answer will offer something in the way of hope.

Hope is the eager expectation that things will turn out well. Since we live in a predominately Christian culture, it's difficult to divest ourselves of the idea that hope is a good thing, which is why we tell the Greek story of Pandora's box to children. But Christian hope is distinct from the Greek hope that lay waiting under all the terrible things—cancer, AIDS, cruelty, ennui—that Zeus had packed into the box.

Zeus was just as omnipotent as Jehovah, but he wasn't particularly good. Like other pagan gods, the Greek gods sometimes helped human beings and sometimes hindered them—but they often just messed with them. So Zeus didn't put hope in the bottom of that box as an antidote to the evil the inquisitive Pandora was sure to let loose in the world. He put it in to *amplify* it.

Hope keeps us attached to the world in spite of its torments. Hope prevents us from just giving up and refusing to play the game we're bound to lose.

Zach and Erin's son, my grandson, Andrew Michael Griffith, was born about ten days before his due date. The pregnancy had gone well, and there was every expectation—we didn't even have to think of it as hope then—that his would be an uncomplicated birth with what we are now so privileged to think of as a normal, that is, healthy outcome.

Instead, Baby Drew was subjected to what is known as a catastrophic cord accident: his umbilical cord was compressed during labor and, as he was emerging into the world, actually broke. Drew lost half of his blood volume. His oxygen supply was cut off for what could only be assumed was too long.

These days, however, a good life can sometimes be salvaged even from so calamitous a beginning as this, so my grandson was whisked off to the neonatal intensive care unit where his small life would be sustained by various instruments and tubes for the next five days.

If hope is a thing with feathers, it is not a soaring raptor but a fallen sparrow, one that accidentally hurled itself against what it thought was clear air but was really an unforgiving window: bewildered, ignorant, bleeding at its beak, it staggers beneath the treachery of clean glass. It tries to sing with a broken voice and tries to fly with broken wings. There is heroism in hope, but mostly there is pathos.

Please? The hopeful sparrow peeps. For you all things are possible.

Please?

If the bird is lucky, its injuries allow it to get airborne before some predator — a hawk, perhaps — comes along and counts it as a lucky meal, the answer to its own prayer.

Christian hope is defined as the anticipation of a future in which God's purposes are fulfilled according to God's covenant faithfulness and the resurrection of Jesus Christ, all of which is prefigured by the work of the Holy Spirit through the church and, presumably, churchgoers.

If the daughter of a Roman official, or a widow's son, or even Lazarus, is resurrected as a sign of what is to come, why not your daughter, your son, your father, your friend? *Why not my grandson?*

Yo! God! A little miracle here in the University of California at San Diego Neonatal Intensive Care Unit would do a hell of a lot for your reputation among the skeptical, rational materialists of the twenty-first century USA. You've done it before. You can do it again.

Not my will but yours be done, of course. But Jesus, I'm just saying...

Please?

I was having lunch one day with a clergy colleague and as she distributed salad onto our respective plates, she asked me what theological questions I am most apt to see raised in my work. "Well," I said, "there's the theodicy problem, of course. You know, how can a good and loving God allow evil and suffering..."

As if I'd pressed a button, my colleague lit up, opened up, and gave forth her answer. Human agency, choice making, free will are all meaningless without the freedom to choose badly, etc.

When a given disaster too clearly lacks a connection to any genuine human agency, we fall back on the Mystery and on Christian hope, the promise that even if our human lives are presently made unbearable, everything will be fine, every tear dried, every frown turned upside down when the last days come.

I can't be too hard on my colleague: I, too, have buttons that can be pressed. The files in my clever head pop open and there are all the answers I am far too quick to offer to questions that haven't actually been asked.

I wasn't a chaplain in the Neonatal Intensive Care Unit in San Diego. I was the anguished grandmother of a baby boy, mother to a son and daughter-in-law whose hearts were courageous and breaking. But the hospital had a chaplain, and he came to visit.

"It must be difficult to understand how God could let something like this happen to your little baby," he said sympathetically. "God's ways can be hard to understand at times like these."

He was a good guy, sincerely eager to offer solace and to be of help. My son and daughter-in-law listened politely to him, and I blew my nose and said hello with considerable sympathy: I know what it is to show up in the tunnel when the light at the end is fading to black.

"Does prayer work?" Dr. Oz asks hopefully.

I must answer honestly: no.

But also: it depends on what you are expecting prayer to do.

Oh, I know what we want prayer to do. We want there to be a Santa God sitting on a cloud in that grand, celestial department store in the sky.

Who, if His child asks for bread, will give her a stone?

If we had what we prayed for, life would be all bread, all the time. Is it only me who notices all these stones? Surely not.

Why do we cling to a notion of God that is so utterly useless in the face of something as ubiquitous as death, and as common as pain? Why do we worship a God who can't comfort us when there is no hope? My particular ministry might seem like all-death-all-the-time, but surely theologians, being human, have smacked up against a few hopeless moments, too? Have they never listened to the cries of the bereaved? God, as too many describe Him, offers no recognition of the reality of loss, no explanation, only the cruel demand that we go on hoping, for a "miracle" and, when we get the stone instead, for some unseen, intangible abstraction: *I am the way, the truth, and the light, whosoever believeth in me…*

The Word is an IOU scribbled in invisible ink on foolscap, and this is supposed to take the place of the warm and necessary dear one we will never see again.

It doesn't work. It—the Gospel, the Revelation—might even be true, somehow, but it doesn't work.

Jesus found this out: in the face of loss, even Jesus had to shut his mouth and stand there, weeping with Mary in the dust and sorrow he found on the road to Bethany.

When Zach joined the Marines, I was afraid he would be changed into a monster and the change would be forever. I was afraid he would be sent into combat, traumatized, maimed. And I feared death.

His death. Never his infant's.

My brain knows that babies die, just as my brain knows that earthquakes happen. But the earth in Maine remains unmoved beneath my feet and all the newborns I'd seen were hale and hearty so my heart was not prepared for California or this: clad in a desert-brown T-shirt and desert fatigues, his belt buckle carefully aligned with his zipper, my son was on the phone arranging for the cremation of his son.

I was knitting on the couch in Zach and Erin's sunny apartment in San Diego. Jets from the nearby military base at Miramar streaked through the pale sky. When area residents call the base to complain about the noise, Erin told me, they are politely informed, "Ma'am, that is the sound of freedom."

Simon was there with me, sharing the guest room that should have been our grandson's nursery. Aunt Mary would be flying in from Georgia soon. Every few minutes a cell phone rang: It would be one of the baby's grieving aunts and uncles, or Tonya. It would be a Maine game warden, a trooper, or a concerned Marine calling from Camp Pendleton with an offer of food. Reverend Jenks called to let me know that several of his parishioners mentioned Zach, Erin, and Baby Drew during the Prayers of the People and that everyone in Maine who loved us was simultaneously sending great prayerful plumes of love billowing up into the clear Maine sky. Caught by the wind, their love could travel all the way to California, so I told the reverend this must be why I kept catching whiffs of balsam fir, beach roses, and the mnemonic salty smell of tears on the westward breeze.

The hospital provided a list of area funeral homes. Zach and Erin selected one. The woman who answered the phone was kind. She said that the cremation wouldn't take long, and that the crematory would provide a temporary urn, made of plastic and "suitable for a loved one weighing up to seven pounds."

"My son weighed six pounds, two ounces," said Zach.

"Yes. So that will be fine. You can pick him up tomorrow," the funeral director replied.

Erin signaled urgently to her husband: *the airport?*

"Oh yes...excuse me, ma'am, but can the urn go through airport security?" Zach asked. "We're taking him home to Maine for the funeral."

"It can. It will have to go through the X-ray scanner, but they won't need to open it."

"Thank you, ma'am."

My hands went on knitting. Another fighter jet roared by, making the hullabaloo of freedom.

"What are you knitting?" Erin asked me.

"I don't know," I said. Then I did: "It's an urn cozy."

It would be a little drawstring bag, about five inches tall, made of the California handspun I'd found at a street market in San Diego's Balboa Park and the Maine-made yarn I brought with me from home. It would end up being sort of baggy, just like all the sweaters and hats I'd made for my grandson, all the things my hands have ever knit for those I love.

My husband Simon says that the highest praise he ever hears me utter of something is that it is "useful."

"Does prayer work?" the radio interviewers ask, and I know what they are asking.

"Prayer doesn't work," I reply. "But prayer is useful."

We want prayer to alter reality, and prayer won't do that. What prayer can do is open our eyes to reality: prayer can help us to see what is actually happening all around us. Our prayers let us see God in what is, and prayers can reveal that God is love.

So where might God be seen in this, the story of the short, hopeless life and inevitable death of one of God's fallen sparrows, this little baby boy in San Diego?

God was *everywhere*. God was all around and beyond: God was the tenderness in the hands of the doctors who removed the respirator from Drew's little mouth, God was the tears in the eyes of the nurse as he adjusted the anesthetic, God was the woman who gave me a Kleenex and put her arms around me when I broke down — it turned out that she was the neonatologist who had been present at Baby Drew's birth — and God? Oh God, your miraculous love was my daughter-in-law's strength as she sang to the son that lay in her arms; You were the song he heard as he died.

I wanted Baby Drew to have life. It would have been such a good life, in a good world.

"It was a good life," says my son the Marine. "A good life in a good world, a life filled end to end, womb to tomb, with love."

Does prayer work?

No.

And: yes.

Oh yes.

CHAPTER TWENTY-EIGHT

As they've grown older and begun to realize the implications of having a mother who writes books, my offspring now assert their rights to their own material. Over a family supper my son Peter might start telling us about his band's most recent gig at a seedy bar somewhere in Maine:

"...so then this elderly waitress in a low-cut blouse started handing out complimentary Jell-O shots... And a girl got drunk and threw what all the guys in the band kind of hoped were her underpants onto the stage, but it turned out to be a Kleenex..."

Glancing over at his mother, Peter will see the glint of literary avarice in her eye. Quickly, loudly, he'll declare: "COPYRIGHT! This one's mine."

"Awwww, Peetsie! C'mon!"

"Really, Mom-Dawg. You can't have it."

Ellie, who has serious plans to become a playwright and

novelist, felt the need to draw a boundary around the whole, fabulous gold mine of stories she gained in the year she spent in Russia as an exchange student. I'm not allowed to even write the words "Russia" and "daughter" in the same sentence, nor compose my own Russian saga out of ten days I spent visiting her. (What makes this a particularly onerous restriction is that my brother was with us, and he always makes a story better just by being in it.)

So I had to request special permission from my own daughter to tell the following anecdote:

Ellie, at sixteen, traveled to Russia and lived with a family in a remote Siberian city. Every weekend, the host family would bring my daughter with them when they went to visit their grandmother. The grandmother was called Babushka and spoke only Russian.

To begin with, Ellie's interactions with Babushka were minimal, confined to polite smiles and gestures. As Ellie's was a near-total immersion in the language, however, her Russian developed fairly quickly. At last she and Babushka could have a chat.

Babushka naturally asked Ellie about her family.

"I have a mother, a father, three brothers, and two sisters," Ellie said carefully.

Then Babushka asked about her religion.

Ellie answered: "My family is Unitarian Universalist."

Not surprisingly, Babushka had no idea what this was, so Ellie offered a concise explanation, after which Babushka decided that this American girl's religion was false, disgusting, and satanic.

She harangued Ellie at length in Russian about the damnation and eternal agony that awaited Ellie, her parents, her brothers, and her sisters, and when Ellie didn't respond as expected (whatever the expectation was—a grateful, weeping conversion to Russian Orthodoxy?), Babushka repeated this aggressive attempt at evangelization every weekend thereafter.

"It's annoying," Ellie said, with classic understatement, in one of the rare telephone calls she could manage to make from the other side of the planet.

"I should think so," I said crossly. "Honestly, Ellie—how miserable for you!"

"Yes, well," said Ellie. "You know, Mom, in my spare time here I've begun writing a play."

"Ah, yes?"

"Yes. It's about a girl who goes to Russia as an exchange student," said Ellie. *"And I know who is going to die at the end."*

"If it's a good experience, great!" my father used to say. "If it's a bad experience, it'll be a story." If it's your experience, I would add, it's your story.

Ellie owns her stories of Russia, just as Peter owns being a drummer in a rock-and-roll band, and Cobus owns law school, and Ilona owns her experience of sliding an intravenous line into a patient's vein. My story of Baby Drew is merely a grandmother's tale: it is Zach's wife, not his mother, who owns and shares the parents' tale with Zach.

I suppose Woolie owns her own stories, too, though these are especially hard to keep my hands off. She's the youngest and, as if the nickname "Woolie" weren't infantilizing enough, I am inclined (still) to call her "Wooglet," "Woogie-Piggie," and any number of indulgent variations, because I think she's adorable (and I adore her).

She was the last to leave home and so, when I noticed that our bars of soap were turning mushy, I assigned blame to Woogie-Piggie and her long, contemplative ablutions.

The best thing would be to put a new, wire-mesh shelf into the shower stall where the soap could stay out of the spray and keep relatively dry. Though Simon is usually in charge of home improvements, I bought such a shelf and installed it myself.

"Installed" might be a slight exaggeration: the shelf came with suction cups. All I had to do was step into the shower, decide where I wanted the shelf to be, hold it in position, and push until the suction cups sucked. After a few experiments, I chose my spot, about ten inches higher than my own head and six inches to the left of the shower nozzle. Press. Suck. *Voilà!*

Standing back to admire my handiwork, I was visited by a sudden rush of motherly concern: is Woolie going to be able to reach that high?

I imagined, for that half second, a tiny, curly-haired creature jumping for the soap, but on the day that I stuck that shelf up in the bathroom, my youngest child was two inches taller than I am.

At twenty-one, having passed the written exam and the physical assessment test (push-ups, sit-ups, running a mile and a half), Woolie matriculated at the Maine Criminal Justice Academy for the first phase of the training necessary to become a law enforcement officer in the state of Maine. She studied the laws of Maine, learned to operate a police radio and the lights-and-siren, and how to apply handcuffs. She has been pepper-sprayed and Tased (it's horrible, she says, laughing uproariously). She has sworn on her honor to serve and protect, and to uphold the Constitution. She has learned to keep her gun hand free.

It was Warden Chris Dyer who instructed his chaplain's daughter in basic defensive tactics on the blue mats in the academy gym.

"She's a fiery little thing!" he told me afterward. "She can take a punch, and she never gives up. You can tell she had big brothers."

When my darling Woogie-Piggie signs on, it is not as her father's daughter (412-B) nor even as her mother's little girl (2107-B). She has her own call number, her own power, her own responsibility.

"At last, I'm useful!" Woolie crowed, the day she was sworn in.

Her chief called to ask me if I was okay with my daughter's career choice. "I don't generally ask the moms," he said. "But you have history. Are you scared for her?"

"Witless," I said, smiling from ear to ear.

*   *   *

The National Law Enforcement Officers Memorial in Judiciary Square is enclosed by granite walls that curve like cupped hands. These walls are engraved with the names of police officers who have died in the line of duty. On panel 25-E, line 20, you can find my husband's name. Every time I see it there, it always somehow surprises me: *Good heavens, Drew! What are you doing here?*

Some of the names on the wall are there because someone forgot to keep the doorjamb of the car between the body and a bullet. Other names are on the wall because someone didn't search a suspect carefully enough or stepped away from an accident, distracted, into the roadway, or because a depressed teenager who jumped off a bridge started shouting for help when she hit the water.

After a decade's worth of brave and lucky interactions with the drunk or drugged, the violent, the despairing, the self-damned, Drew forgot to turn his head one more time when pulling out after a speeder. He didn't see the ice truck bearing down on him and so his name is on the wall at Judiciary Square.

Inspiring quotes have been engraved alongside the names: *"In valor there is hope"* (Tacitus) and *"The wicked flee when no man pursueth: but the righteous are bold as a lion"* (Proverbs 28:1). Then there's this, from the first President Bush: "Carved on these walls is the story of America, of a continuing quest to preserve both democracy and decency, and to protect a national treasure that we call the American dream." These are fine, but I'm glad the designers of the memorial included this one, too, from Vivian Eny Cross, the widow of a police officer: "It is not how these officers died that made them heroes. It is how they lived."

God, what do you want for your children?

It is the question that we ought to ask whenever an opportunity for divine interview (even an imaginary one) presents itself. If God were what we wish God could be, the answer would be: *Oh, my little ones, I want you to be safe, to live long and prosper.*

Because God is what God is, the answer comes in the form of a story, the one we've been struggling to tell ever since we descended from the trees and shaped our hands around a rock, our lives around one another, and our disarmed mouths around the Word.

There is widespread agreement among historians (secular as well as religious) that, indeed, a Galilean Jew named Jesus was born to a woman named Mary somewhere between 7 and 2 BCE and died between 30 and 36 CE. Between those two rough dates, Jesus was fed, housed, and protected by his mom and stepdad, taught to walk and speak, love and serve. Baptized by John, he had a brief career as an itinerant preacher countercultural enough to attract the attention of the Roman prefect Pontius Pilate. Pilate executed Jesus by the means and for the motives common to that time.

Neither I, nor the Gospel writers, nor the innumerable artists who have painted the scene at the foot of the Cross have imagined the Virgin Mary as being "okay with" her son's suffering and death. She is certainly never pictured as proud of him, serenely confident that his death was a fine thing. She is devastated. The very salvation of the world could not be worth so dear a price.

Given time, Mary surely healed, and would eventually have been able to articulate what loving her son meant, now that he was gone. She could probably have done this at least as eloquently and powerfully as the Acts of the Apostles or the Letters of Paul. Maybe one day, a desert cave in the Levant will yield a fresh cache of scrolls: *The Gospel According to the Mom*. I'd hazard a prediction that Mary's version won't be told as if Jesus's death were the sum and meaning of who he was. The lesson would, I think, come far closer to this: *It is not how my child died, but how he lived that made him a hero.*

Maybe if Simon and his first wife, and Drew and I and the helpful village, had not conspired to raise children who are quite so dangerously service-oriented, Zach, Peter, Cobus, Ellie, Ilona, and Officer Woolie would be, if not safe, at least safer.

They are not safe. *But they are useful.*

—〰—

Dear Children,

Never pass up using a clean bathroom.
    But seriously, this is what I want for each of you: a life of courage, kindness, and dangerous unselfishness:

may you be songs for the silence, poems for an empty page. As the Torah says, may you be lights in the world.

Love, Mom

———

Though I'm agnostic about Heaven as a reality, heaven as a metaphor can be useful. Here's a paradisiacal image that reliably makes me smile: A little baby boy named Drew, six pounds, two ounces, floats gently skyward through warm shafts of sunlight. There with his shiny trooper boots planted on a cumulus cloud, his grandfather, Big Drew, awaits. He is ten feet tall and his wings are unfurled, his experienced father's arms are open and ready to receive this jewel into his keeping.

"Come on, little buddy," he is saying. "I'll change that diaper and then I'll tell you a story."

Acknowledgments

To that ubiquitous, social-occasion inquiry "what do you do?" I could reply that I'm an author, but I never do. It is an answer that tends to let the air out of any conversational balloon.

Q. What do you write?

A. I write creative nonfiction... memoirs, mostly.

Q. (politely) Oh.

An aversion to boring people might be sufficient explanation for why I don't talk a lot about my writing, but there is another reason. Simply: I'm a minister and law enforcement chaplain. Truly: it's what I do and what I am. Writing serves my ministry rather than the other way around.

Any minister, of whatever denominational affiliation, must negotiate between two inescapable and occasionally incompatible duties.

First, he or she provides personal, pastoral succor to those in need: *Show up, shut up, and be.*

Second, he or she must name, proclaim, and bear public witness to the work of God in the world: *Stand up and holler!*

As a minister who writes, I do my best to protect the privacy of others even as I bear witness to love as it is revealed, among other places, in the world and works of my favorite armed men and women, the game wardens of Maine.

Any game warden or other person identified by name in this book has given his or her permission. All others have had their names and other identifying details altered.

Some of the themes in *Anchor and Flares* were developed for the Fall 2014 Minns Lectures. The Minns are an annual series of lectures on religious topics conducted under the auspices of First Church and King's Chapel in Boston. Since 1942, thinkers within the Unitarian Universalist tradition have been given a chance to speak at length on significant topics. I was proud to be included among them.

Thanks are owed to patient readers of the early drafts of this manuscript—my agent, Sally Wofford-Girand, and her stalwart assistants, and my friends Marie, Cindy, and Joel and Kelly.

Along with teaching my boy to blow things up, the United States Marine Corps honed my son W. Zachary Griffith's skills as a writer and editor to such a degree that Zach was able to read a book written *about him by his own mother* with a dispassionate eye for both the good phrase and the misplaced comma. As I write, he is hard at work on his own first book. His *morfar*, Peter Braestrup (writer, editor, and Marine), would be so proud.

Anchor
&
Flares

QUESTIONS AND TOPICS FOR DISCUSSION

1. The Maine Warden Service's handbook for boaters reminds those heading out on the water to keep an anchor and flares aboard at all times. In an emergency, boaters need something to keep them steady and to draw help. How, according to Braestrup, does this wisdom apply in other facets of life?

2. After Zach's birth, Braestrup asked her relatives for pieces of parenting advice that she could use and compile into a parenting manual. If you were asked for a contribution, what would it be? Is there a particular piece of advice—parenting or otherwise—you received that has stuck with you? Have you ever received any truly terrible advice? Do you have any memories of interactions with your children or parents that you still revisit with horror? What, if anything, did you learn from those moments and the subsequent memories of them?

3. Throughout the book, Braestrup discusses gender and the role it played in both her childhood and that of her children. How do you think her upbringing regarding

her gender informed how she decided to raise her own children? Did gender play a big role in your upbringing? Did you raise your children to think about gender the same way you were raised, or did you take a different approach?

4. Discuss Braestrup's thoughts on disciplining children. Do you have a set way to discipline your children? Are you always able to follow that guideline? What do you think your style of discipline teaches your children?

5. How would you react if one of your children decided to join the armed services?

6. Braestrup has four children and two stepchildren, and she seems to have raised them all a bit differently. If you have multiple children, did your parenting style change with each child? Were you one of multiple siblings? If so, do you think you were parented differently than your siblings?

7. Braestrup struggles with the issue of violence and her desire to raise her children to be nonviolent. Is this something you have thought a lot about? If so, how do you put it into practice?

8. How do you think Braestrup's religious belief has shaped the way she views grief and how she grieves? What role does religion play for you in the face of tragedy or despair?